P9-CDY-891

THE REPLY TO HAYNE

From the original painting in Faneuil Hall, Boston

E340.W4B35 79980

LIBRARY
EMORY & HENRY
COLLEGE

WITHDRAWN

EMORY, VIRGINIA

Given by my Mother
Dec 25, 1929
Christmas eve.

DANIEL WEBSTER

DANIEL WEBSTER

*A hitherto unpublished portrait made for his daughter Julia
and now in the possession of Lewis A. Armistead of Boston*

DANIEL WEBSTER

Allan L. Benson

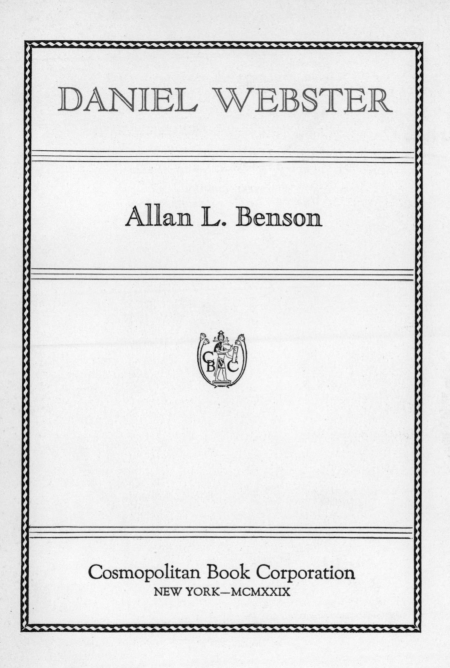

Cosmopolitan Book Corporation
NEW YORK—MCMXXIX

COPYRIGHT, 1929, BY
ALLAN L. BENSON

ALL RIGHTS RESERVED INCLUDING THAT
OF TRANSLATION INTO FOREIGN LAN-
GUAGES INCLUDING THE SCANDINAVIAN

PRINTED IN THE U. S. A. BY J. J. LITTLE
& IVES COMPANY, NEW YORK

FIRST EDITION

E
340
.W4B35

EXPLANATORY

IT is a great experience to take a man who has been dead seventy-seven years, turn back the clock with him, be ever afterward at his side—through childhood, through boyhood, through all the great and little moments of manhood—and then, in his old age, put him back into his tomb.

This experience, in the case of Daniel Webster, is without precedent in my forty years of writing. I have never written anything that I so enjoyed writing as I have this book; and if it be not written too poorly, some of this satisfaction will get through to the reader. I have written about men who were living—men with whom I had spent months or years and knew well—without feeling that I had drawn so near to one of them as I have to Webster. I saw each of these living men from but one point of view—my own—whereas, in studying Webster, I saw him from each of the angles in which he appeared to the various close friends who wrote books or made statements about him. I have tried, in this book, by blending the incomplete pictures of Webster's friends, to present a complete portrait, not merely of Webster the statesman, but of Webster the man, with all his delightful drolleries, and not without some attention to his weaknesses.

Also, I have tried to show that the historians of his day never gave him his due, and that later writers have but followed the errors of their predecessors. He seems to me to have been the only American statesman of his

v

79980

EMORY AND HENRY LIBRARY

day who advocated a course that, if followed, would eventually have done away with chattel slavery without a civil war. Clay, too, had vision, but not so much as Webster. Lincoln was not of Webster's day, but when he arrived he took a position with regard to the problems presented by slavery that was identical with that of Webster.

There is no end of books in which Webster plays a part—in fact, the history of the forty years lying between 1812 and 1852 cannot be written without him. But the following books are the ones upon which I have drawn most heavily.

Webster's Private Correspondence, edited by Fletcher Webster, published in two volumes, by Little, Brown & Company of Boston, consists of more than nine hundred letters written by him, and about one hundred and fifty written to him. It is a great reservoir of information covering his entire life.

The Life of Daniel Webster, by his friend George Ticknor Curtis, published in two volumes by D. Appleton & Company, New York, is the best formal biography. It contains a wealth of material, including frequent extended quotations from the *Ticknor Manuscripts,* is strong on the historical, but weak on the human side.

Reminiscences of Daniel Webster, by his old friend Peter Harvey and published by Little, Brown & Company, Boston, is not a biography at all, but an extraordinary accomplishment in presenting Webster, from childhood to death, in all of his various moods and phases. It is the most human of all the Webster books.

The Private Life of Daniel Webster, by Charles Lanman, and published by Harper & Brothers within a few weeks of Webster's death, was a little labor of love performed in humble tribute to his memory by his secretary. It is slight and amateurish, but touching in its loyalty and illuminating to the extent that it goes.

The Works of Daniel Webster, edited by Edward Everett, containing a biographical sketch of Webster by him and published in six volumes by Charles C. Little and James Brown, Boston, consists of Webster's speeches and orations.

Famous Americans of Recent Times, by James Parton, published by Field, Osgood & Company, Boston, contains a highly biased but readable sketch of Webster, which is valuable only because it has in it perhaps the best existing statement of what Webster's enemies said about his drinking habits.

Daniel Webster, the Expounder of the Constitution, by Everett Pepperrell Wheeler, published by G. P. Putnam's Sons, New York, goes deeply and well into the great law cases of Webster. It is authoritative, illuminating, and readable.

The Diary of Philip Hone, edited by Allan Nevins and published by Dodd, Mead & Company, New York, contains many interesting entries concerning Webster, and his convivial New York friends, one of whom was Hone.

The Autobiography of Horace Greeley, published by E. B. Treat, New York, and *The American Conflict,* by Horace Greeley, published by O. D. Case & Company, Chicago, contain interesting sidelights obtained by Greeley as a newspaper correspondent, together with historical facts concerning the period in which the Civil War was brewing.

Perley's Reminiscences (two volumes), by Ben Perley Poore, published by Hubbard Brothers, Philadelphia, is a moving picture of Washington political life as seen during a period of sixty years by a newspaper correspondent. It is helpful in contributing to the understanding of Washington political and social life in Webster's day, but too much dependence should not be placed upon some of its statements. It is pungent, however, and, in some respects, in a class by itself.

A. L. B.

Yonkers, New York,
April 22, 1929.

ILLUSTRATIONS

DANIEL WEBSTER   *Frontispiece*
                                                  FACING PAGE
THE HOUSE IN WHICH DANIEL WEBSTER WAS BORN   20

GRACE FLETCHER WEBSTER   56

WEBSTER AT THE AGE OF THIRTY-EIGHT   84

WEBSTER IN HIS PRIME   108

WEBSTER'S HOME AT MARSHFIELD   142

CAROLINE LE ROY WEBSTER   182

                                                  BETWEEN PAGES
FACSIMILE OF WEBSTER LETTER   190-191

                                                  FACING PAGE
COLONEL FLETCHER WEBSTER   200

WEBSTER AT SIXTY-THREE   226

MAJOR EDWARD WEBSTER   300

DANIEL WEBSTER AS SECRETARY OF STATE   348

THE "BROTHER AND SISTER TREES"   378

Websters life as a public man, was an Epic.
full of the most brilliant and dramatic scenes,
covering a period of fifty years. And Webster
"still lives" and will live in all the future of
these United States. His far seeing statesmanship
and all-embracing patriotism is the lesson
and the wisdom for this day and hour, as it
was for his own day and hour. Only his devoted
loyalty to the constitution and the Union, became
once more and forever, the common creed of all
our people, North, South, East and West. Bind
and keep us one and make it unpossible for
this "Government of the people to perish from the
earth" The danger which threatened the Union
in his day is not now, nor is ever again likely
to become formidable. "Nullification" and
"Secession" are obsolete words, having only now
historical interest; largely made so by the
titanic Hons of Webster.

                              Curtis Columtia

"In medio tutissimus ibis"

PART ONE

*D*ANIEL, *in the long struggle with poverty and adverse fortune that your mother and I have made to give you and Ezekiel an education, we have often talked over these sacrifices, and the prospects of our children. Your mother has often said to me that she had no fear about Ezekiel; that he had fixed and steady habits, and an indomitable energy. . . . But as for you, she did not know. Either you would be something or nothing, she did not know which. I think . . . you have fulfilled her prophecy. You have come to nothing."*

—EBENEZER WEBSTER.

Salisbury Feb 13th
1801

"Come. Ripley, throw your volumes by,
You love to chat, and so do I;
Now let us put our heads together
and talk of woman, war and weather, —
All hackneyed subjects, it is true,
But just reverse them and they're new.
So when our topics are run out,
Then gravely make a new beginning,
And talk of weather, war and woman.

* * * *

(sig) Daniel

DANIEL WEBSTER

I

Daughter
Grave died in
her fathers
arms 1817

Buried his
wife 1828

Brother
Ezekiel
died 1829

Son Edward
killed in
Mexican War
1845

THE lightning of death was always playing around the Webster family. It played around Daniel all his life, and after his death struck down in a battle of the Civil War his only surviving son. Yet, if it had not been for such a bolt, Daniel never would have been born at all. If the elder Webster's first wife had not suddenly died, when she was barely out of her twenties, there would have been no Daniel Webster. There might have been a ninth child, but he would have lacked half of the ingredients that made up the man who looms so large in early American history.

"Excellent, excellent parent," Daniel once exclaimed in speaking of his father, yet if the facts be studied, it may be suspected that Daniel's mother was the excellent parent. The father, old Ebenezer, had, as we shall see, his points, but it was Abigail Eastman who put into the Webster blood something that made it yield power. The first wife's five children, and the first three of the second wife's offspring (so strong, apparently, was the Websterian influence) amounted to nothing. As Balzac many years later said, in describing a certain kind of persons: "They seemed to have been created to make up the crowd in the world." Ezekiel, the eighth child, had better stuff in him, though he never became a great man.

Then on January 18, 1782, in Salisbury, New Hampshire, came Daniel Webster.

Old Ebenezer finished off his second family with a

daughter who, fashioned after the Webster pattern, was just "one of the crowd."

Daniel Webster once wrote an autobiographical sketch in which he told much about his father but nothing about his mother. The sketch contained only two or three casual references to her, and one of these related to the fact that she was buried on the old farm beside his father and some of his brothers and sisters. More than nine hundred letters written by Webster and more than one hundred and fifty written to him have been published, but not one of these letters was written by his mother or to her. She lived to be seventy years old, by which time he was in Congress, but there is no evidence that she and her distinguished son ever exchanged a letter. Nor in all the letters that Webster wrote to others is there more than a left-handed reference to her—except one, and that was when she died. Nobody now knows why. There is nothing whatever to indicate that they were ever on bad terms. Whatever the reason, it is forever buried in the hills of New England.

There is no doubt, however, that Daniel considered his father to have been the intellectual superior of his mother. Writing to his son, in 1840, Daniel said: "I believe we are all indebted to my father's mother for a large portion of the little sense and character that belong to us."

It was a preacher's daughter, Daniel Webster's paternal grandmother, who put black hair and swarthy skins upon some of the Websters. She was the daughter of the Reverend Stephen Batchelder, a man of some little reputation in his county of Rockingham. Before she came into the family the Websters all had light complexions, sandy hair, and bushy eyebrows. After she entered it, there was a change. Two of her sons were like the usual run of

Websters, but the one who was to become the father of Daniel Webster looked like her. Of Ebenezer's children, only one son besides Daniel had the Batchelder complexion, and he was Ezekiel, the only one of the Webster children besides Daniel who amounted to anything.

Perhaps Daniel was right in giving more credit for what he was to his grandmother than he did to his mother. But whatever old Ebenezer may have been, he did not begin having children that were more than ordinary until Abigail Eastman came into the family.

Two wives and ten children, to the end of their days, stood almost in awe before Ebenezer Webster. His neighbors, for miles around, soon learned to follow his leadership, compelled sometimes by his gentle tyranny, but most frequently by affection for him and faith in his superior wisdom. Ebenezer Webster was the background of his great son's life and, as such, must be understood by everybody who would understand Daniel Webster.

We first see him in 1760 as a young soldier, off for the French and Indian War. Twenty-one years old. Six feet tall. Coal-black hair and eyes. Broad shoulders and a deep chest. Large features. A Roman nose. Never had been in a schoolhouse as a pupil a day in his life. Knew nothing except what he had heard people say. Why he went to war may therefore seem a mystery. It is not. He went to war because fear of Indians was a daily experience of his life. Farming was not safe because of the foes that lurked behind trees. Being a woman and working in a house was not safe. Red men crept up when the men were absent and slew the women. All these things young Ebenezer knew, and he also believed that the French, who owned and ruled Canada, incited the Indians to make war upon the whites.

Yet we need not assume that, as a young man, he took

even these things too seriously. At his age war was a game, a great adventure—a man-hunt. It was probably quite interesting for this youth occasionally to match wits with an Indian, to ascertain which could shoot at the other —from behind a tree—with the greater accuracy. Nor were Ebenezer and his companions shooting at Indians all the time. There were long weeks and even months when, care-free, so far as earning a living was concerned, they roamed the forests by day, taking a shot now and then at any bird or animal that, a little later, might smell good as it was being roasted on a spit over a camp-fire. There were almost a thousand nights, during most of which they assembled in their tents or around their fires, recounting the adventures of the day, telling stories and talking about the girls at home—as young men, in such circumstances, have always done and always will do. Certainly, as we shall soon see, Ebenezer never forgot that he had left a girl behind him.

If there be any such thing as "glorious war" that war, at that time and place, was glorious. It was full of adventure and pleasant exercise with little personal danger. The nature of the conflict may be further inferred from the fact that Ebenezer and his companions fared forth equipped with skates and snowshoes. In winter along Lake George, upon the banks of which some of the fighting was done, skates came in handy. Skates were the rapid motor-trucks of the day, facilitating the movement of troops.

Webster, under Stark and Putnam, who afterward became famous in the Revolutionary War, fought and skated his way into Canada and, under General Amherst, assisted in the taking of Ticonderoga and Crown Point. The French power crumbled. In 1763, peace was signed. France ceded Canada to England. Webster went home.

Three years in the army fighting Indians had brought about great changes in Ebenezer Webster. Something half boy and half man had gone away; something like a man and a half came back. He had developed the military carriage which remained with him throughout life. Indecision never afterward bothered him. He carried his head high, was positive, emphatic, full of plans for the future. What he wanted at once was a farm and a home. Circumstances soon opened the way before him. A grant of land in the wilderness near the center of the state of New Hampshire was offered by Benning Wentworth, the colonial governor, to veterans of the war.

"My father joined this enterprise," said Daniel Webster. "He had the discretion to take a wife along with him, intending, whatever else he might want, to have good company."

Ebenezer had taken along with him Mehitable Smith, whom he had married in 1764. They traveled as far as the road went and then struck a little farther into the wilderness. When the others stopped, Ebenezer and his young wife continued onward a mile or so toward the north.

"When my father had built his log cabin and lighted his fire," said Daniel, "his smoke ascended nearer to the North Star than that of any other of His Majesty's New England subjects. His nearest civilized neighbor on the north was at Montreal."

From the modern point of view, not so good a place for a young wife. A hut for a house and made of logs at that. Woods all around. Trees to be cut down and stumps to be pulled or cut out before even a garden could be started. Mountainous country, too. Deep snow during the long winters. Perhaps Mehitable Webster did not much care. Life as she found it there was not so very different from the only kind of life she had ever seen human beings

A company of pioneers headed by Colonel Stevens - The township was called stevenstown. Ebenezer Webster selected the most northerly plot 4 miles wide, 9 miles long.

live. Whatever may have been her feelings, during the next ten years she became the mother of five children. Olle, a daughter, and Ebenezer, a son, died young. Susannah, born third, lived to become the wife of John Colby. David and Joseph came next and last. There could be no more for the present, because Mehitable Webster was dead, ten years from her marriage day.

Five months later, Ebenezer Webster had a new wife. Abigail Eastman this time. She, too, soon began to have children. The first one was a girl. What should be her name? A thousand guesses, if one wishes them. She was named Mehitable, after Ebenezer's first wife.

Only a very unusual woman would consent to name her first-born after her husband's first wife. Ebenezer, as a man of honor and keen sense of justice, made it up to her the next year when he built her a better house than the first wife had had—a house not of logs but of boards. Ebenezer knew that it does not take much to appease a woman if one chooses the right thing.

Ebenezer, in fact, was more than just. He permitted the second child, a girl, to be named Abigail, after her mother.

The third child, Ezekiel, was a brother whom Daniel so loved that in dedicating one of his books of speeches to two of Ezekiel's daughters, years after their father's death, he expressed "a desire that the name of my brother, Ezekiel Webster, may be associated with mine, so long as anything written or spoken by me shall be regarded or read."

Daniel was the fourth child of the second edition of Websters, and Sarah, the fifth and last. Mehitable and Sarah were never married.

The children of the middle-aged and the old are less likely than the offspring of the young to survive infancy, but if they do, they are more likely to live to be old. Benjamin Franklin, the fifteenth child of his father who had two wives and seventeen children, was the youngest son—the youngest son of the youngest son for five generations—and reached the age of eighty-four. Daniel Webster, ninth of his father's ten children and born when his father was forty-three years old, was at the age of fifty-seven the only survivor of his father's two families of children, not one of whom lived to be as old as he was then.

Physically, Daniel Webster had so poor a start that he did not, until he was about twenty-five years of age, develop dependable health. His mother, however, soon perceived in him, as every mother perceives in her son, signs of impending greatness. His big black eyes were considered to have a very solemn expression, indicating, perhaps, that he might grow up to be like his father, who later became a judge. An expansive forehead added to the hope of fame. The poor lady did not know that the eye itself has no more expression than a doorknob, and that a prominent forehead is more likely to be the product of rickets suffered in childhood than an indication of brain power. It is the manner in which the eyelids are held and the presence or absence of wrinkles about them that create what is called the eye's expression. Prominent foreheads are usually caused by rickets which attack children before they are two years old who have been fed badly and given too little sunlight. The Webster house was a place in which rickets might be expected to appear. In those days it was not considered good sense to waste much money on window glass. With long, cold winters, Daniel was apparently permitted to remain in the house and develop rickets and a big forehead when he should have been bundled up and put out in the sunlight.

In 1791 Ebenezer Webster procured the position of Judge of the local court. Salary 3 or 400 dollars a year.

The first family of five Webster children was produced in ten years, the second family of five in twenty
years. But while the second family was coming, the Revolutionary War was proceeding, and Ebenezer was taking
part in it. Being a militiaman instead of an enlisted or
drafted man, he fought when there was nothing to do on
the farm, which enabled him to spend some time at home.
Yet he took his soldiering seriously, and was away with
the troops many months of each year. With one hundred
neighbors who had elected him their captain, he took part
in nearly every campaign of the war. He was among the
first to scale the Tory breastworks at Bennington and,
when he came out of battle, was so covered with dust
and powder-smoke that he could scarcely be recognized.

Daniel Webster was always very proud of his father's
service in the Revolutionary War. The facts of course
came to him, in the first instance, from his father, but to
the day of his death he never tired of hearing the same
stories from others. While walking along a country road
in New Hampshire in 1840 Daniel was overtaken by a
man more than eighty years old who asked him to ride
with him. Conversation shifted from one subject to another and finally the old man, who did not know who it
was who sat beside him, remarked that he had known
"Old Judge Webster, the father of Daniel." "We were
out in the Continental War together," he said. Early
Americans always spoke of the fringe of colonies along
the Atlantic as if they were the Continent.

As the horses slowly wormed their way along the
rocky road, the old man spun his tale to the silent man at
his side. He and old Judge Webster were at Dorchester
Heights when General Washington had his camp there.
A detachment of Webster's company was delegated to
guard duty around Washington's tent. The spinner of the

tale was one of the company. Early on a frosty morning he was walking briskly back and forth before the tent when the flaps parted, and the tall figure of Washington stepped out. Washington first looked at the sky to see what kind of day it seemed likely to be. Then he turned to the sentry and asked him who was in command of the company on guard. The sentry (now the old man, the spinner of the tale) replied that Captain Webster was in command. Washington told him to tell Captain Webster to call at his tent early the next morning.

Early next morning Captain Webster called. Washington sought information. What was the feeling in New Hampshire? Had the people counted the cost of resistance to the British? Were they willing to throw away the scabbard and spend and be spent in the cause? Washington talked an hour with Webster and, when he had finished, thanked him and shook him warmly by the hand.

Nor was this the only occasion when Ebenezer Webster stood guard over the tent that sheltered George Washington. The second time was at West Point. It was the evening of the day that Washington learned of Arnold's treason. When the time came to station a guard for the night, Washington sent for Webster, told him what he wanted and said with a smile: "I believe I can trust *you*."

Ebenezer Webster said that Washington paced up and down in his tent or wrote at his camp-table until daylight.

In telling these stories, years afterward, to his son Fletcher, Daniel Webster said: "I should rather have it said on my father's tombstone that he had guarded the person of George Washington, and was worthy of such a trust, than to have emblazoned upon it the proudest insignia of heraldry that the world can give."

Upon such thrilling narratives as these was Daniel Webster reared. We see him, with his solemn black eyes, listening intently. Have the vibrations already started in his brain that later are to resound around the battle monument at Bunker Hill and shake the senate chamber as he replies to Hayne? An intelligent boy's brain is a wonderful thing, and Daniel Webster, who was born a year before the Revolutionary War was officially ended, who was five years old when the Constitution was drafted and seventeen years old when Washington died, felt very near to the Revolution, to the Constitution, and to Washington.

?

Constitutional Convention 1787 1788

Had not his father twice stood guard at the door of the great commander's tent?

II

EBENEZER WEBSTER, at the age of forty-four, returned from the Revolutionary War. Daniel, a puny child a year old, was in his cradle, beside which his mother often cried because a neighbor had expressed the opinion that the baby was too weak to live. Abigail herself was well, but with two broods of children tagging at her heels she was tired. A year later her final child was born —little Sarah to whom had been given enough vitality to last only a little more than twenty years.

Ebenezer Webster returned from the war, not exactly a hero, but a well-beloved man. The note of veneration began to creep into the opinions of him that his neighbors expressed. Whatever offices they had at their disposal were given to him. He had never been to school but had taught himself how to read and write. He had never read much, because there was not much to read, but he had done what he could. Nothing of this sort mattered. His neighbors sent him first to one house of the legislature and then to the other. They elected him to the state convention that was chosen to accept or reject the Federal Constitution that had just been submitted by the Philadelphia·convention. Although he did not know a word of law, they elected him a judge of the court of common pleas of his county. "Book larnin'" was not what they wanted. They wanted common sense and felt that old Ebenezer Webster had it.

It was fortunate for Webster, when he returned from the war, that his neighbors thus idolized him. It was fortunate for him because the tyrannical nature with which he had been born was now at its height. He had a way of stamping into a public meeting, standing it on its head, so to speak, commanding it to reverse itself and do what he wanted done. Confronted by a crowd of churchmen, met to ordain a minister, but deadlocked upon a point of doctrine, old Ebenezer arose and said: "Gentlemen, the ordination must come on *now,* and if you cannot assist, we must try to get along without you. The point under discussion must be postponed to some other day." Whereupon the ordination ceremonies proceeded without further delay!

As a delegate to the state convention chosen to pass upon the Federal Constitution, Ebenezer was instructed to vote against it. Although Webster could not go back to the electors who had chosen him and obtain their permission to vote for the Constitution he managed to convince himself that he was justified in voting as he pleased and voted for it. The fact that Washington's signature was at the bottom of it was enough for him.

For the most part, Webster's high-handed methods were apparently rather liked by his constituents, whose

admiration for his independence was perhaps as great as
their faith in his common sense. But his gentle tyranny
occasionally got on the nerves of some of his neighbors.
Once, for instance, a rumor began to circulate around
the countryside that Judge Webster had been seen in a
dancing hall. For a judge and a churchman to go to such
a place shocked the community. A copy of the New
Hampshire Statesman of the day tells the rest of the story:

> A member of his church entered a complaint,
> requiring satisfaction for this reproach. Parson
> Worcester suggested a written acknowledgment.
> Judge Webster replied that he would put nothing on
> file, but that he would make an oral confession be-
> fore the congregation. Accordingly, on the next Sun-
> day, after the forenoon exercises were closed, he rose
> in his place and said:
> "A few days since I had some business with my
> nephew, Stephen Bohonon; went up to his house,
> found him in the hall of the tavern instructing the
> youth in dancing. They were in the midst of a dance
> when I entered the hall. I took a seat and waited
> until the dance was closed; took the earliest oppor-
> tunity to do my errand with Stephen; found the
> young people civil and orderly; saw nothing im-
> proper. Now, if in all this I have offended any of
> my *weaker* brethren, I am sorry for it."

The last office that Ebenezer Webster held was the
judgeship of the court of common pleas. The court consisted of three members. The presiding judge was always
a lawyer. The two "side justices," as they were called,
were usually farmers noted for their honesty and horse-
sense. Ebenezer was a side justice. In one respect, at
least, it must have been a sort of comic opera court,
though perhaps it yielded as much justice as any. The
side justices, though they knew nothing of the law, had

the power, as did the presiding justice, of declaring to the jury what was the law bearing upon the case in point. Sometimes the learned judges agreed as to what was the law and sometimes they did not. When they did not the juries probably forgot the law altogether and did what seemed best.

Daniel Webster, as a young lawyer, argued his first case before the court upon which his father sat. It was a proud moment for both of them.

All the years that Ebenezer Webster was holding public office he was working hard on his sterile farm to eke out the barest living. In 1795, when he was fifty-six years old, he and Daniel were working together in the hayfield, one hot day in July, when they looked up and saw a visitor approaching. The visitor was the member of congress from their district, the Honorable Abiel Foster who lived in Canterbury, six miles distant. He was out looking after his political fences and wished to make sure of the support of Ebenezer. He did not remain long and, after he had gone, the old judge called Daniel to him and together they sat down upon a haycock, under an elm.

"My son," said Ebenezer, "that is a worthy man. He is a member of congress. He sits in congress and gets six *at Philadelphia* dollars a day while I toil here. It is because he has had an education. He went to college and later became a minister, but he has not much natural power. His education is what has put him where he is. If I had had his chance, I could have been where he is. I came near it, as it was, but I missed it and now must work here."

Daniel, when he was a lad, was easily moved to tears. The thought of his father slaving on the farm was too much for him and he wept. He told his father that he should work no more, that he and Ezekiel would do the work. The father should rest. *Daniel from all reports was considered an exceedingly poor farmer.*

"It is of no importance now," continued Ebenezer. "I now live but for my children. I could not give your elder brothers the advantage of knowledge, but I can do something for you. Exert yourself, improve your opportunities, learn, learn, and when I am gone, you will not need to go through the hardships that I have undergone, and which have made me an old man before my time."

No father ever sacrificed himself for a more appreciative son. Forty years afterward Daniel Webster said:

"My father died in April, 1806. I neither left him nor forsook him. My opening an office at Boscawen was that I might be near him. I closed his eyes in this very house. He died at the age of sixty-seven, after a life of exertion, toil, and exposure; a private soldier, an officer, a legislator, a judge, everything that a man could be to whom learning had never disclosed her 'ample page.'

"My first speech at the bar was made when he was on the bench. He never heard me a second time. He had in him the character of some of the old Puritans. He was deeply religious but not sour. On the contrary, good-humored, facetious, showing even in his age, with a contagious laugh, teeth all as white as alabaster; gentle, soft, playful, and yet having a heart in him that seemed to have been borrowed from a lion. He could frown; a frown it was; but cheerfulness, good humor and smiles composed his most usual aspect."

The little world in which Daniel Webster began to move about was unusual, even in his day, and now is as dead as ancient Egypt. The two parents and the ten children were devoted to each other. The parents asked nothing more in life than opportunities to sacrifice themselves for their children. The children loved their mother and idolized their father. All of them were very emotional. Somebody was always "bursting into tears" over an event that would touch the modern boy little if at all.

Between Daniel and Ezekiel, two years his senior, was an attachment the like of which is seldom seen at any time or in any country. Daniel had three other brothers and five sisters, but so great was the love of Dan and Zeke for each other that neither of them, in recounting the events of his childhood, often mentioned any of the others. Daniel's stories were always studded with references to "Ezekiel and Father," Ezekiel's with comments upon "Father and Daniel." Daniel's heart nearly stopped beating the morning he was awakened at two o'clock and told that Ezekiel, then forty-nine, at the very moment of his conclusion of an argument in court, had dropped dead. To the day of Ezekiel's death, Daniel sought his advice with regard to law and politics, and after the delivery of the reply to Hayne, Daniel grieved that Ezekiel had not lived to hear it. The plaudits of the country were not enough. Daniel missed the approval and the appreciation of his brother.

To speak in terms of paradox, the two boys began to draw close to each other when Daniel was sent away to school, preparatory to going to college. The father, because of his poverty, had not been able to do anything for the other boys (girls, in those days, were not mentioned in connection with education) but with "three or four hundred dollars a year" coming to him from his judgeship, he thought he could do something for Daniel.

The other brothers banteringly said that Daniel was to be sent to school "to make him as smart as the rest of us." Old Ebenezer for a time was perplexed because Ezekiel seemed more likely, in some respects, to do something with an education than Daniel. "Ezekiel cannot tell half he knows," said the old man one day, "while

Daniel can tell a good deal more than he knows." A politician was developing before their eyes but no one knew it! Daniel was chosen because he could best be spared from the farm. He was weak, sickly and not of much account, while Ezekiel was strong.

The decision to send Daniel away to school was suddenly communicated to him a few months after he was thirteen years old. The father and mother had of course been thinking about it a long while, but Daniel was kept in the dark until one day in May, 1796, the father mounted a horse, told Daniel to get on another, and away they went to Phillips Academy, a preparatory school.

Exter

Nobody ever more needed to go to a preparatory school than did Daniel. What he knew was only a little, and he was not sure of that. It was not his fault. The country schools were poor, and, poor as they were, he was not able, because of illness, steadily to attend them. He never could remember a time when he could not read the Bible. He had a passion for reading, but very little to read that was suited to his years. Addison . . . the Spectator . . . Dr. Johnson . . . Pope's "Essay on Man." All of these he brought home from a circulating library and read them, not once or twice, but many times. "We thought they were all to be got by heart." Pope's "Essay" he could repeat from beginning to end. He could read better than his teacher. The teacher taught nothing but reading and writing—that was all the boy got for wading three miles each way through the snowbanks in winter—yet because Daniel was a miserable penman, a teacher once told him that he "feared his fingers were destined for the plow-tail."

Daniel's passion for books once almost caused him to burn his aged grandmother to death in her bed. The close of the year had brought the new year's almanac.

Daniel and Ezekiel rushed for it. Before night they had mastered it. They had read and laughed at all the jokes. They had got what they could out of its moral teachings and its sentimental expressions. Above all, they had committed to memory each of the four-line verses that appeared at the top of each page. They awakened in the middle of the winter's night and got to talking about the verses. They disagreed in their recollection of a word in the third line of the verse for the month of April. There was no way to prove which was right except to get the almanac. The thing could not wait until morning—it must be settled at once.

Daniel undertook to settle it. He lighted a candle and stealthily picked his way, in his bare feet, to his grandmother's bedroom where was the precious almanac. With it he crept back to Ezekiel. The almanac was hastily consulted. Ezekiel was found to be right. A little gloating from the elder brother. A puff at the candle from Daniel. Darkness! Silence!

But Daniel could not go to sleep. A little humiliated, perhaps. He was beginning to get drowsy when he saw what appeared to be a light under the door of his grandmother's room. The grandmother was too old to have arisen and lighted a candle. It must be that he had lighted something there himself. A hop out of bed and a few quick steps brought him to the door which he threw open. Fire! It seemed to young Daniel as if there were nothing else in the room. At the top of his voice he shouted. Everybody in the house responded. Old Ebenezer, clad in his underclothes and shirt with a nightcap upon his head. Mrs. Webster, Sally, Ezekiel—all of them. No volunteer fireman ever worked more rapidly than did the old judge. While others rushed for water, Ebenezer set to smothering the flames with woolen blankets. Daniel said it was his father's work that saved the house—that and the fact that the fire was discovered just when it was. In two or three minutes more, nothing could have saved Mrs. Webster's mother—and nothing could have saved the house. All of them might have been burned alive.

Daniel, at the country school, had learned nothing but reading, writing and spelling. At the preparatory school he was placed in the dumb-bell class with five other boys and set to studying grammar, writing and arithmetic. He was so "overpowered," he said, at being in preparatory school at all that he could hardly retain the mastery of his own senses, among ninety boys "who knew so much more" than he did. Nor did the other students fail to notice his "rustic manners and raiment." Some ridiculed him. Daniel winced but worked. Others called it work. He called it play. He did not have to study. What he read once became his own. In a month he was promoted. "Webster," said his instructor, "you will pass into another room and join a higher class." Turning to the pupils, the instructor said: "Boys, you will take your final leave of Webster. You will never see him again."

One thing Daniel could not do at that time was to speak before the school. The "kind and excellent Buckminster," would gently plead and urge, and Daniel would try, but when he faced the school, what he had learned by heart and declaimed in his room evaporated. "Sometimes my instructors frowned," said Daniel, "sometimes they smiled." He went home and "wept bitter tears of mortification."

Daniel was still so much of a boy that when he went back to the farm, for his summer vacation, he mostly forgot all of his fine promises about helping his father and loafed on the old man most outrageously. Sent out in the morning to pitch hay, he soon threw down his fork, looked

The House in Which Daniel Webster Was Born

This drawing was made from Webster's description and approved by him

Daniel was never fond of physical effort, and one day when the father left home he gave the two boys Zeke and Daniel, directions to perform some specific work which he found untouched upon his return.

With a frown on his face he asked the elder boy what he had been doing all day? "Nothing, Sir, "replied the son.

"Well Daniel, what have you been doing?"

"Helping Zeke, Sir" was the quick reply.

up his little sister Sally, and the two went away to pick whortleberries. Neighbors thought he was lazy and, when they saw him loafing, laughed at him. College boy! Inferior stuff! Daniel had not yet learned to work, but more important, he did not feel well. He dearly loved to play and he was a lovable youngster, who easily made friends in the neighborhood among old codgers who liked to talk. Daniel himself speaks:

A character of this sort, one Robert Wise, with whose adventures, as I learned them from himself I could fill a small book, was a near neighbor and a sort of humble companion for a great many years. He was a Yorkshire man; had been a sailor; was with Byng in the Mediterranean; had been a soldier, deserted from the garrison at Gibraltar; traveled through Spain and France and Holland; was taken up afterwards, severely punished and sent back to the army; was in the battle of Minden; had a thousand stories of the yellow-haired Prince Ferdinand; was sent to Ireland and thence to Boston, with the troops brought out by General Gage; fought at Bunker Hill, deserted to our ranks, served with the New Hampshire troops in all the succeeding campaigns, and at the peace built a little cottage in the corner of our field, on the river's bank, and there lived to an advanced age.

He was my Isaac Walton. He had a wife but no child. He loved me because I would read the newspapers to him, containing the accounts of battles in the European wars. He had twice deserted from the English King, and once at least committed treason as well as desertion, but he still had a British heart. When I have read to him the details of the victories of Howe and Jervis, etc., I remember he was excited almost to convulsions and would relieve his excitement by a gush of exulting tears. He finally picked up a fatherless child, took him home, sent him to school and took care of him, only, as he said, that he might have someone to read the newspaper to him. He could never read himself.

Alas, poor Robert. I have never so attained the narrative art as to hold the attention of others as thou, with thy Yorkshire tongue, hast held mine. Thou hast carried me many a mile on thy back, paddled me over and over and up and down the stream, and given whole days in aid of my boyish sports and asked no mead but that, at night, I would sit down at thy cottage door, and read to thee some passage of thy country's glory. Thou wast, indeed, a true Briton.

What boy could work with such a man around?

Daniel remained at the academy only nine months and left because his father had found a cheaper place that he believed would do well enough. The cheaper place was the home of the Reverend Samuel Wood, in Boscawen, six miles distant from the Webster home.

It was on the way to Mr. Wood's place that Ebenezer told Daniel that he intended to send him to college.

"I remember," Daniel wrote many years afterward, "the very hill which we were ascending, through deep snows in a New England sleigh, when my father made known this purpose to me. I could not speak. How could he, I thought, with so large a family, and in such narrow circumstances, think of incurring so great an expense for me? A warm glow ran all over me and I laid my head on my father's shoulder and wept."

The same boy who left the hayfield to pick whortleberries! Yet it should be said that Daniel, in after years, redeemed every one of the promises that he made to his parents. He paid his father's debts and took turns with Ezekiel in supporting their mother after she became a widow, though the mother seems to have preferred to live with Ezekiel most of the time.

The Reverend Mr. Wood, to whom Daniel was now sent, had not much learning himself, but greatly loved it. He was just an ordinary New England clergyman of his day. What he lacked in scholarship, however, he made up in conscientiousness and enthusiasm. If each of his pupils, instead of paying him a dollar a week for board and tuition, had paid him $100, none of them would have received more than he did. Mr. Wood, for a dollar, gave each of them all he had. Daniel quickly got in touch with another circulating library and, in addition to his studies, read a good deal. He said he read "Don Quixote" at one sitting, but how he could have done so, unless he read continuously for three or four days and nights, is difficult to understand. Perhaps what he read was something that had been cut down and compressed for children. Daniel remained with Mr. Wood only six months, at the end of which time, at the age of fifteen, he entered Dartmouth College, "miserably prepared," as he himself afterward said. That was in the fall of 1797. *Age 15.*

He was not well prepared for his collegiate work, and in truth he never could correctly be called a scholar. He was passionately fond of reading and had a wonderful memory.

III

DARTMOUTH COLLEGE was destined to cut a great figure in Daniel Webster's life, not because he went to it to study, but because, a few years later, he made before the Supreme Court of the United States, in defense of this small college's rights, an argument that was both blood-stirring and law-making. The reasoning that he used then is a part of the law of the land now, which we all feel, though we seldom recall whence it came.

Dartmouth, at that time, was not much of a college. We are told that it "had no provision for teaching modern languages." It taught the dead ones though, and Webster learned so much of them that when he was a United States Senator and a famous orator, he paid a man to go over some of his prepared speeches and cut from them some of their Latin words and phrases. Throughout life, Webster could not make a speech without succumbing to the temptation to salt it heavily with Latin. A thing which now would be regarded as ridiculous, the farmers then liked. Understanding no such words themselves, they were proud to vote for men who could use them. Webster, at Dartmouth, became a very good Latin scholar, and, if caught in a tight place, could write a little Greek.

Dartmouth's course in mathematics and the exact sciences was also, we are told, "very meager." Years afterward, Webster said that all he ever learned about higher mathematics "could be placed upon the ball of a gnat's eye without making it wince."

Webster, as a college boy, comes to the imagination. Tall, slim, swarthy. Coal-black hair and big black eyes. Dignified, yet very friendly and full of fun. Punctual in his attendance. A good student, a good fellow, and beloved by everybody, though the girls regarded him as bashful. The characteristics that remained with Webster throughout life were a part of him then. In his intercourse with others he was the soul of courtesy and consideration. He had a sense of humor and liked to laugh. He was a real fellow.

During his first two years, he was a good student, but nobody ever thought of saying that he was the best in his class. The college faculty held him in no higher repute. "At his sophomore exhibition," we are told, "neither of the two principal appointments was assigned to him."

The young gentlemen to whom the assignments were

made have not been heard from since. Webster appears to have done in college about what would be natural to a boy who had it in him to accomplish all that he did as a man. He plunged on the things he liked best and gave the others only just enough attention to pass him with credit. The subjects he liked best happened to be those of which, later in life, he made the most use—literature, history, oratory. Of the long, rolling sentence, he was so enamored that it became a nuisance. "While in college," he said, "I delivered two or three occasional addresses which were published. I trust they are forgotten; they were in very bad taste."

When a puppy first realizes that it has a tail it sometimes whirls rapidly around in an attempt to catch it. Webster's letters, written while he was in college and for some years afterward, remind one of such a puppy. The lad had learned that there are such things as words, and that it is possible to make of them many amazing combinations. Always, too, he was both whimsical and humorous. Once, at least, he began a letter with a postscript, merely, as he said, because nobody had ever done so before. Sometimes he would address a chum as "Good Hervey" or, in the case of his brother, as "Good Zeke." Sometimes, as "Lovely Boy." Never, however, was missing the note of ardent friendship. "Good-by, Jemmy! Always Your Daniel Webster." A little of the village cut-up, a little of the puppy chasing its tail, a good deal more of the honest young fellow bearing witness to his capacity for friendship.

"Jemmy," by the way, was James Hervey Bingham. They were equals then. When Webster was secretary of state, Bingham was a clerk in his department and looked up to him as if he had been a god.

Girls were apparently upon his horizon a good deal

more than he cared to admit, the proof of which is that
he could not keep them out of his letters. One girl had
said that he was bashful. He declared that he would
never do anything to change her opinion. Another girl,
as she was leaving a room in which he was seated, made
an unpleasant remark about him that he overheard.
Webster tried to freeze her with a frown—a "dirty look,"
as we should say today. At a distance down the street,
Webster and a companion saw a girl in a buggy who
looked good to them. Each stood a little more erect, as
they drew near her, prepared to make an interesting discovery. They did. The lady was Webster's sister, dressed
up so that he did not know her. Just before a ball, another young lady stepped on a hoe or an ax and cut her
foot. In the next letter that Daniel wrote to her, he
proceeded to immortalize the event in verse:

> Rust seize the axe, the hoe or spade,
> Which in your foot this gash has made,
> Which cut through kid and silk and skin,
> To spill the blood that was within;
> By which you're forced to creep and crawl
> Nor frisk and frolic at the ball.
>
> But, Clara, Clara! were thy heart
> As tender as thy pedal part;
> From thy sweet lips did love but flow,
> Swift as blood gushes from thy toe,
> So many beaus would not complain
> That all their bows and vows were vain.

Webster could write much worse verse than this and
often did it. Once he wrote a "poem" extolling chewing
tobacco. Usually, however, his subject was girls.

Yet in Webster's boyhood letters was oftentimes much
more than verbosity, rhymed and unrhymed nonsense.
When he was only sixteen or seventeen years of age he
communicated voluminously upon world-politics and

See page 2.

affairs of state. He could not see Napoleon at all—a mere "gasconading" swashbuckler. When old John Adams, who was then President, did right, young Daniel was quick to commend him, but when the President's foot slipped, Daniel was there to set him back on the path. The prospect of Jefferson's election, when it arose, filled the bosom of the stripling with the direst forebodings. As the son of an old Federalist, he had swallowed all of the nonsense about Jefferson's atheism and regarded him as a dangerous character.

Beneath the humor and the whimsicality of Daniel's letters, however, was a heart that was becoming increasingly sad. There he was at college, fixing himself for life, while back at home was his brother, "Good Old Zeke," wrecking his career in the cornfields. The next time he went home, he told Zeke how he felt. They lay in bed together and talked about the matter all night. Zeke would like to go to college, but how could he go? Old Ebenezer needed him to work the farm. The other brothers had all married and gone away. The father, growing old, was less than ever able to do the work himself. The farm had already been mortgaged to send Daniel away. Perhaps a little more could be raised on a mortgage, but would it be right so to load their old father and mother with debt?

Zeke thought it would not be right. Daniel thought it would. Daniel believed that he and his brother, by going to college, could sufficiently increase their earning power to make it possible for them to look after their elders in old age. But it was a hard thing to ask their parents. Zeke did not want to ask.

Daniel had the nerve to go to the front for his brother. As soon as he met his father the next morning, he told him at great length how he felt about Zeke.

Old Ebenezer heard his son in silence. He cared nothing for life except to do for his children. But there were the mother and the two maiden sisters—now growing a little old—who must be considered. Ebenezer finally settled the matter, so far as he was concerned, by saying that the mother should decide. If she was willing to take the chance, he would do so.

Abigail listened while the broken old man, within less than six years of the grave told his brief story. Dan wanted Zeke to go to college. To raise the money to send him would bring them within sight of the poorhouse. She should decide.

Abigail Webster for a moment was silent. Then she replied that she had faith in the boys and that if they would agree to see that the family did not, in later years, come to want, she would consent.

When the neighbors heard what was going on over at the Webster house there was not only criticism but deep resentment. It was bad enough to send Dan to college, but what did old man Webster mean by sending big, burly Zeke, too? Was he trying to put on airs before the neighborhood? Were his children too good to remain on the farm and do the work that other folks did?

Such talk sounds strange now. It was the common thing then, at least in the neighborhood where the Websters lived. The farmers of that day and place were the enemies of liberal education, believing that it tended to create an aristocracy. It was wrong, in their opinion, to seek to elevate by education one member of a family to the comparative disparagement of the others. Every able-bodied young man should be kept on the farm, and colleges maintained solely for the weak and the sickly.

Old Ebenezer, the aging old lion, could not roar and command silence as once he had done, but at least he could hold his ground. Regardless of what the neighbors said, Zeke was forthwith sent away to preparatory school and in 1801 entered Dartmouth just as Daniel was quitting it. In due time, Zeke was graduated, studied law, and became a very good country lawyer.

Daniel Webster left Dartmouth in a blaze of glory, so far as the student body was concerned. But the faculty, in distributing the honors at the commencement exercises, could not quite place Daniel. There were four honors to be awarded, but in each instance there seemed to be a reason why somebody else should be chosen. It was an unfortunate muddle for which perhaps nobody was to blame, though it is obvious that, in this case, the quick insight of the student body was more penetrating than the seasoned judgment of their instructors. It is definitely known that Daniel did not attend the commencement exercises, though the tradition that he tore up his diploma in the faces of the members of the faculty is probably untrue. Even as a boy he had better control.

Through with college forever, Daniel returned to the old home for a few weeks of recreation. In the course of his wanderings about the countryside, he came upon the log house of old John Hanson, at whose home he had nearly starved to death a few years before, because the family had nothing to eat but grass fried in hog lard. The old man received him warmly, talked to him at length, told him what a good boy he was and how good his father had always been. Also he told Daniel what to do.

First, he should avoid the mistake that is made by most college graduates. He should not become a clergyman, a doctor, or a lawyer. Preachers made barely enough to keep them alive. Doctoring was a miserable profession, first because it flourished upon the misfortunes of others

and also because doctors were kept up nights and given
no peace. The law? He would not suggest that to anybody.

Mr. Hanson believed that a bright boy like Daniel,
who had book larnin', could do well if he would follow
in the footsteps of a man who lived where he did when
he was young. That man, by consulting his books, could
find lost property. Farmers who had lost a horse or a
cow willingly paid him three or four dollars for telling
where to find them.

"Daniel," said the old man, "there is not a conjurer
within a hundred miles of this place. The best thing you
can do is to study that and be a conjurer!"

He said, "soon after he left college that he was credited with
more scholarships than he deserved, because of his ability to tell
all that he did know, to the best advantage, and also that
he was careful never to go beyond his depth.

IV

DANIEL WEBSTER decided to study law. In reaching this decision he was moved neither by ambition
nor by a desire to take part in the administration of justice. Poverty had so cowed him that he was content to
keep his aspirations close to earth. What he wanted most
was a living. He knew business might give him not only a
living but riches; on the other hand it might put him on
the sidewalk, while the sheriff placed a padlock upon his
door. Webster preferred something that he believed could
be depended upon, year in and year out, to furnish bread
and butter. And at that, during the next three or four
years, he twice wavered so violently that the law came
near losing him. Whoever believes that Daniel Webster,
from the beginning, always walked, under the light of his
luminous eyes, straight toward his destination, does not
know his Webster. For a time, he was one of the world's
worst wobblers.

Moreover, there is reason to suspect that Webster, from the time he was born to the day of his death, was always a little lazy. There is a type of very able men who do brilliantly—and easily—the big things that are fitted to their abilities—and then go fishing. Webster was apparently one of this type. The things that ordinary men cannot do at all, he did with a flourish and did supremely well. Lesser tasks, the doing of which is necessary to the demonstration of a man's full power, Webster left untouched because they did not interest him.

To show how lightly ambition had touched him, and how utterly inadequate was his estimate of his own latent powers, a story may be told. Near the Webster home in central New Hampshire lived a country lawyer whose plodding practice brought him an annual income of about $1,500. While Webster was studying law, he told a group of young friends that if he could ever become as successful a lawyer as was this country barrister he would be satisfied. His companions sharply remonstrated with him. Such an aspiration was absurd. Had he not been the most brilliant student at Dartmouth?

Webster promptly replied that he had not been the most brilliant student at Dartmouth. There was a lot of nonsense about what he had done at college. Many students were better informed than himself. He had achieved his unwarranted reputation, not intentionally, but by the exercise of a little quiet prudence. When he had told all he knew about the variety of subjects upon which he was superficially informed, he stopped. The other students assumed that he could have said much more. He couldn't. Such was Webster's modest estimate of his abilities as set forth in justification of his small aspirations.

No man ever undertook the wooing of the mistress

Law with much less ardor than did Daniel Webster. If his father and his friends had not urged him, and the law had not seemed likely to assure him a fairly certain living, he would have turned to literature, for the study of which he had a genuine liking. But literature promised neither bread nor meat, so Webster, in his own home town of Salisbury in August, 1802, when he was not yet quite twenty years of age, began the study of law in the office of his father's friend Thomas W. Thompson.

Not long after the young student entered the office, one afternoon when Thompson was out, a client came in. He was a young fellow who wanted to "put the law" on a neighbor. The neighbor was a crusty old gentleman who, not happening to fancy the music that the young man made on a violin at a husking-bee, suddenly had seized the musical instrument and crashed it against a wall, to the great injury and damage of the plaintiff. Webster brought an action of trespass for breaking the violin. It was his first case.

As the fall days wore on, Webster made out writs, read law, read history, the English classics, and Latin, and finished many an afternoon with his dog, his gun, or his fishing-rod. He was beginning to indulge a fondness for outdoor sports that remained with him throughout life. Sometimes he went abroad without dog, gun, or tackle. He liked to sit in an open field, look up at the sky, and let his mind run wherever it would. This tendency too, continued with him throughout life. While Webster had a great capacity for friendship, he liked also to be much alone, out in the country, loafing and "inviting his soul."

But such pleasant days were not to last long. Webster's old enemy, Poverty, soon found him out. Zeke, up in Dartmouth, was short of cash. Daniel wanted to cease

studying law for a time and teach school to earn money
to give to Zeke. Old Ebenezer, loath to see Daniel's studies
interrupted, went to see the governor of the state to ask
aid in obtaining a loan. In this way, a little more was
borrowed. It was not enough to last long. Before
winter had fairly set in, it became apparent that Zeke
would soon need money again. Daniel therefore promptly
accepted an offer that had come to him to go to what
is now Fryeburg, Maine—though it was then in Massachusetts—to teach school, at a salary of $350 a year.
He soon obtained a job copying deeds, two hours a
night, four nights a week, for which he was paid two
dollars. This was just enough to pay his board. At the
end of the first quarter he gave his entire salary, about
$112, to Zeke. Moreover, he delivered it personally, mak-
ing the long journey from Fryeburg and return on a horse.

As Daniel returned to his work in the school the lure
of the law slackened its weak hold upon him and he began to wonder whether he had acted wisely in considering
it at all. All of his doubts and fears he put upon paper
and sent to a few of his old college friends. Should he
spend his days teaching school in a kind of comfortable
privacy, or should he go back to the law? What was the
law, anyway? No business for a man like himself. Its
practice was certain to harrow his feelings as he beheld
dishonesty or misfortune. Nor did the idea of "squeezing
his living" from poor folks much appeal to him. He
assumed that he would have to live on poor folks, because
he said "rich folks seldom go to law." The law, he admitted, was calculated to draw forth the powers of the
mind, but what about its effects upon the heart? Would
it bring out the best in a man or the worst? He was inclined to believe that the practice of the law would tend
to make a man callous and unscrupulous.

"The talent with which Heaven has intrusted me is small, very small," he wrote, "yet I feel responsible for the use of it, and am not willing to pervert it to purposes reproachful and unjust; nor to hide it, like the slothful servant, in a napkin."

Daniel was doing some hard thinking. He had to think hard, because the school year was drawing to a close, and the school trustees liked his work so well that they had offered him, if he would remain another year, almost a doubled salary and a house to live in. When the Fourth of July came around, he was asked to deliver a public address, which he did and for which he was paid five dollars. The schoolmaster was popular. But he must decide what he would do.

Webster still did not know. To one friend he wrote that he believed he would drop law and spend his life as a schoolmaster. To another he wrote that he "imagined" he would take one more whirl at the law, praying God, meanwhile, to fortify him against its temptations. At this time, Webster was opening school every morning with prayer, and his conscience was very close to him. Thin as a rail, hollow-cheeked, solemn-eyed, he had the mind of an old man. He would go back to the law, without a thought of eminence to be obtained, praying only that he might always be honest, faithful to his clients and to his conscience.

Webster returned to the law, but he returned to it as a timid keeper would return to a cage of hungry lions. Back in Salisbury again, in the office of Thomas W. Thompson, he laid aside his law book to write to a friend:

"The morality of the profession is, too, a matter of doubt, or rather it is a matter of no doubt at all. Mr. Bennet says that a lawyer who preserves his integrity unspotted deserves a place in the calendar of saints. If this list were entirely made up of lawyers, I fancy it would be a short, a very short list; not so long, if you take the whole world over, as a catalogue of freshmen. And yet this is the profession to which I am devoting myself."

Daniel was taking his medicine, but with a wry face. That he took it at all was probably because of some in-inertia. Food was good for empty stomachs and the law seemed tolerably certain to supply food. A more vigorous character would have kicked over the traces, worked at what he wanted to work, and the Dartmouth College address and the reply to Hayne would have had to be made by somebody else. Because he did not know exactly what he wanted to do, and did know that from time to time throughout life he would need nourishment, Webster stuck to his job, until finally he came to like it.

Webster remained in Mr. Thompson's office two years and then, at the earnest entreaty of Ezekiel, went to Boston in search of a lawyer's office in which to study. [1804] Daniel had thought of going to New York, but Ezekiel told him that the cost of living in New York was too high, that it was a bad town anyway, and that if he would come to Boston, where Ezekiel was teaching in a private school, his brother would help him get started. Ezekiel told him that if he would spend an hour and a half each day teaching Latin and Greek to eight pupils, it would pay him enough for his board in "as genteel a boarding-house as you can wish, or the place affords." Ezekiel was very emphatic about it. Daniel should not hesitate. Another such opportunity might not come to him in his entire life. "Come," finally urged Ezekiel, "and if you don't find everything to your liking I will carry you back to Salisbury with a chaise of six and pay you for your time."

Daniel went to Boston. The first law office that he

visited, craving the privilege of being a clerk, cast him out—didn't want him or anybody. Webster, in after years, smiled at the recollection. In the second office he was more fortunate. It was that of the Honorable Christopher Gore, a man of great renown who had just returned from England where he had served as a commissioner under Jay's Treaty. Webster did not know Gore. Gore, of course, did not know Webster. But Webster had an enthusiastic young friend—a former classmate named Bradley—who may have read of the two nervy young men that visited Franklin when he was Minister to France, each of whom introduced the other, though Franklin had never before seen either of them. At any rate, Bradley introduced Webster to Gore, and Webster introduced Bradley. This done, the friend departed, leaving Webster standing alone in the middle of the floor with his hopes, his fears, and a degree of modesty that amounted almost to diffidence. Gore was looking at him and he feared the worst.

Webster took the situation immediately in hand. If possible, get over the next two minutes without being thrown out. His friend had been kind enough to introduce him, and while he would feel much honored to be permitted to study in Mr. Gore's office, he had not thought of obtruding himself "at this time," without proper letters of introduction.

Gore's face relaxed a little, but he said that his office was hardly the place for a young student, inasmuch as most of his business consisted of consultation. A young man would learn more in an office that had a large commercial practice.

Daniel replied that he was quite sensible of the truth of all that Mr. Gore had said, yet he would nevertheless prefer, if he might do so, to complete the study of his profession right where he was. It would be a great honor.

Gore mellowed a little more. How were Daniel's father and mother and Senator Thompson of Salisbury? All well? Very glad, very glad. Old Captain Eb was an honor to the state, his wife a most estimable woman, and Senator Thompson an ornament to his profession.

"Sit down, Mr. Webster, sit down," exclaimed Gore in the midst of his questions, suddenly aware that his young caller was still standing in the middle of the floor.

Mr. Gore then said that the request made by Daniel was very reasonable and required no apology. He did not intend to fill his office with clerks, yet he might take another. In fact, Daniel might just as well hang up his hat right then, go into another room and begin his reading, sending at his convenience to New Hampshire for his letters of introduction and recommendation.

"You say you come here to study and not to waste time," said Gore. "I shall take you at your word."

Webster entered Gore's office in July, 1804, and remained until March, 1805. He had not been there long when again the temptation came to him to forsake his studies, abandon the law, and do something else. The clerk of his father's court had died and the other two judges, desiring perhaps to please old Judge Webster as well as his son, had offered the place to Daniel. It was the best paid office in the state—fifteen hundred dollars a year. Daniel had no doubt as to what he should do. Manna was falling from the skies.

The next morning his step was springy and his face beaming when he entered Mr. Gore's office.

"You are in good plight this morning," said the seasoned old lawyer to the youth of twenty-two. "Have you good news?"

What a question! Had Daniel good news? He had the best news in the world; news that Mr. Gore, as a warm friend of his clerk would be delighted to hear. Overnight, affluence had flown into his window. No more worrying about the future. A clerkship in his father's court at fifteen hundred dollars a year.

The elder man heard the youth in silence. When Daniel had finished speaking, the congratulations that he expected did not come.

"You are a little excited about this office now," said Gore. "Go into the other room and by-and-by I will have a talk with you about it."

An hour later Gore called him back. The tone of the elder man was now as conciliatory as the younger man's had been when they first met. Mr. Gore could understand perfectly how his clerk felt. After a long struggle against poverty, the salary of the clerkship was a great temptation to him. But had he considered all the facts in the case? His struggle against poverty, however hard, was all but over. Webster had "got up the hill." His education was secure, and he was about ready to be admitted to the bar. A court clerkship was no place for such a man. Gore had an idea that Daniel Webster's mission in life would be to utter words for other men to take down, not to take down the words of other men.

It was a strange situation—a distinguished lawyer who, a little later became governor of Massachusetts and then United States Senator pleading with a young man not to wreck his career. Quickly Gore changed from admonition to flattery. Daniel was such a promising young man! Who could tell what honors might await him? Shifting as suddenly to the voice of command, he exclaimed: "Before you leave me I am going to extort a promise from you to decline it. If in five or six years you do not admit that my advice is good I will make up the difference to you."

Christopher Gore did a good day's work that day. Daniel Webster, much against his own judgment, promised not to give up the law.

The next and most difficult thing to do was to break the news to old Judge Webster. He was an old man with bad health steadily becoming worse. All his life he had suffered from poverty, as he was still suffering from it. Fifteen hundred dollars a year was a colossal sum, as great, a friend of the family later said, as ten thousand would have been in 1850. All of the old man's sons had gone out into the world and he and their mother were left alone. Fifteen hundred dollars a year would place them in comfortable circumstances for the rest of their lives. He had been long looking forward to the time when this offer might come to Daniel, and now it had come.

Daniel Webster, about to undertake the business of placating his father, needed money. He went to a friend and asked for three or four hundred dollars, promising to repay it "some time or other." The money was lent him. Daniel hired a horse and sleigh and started over the hills and down the dales from Boston to Salisbury, New Hampshire.

The sun was just setting when he reached the old home. The father was resting in his armchair in his little room. Before either of them could speak, Daniel noticed how pale his father was, how sunken were his cheeks, and how unusually black seemed his eyes. Old Ebenezer was overjoyed to see the boy and immediately told him that he had got the office for him as clerk of the court. He was particularly pleased that the other judges had, of their own volition, given it to him.

"Thank you, father," said Daniel. "I must go to the other judges and tell them I am much obliged to them."

The tired old man seemed to smell a mouse. He

straightened himself up in his chair. His eyes began to blaze.

"Daniel, Daniel," he exclaimed, "don't you mean to take that office?"

"No, indeed, father," replied Daniel. "I hope I can do much better than that. I mean to use my tongue in the courts, not my pen; to be an actor, not a register of other men's acts. I hope yet, sir, to astonish your Honor in your own court by my professional attainments."

The old man rocked his chair, ever so little. His eyes flashed and then softened, still he did not speak. For a full minute he looked at his son and then slowly said:

"Daniel, in the long struggle with poverty and adverse fortune that your mother and I have made to give you and Ezekiel an education, we have often talked over these sacrifices and the prospects of our children. Your mother has often said to me that she had no fear about Ezekiel; that he had fixed and steady habits, and an indomitable energy. She had no doubt of his success in life. As for you, she did not know. Either you would be something or nothing, she did not know which. I think that your mother was a prophetess, and that the problem is solved tonight. You have fulfilled her prophecy—you have come to nothing."

Daniel took the shot like a man, and stood his ground. Never again was the court clerkship ever mentioned by the father. Daniel had reached that time which comes to every boy when his parents are convinced that he is headed for the rocks. He also had learned, what he had likely long suspected, that Zeke was his mother's favorite son. She had noted, from Daniel's childhood, how eager and ready he always was to stop work on the farm and go fishing, wherefore she admired Zeke's "indomitable energy."

Webster returned to Boston, and in March, 1805, Mr. Gore took him into court, moved his admission to the bar, said that he was the most remarkable young man with whom he had ever come into contact and predicted he would make a great name for himself. Daniel Webster was at last a lawyer. More than that, he was a changed man. There was to be no more talk about the disreputable nature of the profession of the law, because it dealt with the "very refuse and remnant of mankind." Gore's prediction that he would yet make a great name seemed also to give him a different view of himself. Perhaps he could do something worth while in the world. At once he began to take himself more seriously and to work harder.

admitted to the Bar 1805

Webster opened his first law office in the small town of Boscawen, six miles distant from his father's home, which he chose because it was so near his father. For fifteen dollars a year he rented an upper room in a little red shack, the stairs of which were on the outside. The office was remarkable chiefly because it contained less furniture and more books than did the usual office of its kind.

He remained in this office more than two years. He earned less than a thousand dollars during the entire period, but the changes that took place in his mind were worth a fortune to him. Having at last gained respect for his profession, he pursued it eagerly and diligently. What he particularly wanted to lay hold of were the general principles that underlie the law. The details could wait. General principles first. Some of the details never were picked up. But so thorough eventually became his knowledge of the general principles of law that it was his custom, when he had become the greatest advocate in America, to write out what as a matter of common sense the law in any given case should be, and then direct his assistants to look up the books and find it. In this, he developed a remarkable capacity.

Webster's first appearance in court was before his own father. Under the rules of the court he had no right to speak at all, since he had not been in practice two years, but the rule was waived, and Daniel spoke. What the case was about, no one now knows, but the elder Webster said it was a "very creditable effort for which nobody need be ashamed." Most of Webster's cases, in the beginning were little things involving the straying of live stock from one farmer's land to another, but as Webster became better grounded in the law and his cases took on more importance, it began to be noted that his words were tinged with fire. The impassioned orator was stepping forth. Courtrooms rang. Jurors and spectators could hardly believe that such eloquence could proceed from one whom most of them had known all his life. One neighbor said that Webster, when speaking, had "an eye as black as death." The thing that took Webster out of Boscawen and sent him hurrying away toward his destiny was a speech that he made in a murder case before the superior court in Grafton County. The plight of the prisoner was so desperate, because of his obvious guilt, that after hearing the evidence, his senior counsel left it to Webster to address the jury. Webster jumped into the gap, and while he did not save his client, he made so tremendous an effort that before he left the courtroom he was retained in nearly all the cases standing on the docket.

V

DANIEL WEBSTER in 1807 removed to Portsmouth where he soon came into professional collision with Jeremiah Mason, a man destined to have a
very considerable influence upon all his later life. Perhaps
the most important thing that Mason taught Webster
was to use small words, short sentences, and get his
thoughts down to the level of those whom he wished to
influence. Webster had brought with him a florid style,
with a marked tendency to use many more words than
were necessary to bring out an idea. Mason, on the contrary, "had a habit of standing quite near to the jury, so
near that he might have laid a finger on the foreman's
nose," and speaking in a conversational manner, which the
least intelligent among them could understand. Since
Webster's most important business in life was to be the
unleashing of winged words this was an important lesson
to learn.

Mason, years afterward, told how he became acquainted with Webster. Mason had been retained to defend a prominent citizen in one of the neighboring cities,
who was accused of forgery. He had heard that the case
had been prepared for the attorney-general by a wonderfully able young fellow who was "as black as the ace of
spades." Mason thought it well to be careful, but of course
did not worry. When the case came to trial the attorney-
general who was addicted to drinking, was "ill" and the
other prosecutors asked that Webster be permitted to conduct the prosecution. Mason assented to this readily, believing that he ought to have an easy time of it.

"We were introduced," said Mason, "and went at
it, and I soon found that I had no light work on my hands.

He examined his witnesses and shaped his case with so much skill that I had to exert every faculty I possessed. I got the man off, but it was as hard a day's work as I ever did in my life. When the verdict was announced, I went up to the dock and whispered to the prisoner, as the sheriff let him out, to be off for Canada and never to put himself within the reach of that young Webster again."

We shall see so much of Webster and Mason in close conflict, during the next few years that it is well to take a look at them. Webster was twenty-four years old, Mason forty. In stature as in intellect, Mason was a giant. Height, six feet seven inches. Movements, slow and and deliberate. Shoulders always a little stooped as if he disliked to tower so much above the crowd, which, in fact, he did. Head small, in comparison with his body, forehead somewhat retreating, face as heavy as that of Dr. Johnson. Apparently of sluggish temperament. Seated in court, his body was slouched down, though his eyes were always keenly alert. As he slowly arose to address the court it seemed for a time as if he would never cease rising, so tall was he. Of rhetoric he had none, nor any gestures. Pronunciation uncertain and oftentimes quaint, but in simplicity unexcellable; in lucidity and logic superb.

A master of the common law, he was also a master of common sense. Whatever he saw clearly he made jurors see, and few there were who were not moved by the driving force of his reasoning powers. Win or lose, an adversary knew that he had been in a fight. "I have some of your pounding in my bones yet," Webster playfully wrote from Washington in 1830, "and don't care about any more until that wears out."

For many years Webster and Mason were on opposite sides of the most important cases in New England. Once when Mason asked Webster which side of a certain case he was on, Webster replied, "I don't know; take your choice." Mason was in the United States Senate when Webster was in the House of Representatives. Mason lived to be eighty years of age, and at his death Webster delivered a notable eulogy of him.

Webster told Rufus Choate that he would rather meet, combined in a single case, all of the best lawyers he had ever met in the state and federal courts, than to meet Jeremiah Mason single-handed.

A case in which Webster and Mason were pitted against each other and in which Webster exhibited his shrewdness as a cross-examiner was that of a poor shoe-maker named Brown against Matthew Bramble, a rich man of Portsmouth. The rich man was a crook, and it is possible that the poor man was too, inasmuch as Bramble, the man of means, had given to Brown, the man of shoes, a bond obligating Bramble to pay Brown for the duration of his life, one hundred dollars a year to say nothing about a cloud upon a certain parcel of real estate owned by Bramble.

Bramble paid Brown one hundred dollars a year for a good many years, until finally he became tired of it. Would Brown accept a lump sum and call the deal off? Brown would do no such thing. There was nothing to do, it seemed, but to keep on paying, and Bramble continued to pay. But one time, when he was paying, an idea came to him. When it came time to indorse on the bond—as Bramble was accustomed to do, because Brown was un-able to write—the amount paid—he wrote "one thousand dollars," instead of "one hundred dollars," and added: "In full consideration of and satisfaction of this bond." Brown knew nothing about it, not being able to read, and all went well for a year.

At the end of the year, Brown went around to Mr. Bramble to get his money. He did not get it. Money? What was Mr. Brown talking about? Did he not remember that Mr. Bramble, a year before, had paid one thousand dollars in full payment of the bond? Mr. Brown remembered no such thing. Mr. Bramble retorted that Mr. Brown could look upon the bond and see the indorsement which he had witnessed with his own mark. Brown looked, and the indorsement was there. But he knew he had received no thousand dollars. He knew Mr. Bramble was trying to cheat him and he did not intend, if he could help it, to be cheated.

Brown went to Jeremiah Mason to get him to take his case and sue Bramble. Mr. Mason was very sorry but he was Mr. Bramble's attorney and could do nothing for Mr. Brown. The shoemaker made further inquiries and learned that there was a promising young attorney in town named Daniel Webster. He went to him. Webster took his case.

Webster had no actual facts upon which to go, but he felt in his bones that Bramble was dishonest, while the story of the shoemaker impressed him as truth. Webster's first act was to send Bramble a letter that promptly brought Bramble to Webster's office.

The rich gentleman was quite haughty. He would like to know if Webster intended to take up a case of that kind in Portsmouth. If so, the dark gentleman whom he was addressing apparently did not know upon which side his bread was buttered.

The dark gentleman was quiet but firm. Mr. Brown had come to him and told him a story that he believed to be true. Unless Mr. Bramble settled, he would be sued.

Bramble had been gone only a few minutes when Mr.

Mason appeared in Webster's office. He thought Webster had made a mistake. Bramble was a man of influence. It could not be that Brown was telling the truth. Bramble would not do a thing like that.

"Bramble has done just such a thing as that," replied Webster, "and I shall try the suit."

Webster said that when the case came to trial he was never more badly prepared. It was Brown's word against Bramble's. Brown's plight looked so doubtful that Mason, in his opening, said it was a "foolish case."

After Webster had put on his side, which consisted, for the most part, of Brown's testimony, Mason called to the stand a man named Lovejoy. Webster looked up—almost startled. He had seen that man in many and many a courtroom—always a witness for somebody.

While Lovejoy's testimony was proceeding, the court took a recess for luncheon. As Webster walked out of the room a friend of Brown's buttonholed him. "Just before Lovejoy went into court," said the man, "I saw him talking in the hall with Bramble, and Bramble gave a paper to him."

"Very important," said Webster. "Don't say a word about it to anybody."

At two o'clock the judge resumed his place upon the bench, the clerk rapped for order, Lovejoy took his place in the witness chair and continued his story. About eight or ten months before, he said, he had gone to Brown's shop to have his shoes mended. In talking with Brown the subject of the bond came up. Lovejoy asked Brown why he did not sell Bramble's bond back to him. Brown replied that he had already sold it back to Bramble for one thousand dollars. Lovejoy, in mentioning Brown, always referred to him as the "said Brown."

Webster said to himself, "I will now make a spoon or

spoil a horn." He took his pen from behind his ear, strode from his chair to the witness stand and shouted at Lovejoy: "Sir, give me the paper from which you are testifying."

Lovejoy reached into his pocket, started to withdraw a paper, then changed his mind and tried to put it back. Webster was too quick for him. He seized the paper and began to read it to himself.

The room was in a turmoil. Mason claimed for his client the protection of the court. The judge asked Webster for an explanation. Webster who, by this time, had finished reading the paper, read aloud what was on it. It was Lovejoy's testimony, carefully written down for him by Bramble.

Court adjourned, Mason told his client he should make the best settlement he could with Webster. Webster made him give a new bond, amply secured, pay Brown five hundred dollars and pay also a sum equal to Webster's fee, which he made as high as his conscience would permit.

The information that Bramble had been seen to give Lovejoy a paper had made Webster suspicious, but what had sent him into action was Lovejoy's repeated reference to Brown as the "said Brown." That was not the way a witness would naturally speak.

Webster and Mason fought in court but traveled the country roads in peace and amity. Sometimes they traveled on business, sometimes on pleasure; sometimes they hunted, sometimes they fished; but always and wherever they were they talked. The delightful evenings were spent in the barroom of the country hotel. "Barroom" is correct. The word is taken from the record. In speaking or writing about what he did in barrooms, both at this period and during the remainder of his life, Webster usually made it appear that he had gone to the bar to get a pitcher of ice-water or something for his wife. Probably he did sometimes get ice-water for her. Certain it is that he also got fire-water for himself.

Old Christopher Gore got him into the habit when Webster was studying law in his office. Webster, thirty years later, told the story at a small dinner party in New York. Gore had noticed that Webster looked pale and asked him about his boarding-house. Webster said that the meals were not particularly good. Gore advised him to take a little wine with his dinners. Webster replied that he was too poor to buy wine. Gore volunteered to send over a bottle once in a while. Webster drank the wine and liked it. As Webster's income increased he conceded more and more to his liking for tempting food and pleasing drinks. In a few years, this slim young man not only filled out but began to be a little corpulent. Drink and a fondness for rich food played a very important part in the life of Daniel Webster.

Webster's habit of drifting into the barrooms of the country hotels at which he stayed once enabled him to see a great celebrity—old General John Stark, the Revolutionary hero who went into one of the battles of the Revolution declaring that he would, before night, annihilate the enemy "or Molly Stark will be a widow." Stark, at the time Webster encountered him, was about eighty years old, but inasmuch as he was destined to live to be ninety-four, he was still able to get down to the tavern every night and spend a pleasant hour with his friends. Stark lived in Hookset, now Manchester, New Hampshire, and the tavern where Webster stopped was near his home.

It was a cold, rainy night when Webster reached Hookset, put up his horse, had dinner, and then strolled into the barroom. Half a dozen old settlers were sitting around the fire drinking what Webster described as "flip." Stark was one of them.

Webster sat down by the fire. The presence of a stranger brought silence. Webster noticed that "old Stark was getting into a doze and did not seem to notice anything." The others soon resumed their talk. One of them asked another what he thought a certain man was worth. Five hundred dollars was the guess. The other one did not believe it.

The buzz of conversation soon began to arouse the old general. He straightened himself a bit in his chair, blinked his eyes, and said:

"Well, I don't know what *he* is worth, but I know what *I* am worth. They say a thing is worth what it will fetch. If that's so I am worth just forty pounds, for I once fetched that. In the French War I was taken by the Indians, and they took forty pounds as my ransom."

Everybody laughed. The noise aroused the general a little more. Looking around, he saw, for the first time, a stranger sitting at the fire. He bluntly asked Webster who he was, where he came from and where he was going.

The old man's curiosity seemed satisfied for a moment and he lapsed into silence. Still his mind was slowly working.

"What Websters do you belong to?" he asked.

"The Salisbury Websters," Daniel replied.

"Are you in any way related to old Captain Eb?"

"Slightly, sir; he was my father."

At this Stark turned around.

"Are you a son of old Captain Eb? Let me look. Why, I declare! Well, I am inclined to think you may be. In the war we could not tell whether Captain Webster's face was a natural color or blackened by powder. You must be his son for you are a damned sight blacker than he was."

Webster joined in the laugh that followed at his expense and, even after Stark had fallen to sleep again, continued to talk and drink with the others.

Two years before Webster had been teaching school and opening each morning session with prayer. Now Webster, at twenty-five, sipping "flip" with old General Stark and a group of sots, was satisfying his curiosity. Another new experience had come knocking at his door, and he had bade it enter. Very likely he did not care much for the "flip"; it is quite likely, too, that he did not, at the time, care much for the society of the old general and his sots. Such experiences have to be put away in memory and ripened for a few decades before they become delightful. When Webster told the story of that night, General Stark and his companions had been in their graves for many a year, and the young man with the cavernous eyes had become an old man, laden with honors, debts, and physical disabilities; but to the last he loved to tell this story of the aged soldier.

Nothing about Webster was more interesting than the manner in which he crossed the one-way bridge that leads from adolescence to maturity. Instead of running amuck, it seemed as if a great peace had begun to steal over him. Perhaps it was the only peace of the kind that he was destined ever to have, inasmuch as it arose from a sense of financial well-being. He had gained a little upon the dogs of poverty that had tracked him from the cradle, and the dogs of debt that were to run him to his grave had not yet appeared. "I have one hundred and thirty-four dear delightfuls in my pocket," he gleefully wrote to a friend. His younger and favorite sister Sally was

filled with solemn pride when she learned that her big
brother had been paid seven dollars a day for several
days to accompany a gentleman on a business trip. Probably a little better bottle of wine went on the table the
night after he returned home. The wine was for the
weak Webster who, throughout life, we shall see standing
beside the strong one. The weak Webster was at first
so weak that we must wonder whether he would ever have
emerged at all if there had been no Christopher Gore to
keep him at the law. The strong Daniel Webster, during
his young manhood, kept the weaker one under, yet from
the first, he must have loved him a little. Webster was so
strong that he gave way slowly, but his weakness was so
deeply seated that he did give way.

The amazing thing about Webster's youth, however,
was not his drinking, but the velocity and the vigor with
which his young mind went out until it encompassed the
world. We see him when he was twenty-four years old,
writing a political pamphlet addressed to old Whigs,
urging them to stand fast against the possibility of the
election of Jefferson. A few years later we hear his young
voice raised against Jefferson's embargo. Shifting his
mind from Washington to Paris, he fills a letter to a
friend with observations upon the world-shaking revolution engineered by Bonaparte. We hear him making
speeches throughout southern New Hampshire, and note
that his sentences, as they become more compact, are beginning to sizzle. If old Gore taught Webster to drink,
Jeremiah Mason taught him to focus his mind, get his
words down to earth, and shoot them to the exact spot
where he wished them to go. When Webster seized upon
simplicity he was in the way of becoming an orator, and it
was the combination of oratory and statesmanship that
made him. He had a good mind, beautified.

Wrote pamphlet
on the embargo
question

WEBSTER AND WOMEN 53

Webster, at twenty-five, was an able lawyer, rising rapidly in his profession, and at thirty, though he had never cared much about politics, he was in congress.

1812 Elected member of thirteenth congress taking his seat May of 1813.

VI

WHEN Webster was twenty-six years old, he was married to a woman twenty-seven. In his autobiographical sketch, he dismissed the matter in the briefest possible way: "June 24, 1808, I was married." *Married in Salisbury. Grace Fletcher*

What Webster thought of women, love and matrimony was more fully set forth in the letters he had written, during the preceding few years, to some of his close friends.

From the first, Webster attracted women more than women attracted him. Webster incited in women an instantaneous respect, tinged with awe. His appearance was captivating—hair, forehead, eyes—wonderful! His manner was both ingratiating and mystifying. He said a little so beautifully, why did not he say more? Polite, deferential, courteous—but cautious. When Webster had said enough to suit himself he said no more. He was a pastmaster of the art of stopping when there was still time to stop, which to some of his women friends was tantalizing. It is true that he twice took marriage vows, but, so far as he was concerned, with reservations. There was never any scandal connected with his name, but nobody knew better than he did how to enjoy a night off, and these nights became more numerous as he grew older. Webster loved his home; still he did not want to stay in it all the while, nor did he take his wife everywhere he went. He liked to spend much of his off-time with men.

It was when Webster was in college that he discovered

that approximately half of the population was composed of a strange, shy people called girls. He wrote about them frequently and when he was nineteen thought for a brief moment that he would marry one of them. Then the idea of marriage seemed to go out of his mind—at any rate it went out of his letters—until he was about twenty-five, when he discussed it, not with regard to himself but in the abstract. Only once did he draw himself into the picture and then rather crudely.

"The example of my friends," he wrote two years before he was married, "sometimes excites me, and certain narratives I hear of you induce me to inquire why the deuce female flesh and blood was not made for me as well as others; but reasons, good or bad, suppress hope and stifle incipient resolution."

A year later, under cover of what was perhaps supposed to be another general statement, Webster nevertheless disclosed part of his mind with great clearness:

"A wife, I take it," he said, "reverently be it spoken, is like a burning-glass, which concentrates every ray of affection that emanates from a husband's heart. We single dogs have attachments which are dispersed over society, our friendships are scattered all over the world, and we love at a thousand places at the same moment; but you husbands carry all your wares to the same market. You have one bank in which you deposit all your tender sentiments, wherefore I hold you all pardonable for forgetting your friends.

"Now, all of this is very pretty," the letter continued, "but while I thus philosophize, my heart is in my throat and tells me at every syllable that I lie. It tells me that its attachment to any one object, however ardent, however near approaching to adoration, could never sever the ties that hold it to its friends, and that in the commerce of affection there can be no monopoly; it rebels against the doctrine of concentration aforesaid, and kicks the business of the burning-glass to the devil."

The woman who eventually landed the cautious Webster was Miss Grace Fletcher. He met her in 1807 on a visit to his old home town of Salisbury where her married sister lived. Miss Fletcher was the daughter of a preacher. She was very religious, had a good mind, a fine bearing, and was always exceedingly proud of her husband. Sometimes, in after years, upon a notable occasion, tears would glisten in her eyes as Webster's oratory, rising to great heights, so wrought up the emotions of those who heard him that, for the moment, they knew not whether to scream or faint. All eyes were upon him—and he was her man.

A woman with such a husband could do only one of two things—she could idolize him or be jealous of him because nature had done so much more for him than it had for her. Webster's wife never doubted which course to take. If he had kicked his burning-glass to the devil, she had nevertheless taken care to keep her own always near her heart. Nor did she lose by so doing. Webster made her very happy. She was not destined to live to be old, and in due time her place was to be taken by another; but her son Fletcher said that when Daniel Webster died —his second wife weeping beside his bed—he uttered, among his last sentences, the "beloved name" of his first wife, who had then been dead almost twenty-five years.

The five or six years that Webster and his young wife continued to live in Portsmouth were perhaps the happiest of his life. A long time afterward, he referred to them as "very happy years." His law business was flourishing, his health had at last become dependable, the circle of admiring friends ever increasing. The only sorrow that came to him during this period was the death of Sally, the little sister with whom he had fled his father's hayfield to pick whortleberries. Sally died in her early twenties, but her place was soon taken by Grace, the first child of Daniel and the preacher's daughter. She was the image of her father except that she had red cheeks to go with her black hair and big eyes. As she grew into little girlhood, she wound more and more tightly the tendrils around her father's heart. He was pleased, when he came home at night and sat by his own fireside, to have little Grace pull up her small chair and prattle about the pictures in her book.

The long struggle to get an education and gain a foothold in the world had at last justified itself. Every doubt had been dissolved, every question answered. Webster's way, henceforth, promised to be along a strait path—and a country path at that. He would practice the solid profession that in youth he had chosen as most likely to yield him a living—and die, as he expected to live, a country lawyer.

So Webster believed a few months before he left the country forever.

VII

IN November, 1812, Daniel Webster was elected to the Thirteenth Congress as the representative of the Portsmouth (New Hampshire) district, and on May 24, 1813, he took his seat. He was elected as a <u>Federalist</u>, which meant that he espoused the political principles of Washington rather than those of Jefferson. The war with England was in progress, and he was against it. Webster be-

Now Daniel Webster passed through all the stages of the "sophomoric" disease of the mind, as he passed safely through the measles, the chicken-pox and other eruptive maladies incident to childhood and youth. The process, however, by which he purified his style from this taint, and made his diction at least as robust and as manly, as simple and as majestic, as the nature it expressed, will reward a little study.

GRACE FLETCHER WEBSTER

Webster's first wife and the mother of all his children
From a painting by Chester Harding

he mature style of Webster is perfect of its kind, being in words the
press image of his mind and character, — plain, terse, clear,
rcible; and rising from the level of lucid statements and
guments into passages of superlative eloquence only when his
hole nature is stirred by some grand sentiment of freedom,
atriotism, justice, humanity, or religion, which absolutely lifts
im, by its own inherent force and inspiration, to a region
love that in which his mind habitually lives & moves.

At the same time it will be observed that these thrilling
assages, which the boys of four generations have ever been
delighted to declaim in their shrillest tones, are strictly
illustrative of the main purpose of the speech in which they
ffear. They are not mear purple patches of rhetoric,

loosely stitched on the home spun gray of the reasoning, but they seem to be interwoven with it and to be a vital part of it.

Indeed one can hardly decide, in reading these magnificent bursts of eloquence in connection with what precedes and follows them, whether the effect is due to the logic of the orator becoming suddenly morally impassioned, or to his moral passion becoming suddenly logical.

What gave Webster his influence over the opinions of the people of New England was, first his power of so "putting things" that everybody could understand his statements; secondly, his power of so framing his arguments that all the steps from one point to another, in a logical series, could be clearly apprehended by every intelligent farmer or mechanic who had a thoughtful interest in the affairs of the country; and thirdly, his power of inflaming the sentiment of patriotism in all honest and well-intentioned men by overwhelming, appeals to that sentiment.

Perhaps to those sources of influence may be added another which many eminent statesmen have lacked. With all his great superiority to average men in force and breadth of mind, he had a genuine respect for the intellect, as well as for the manhood of the average man.

came as severe a critic of the government as did Lincoln, when a member of congress, during the war with Mexico.

Some men spend their lives trying to get to congress and never get there, Webster made two moves and was in. The first move was a speech. The second was something that he wrote against the war, at the request of his neighbors, and addressed to the President of the United States. The speech (a part of the Fourth of July celebration in Portsmouth in 1812) brought him an opportunity to write the memorial to Mr. Madison and the memorial brought him, almost overnight, a nomination for congress.

Within thirty days after his Fourth of July oration the people of Rockingham County, convinced that something must be done to bring directly to the attention of the President the fact that they opposed the war and wished him quickly to bring it to a close, called a meeting, and a committee was appointed to draft a memorial to President Madison. Webster was placed on this committee. He was almost the youngest one on it, but to him was given the task of putting into written words what the people wanted to say. What he wrote is known in history as the "Rockingham Memorial."

Again Webster showed of what fine material he was made and the amazing extent to which he had so quickly developed. The address that he drafted to the President was couched in the respectful terms that should always characterize an address to the President of the United States. It was dignified, restrained—but emphatic. The administration should not have gone into the war in the first place; if it was determined to go in it should have had the prudence to prepare itself in advance to wage successful war; and having no business in the war anyway, we should seek a speedy, honorable, just peace, rather than continue to play the part of Napoleon's ally.

Webster had said in the address exactly what the people of Rockingham County wanted him to say. A few weeks later they nominated him for congress, and in the November following triumphantly elected him.

In passing through New York on his way to Washington, Webster must have seen that Webster met in the house of representatives two men whom he was destined to know better. One was Henry Clay. The other was John C. Calhoun. Clay was the speaker of the house. Calhoun was gathering the fagots with which to light the fires of the Civil War.

Italian Renaissance Building — The new City Hall just completed.

Webster, when he assumed office, did not choose modestly to take a back seat to give older members an opportunity to perform the pressing business of the day. Nor did he boldly rush in with something half-baked. Instead, he introduced a resolution calling upon the administration to divulge certain very pertinent information. Did or did not the administration, when it declared war against England, have documentary proof that France had withdrawn her inhibitions against American commerce? Or had the administration merely accepted the verbal statement of a French minister? There was a suspicion that France had been lying, and Webster wanted to know. If France had been playing tricks, then it was not true that England was the only offender, in which event the declaration of war against England, operating as it did to the benefit of France, was a mistake.

What Webster said in introducing the resolution was printed in the Washington newspapers the next morning. Chief Justice John Marshall, of the United States Supreme Court, afterward said to Judge Story: "I did not know Mr. Webster then, but I was so much struck with what he said that I did not hesitate to state that Mr.

Webster was a very able man and would become one of the first statesmen in America, and perhaps the very first."

The friends of Madison came to his defense, led by Calhoun. They might as well have saved their breath. Congress had declared war half-heartedly—the house by a majority of thirty votes in a membership of one hundred and twenty-eight, the senate by a majority of six in a membership of thirty-two. The senate, indeed, came within four votes of including France in the declaration. What enthusiasm there had been was subsiding, and both house and senate were in a mood to consider Webster's resolution. As a matter of fact, the speech that he intended to make in its behalf was never uttered. The push that he could have given it was not required. The house passed it, and so did the senate.

What followed was bad for the administration. Madison's secretary of state was forced to respond to the resolution by declaring that it was a month after war was declared against England before proof was received that France had withdrawn her inhibitions against American commerce. And the "proof," when it came, convinced nobody who did not want to believe it. Madison was not fooled. He knew that Napoleon had been trying to deceive him. He said so.

Calhoun endeavored to save the situation by putting through a resolution indorsing the administration's war record, but the house ignored it, and on August 2, 1813, congress adjourned until the following December.

Webster returned to Portsmouth to greet a son, ten days old—Daniel Fletcher. The first name was soon dropped. Fletcher Webster was the son who was killed in 1862 in the Second Battle of Bull Run.

VIII

WHEN Daniel Webster, in December, 1813, returned to the house of representatives, he was a marked man. During a short midsummer session he had shown that he knew how to catch the Madison administration by the ear and stand it on its tiptoes. He was acting upon the advice that old Christopher Gore had given him when he was a law student—"Be useful to your friends and a little dangerous to your enemies, and you will get on."

Webster had already become more than a little dangerous to his enemies. Nobody could say that he was not scrupulously fair in his attacks upon the acts and policies of the President. Nobody could accuse him of the use of immoderate language. Webster always used moderate language when no other kind of language would serve him so well. But when the time came, he knew how to draw a deadly bead upon his adversary and lay him low. Sometimes he would do this with a closely reasoned speech. Sometimes he would do it with an explosive phrase, which would reverberate throughout the country long after his speech had been forgotten. Such a phrase was employed when he said:

"Utterly astonished at the declaration of war, I have been surprised at nothing since."

A second shell immediately followed the first:

"I saw how it would be prosecuted when I saw how it was begun."

The third in a quick, crashing series:

"There is, in the nature of things, a relation between rash counsels and feeble execution."

These sticks and stones broke bones, because the unkind words that propelled them were true. Madison had done exactly what Webster accused him of doing. Desiring peace, but believing that England's attitude gave him no choice, he had rushed into war—and a little later for the Virginia hills. Congress had rather reluctantly started something that it might not be able to finish. The war on land was going badly, and there was no navy worth mentioning with which to make war at sea. The country was becoming restless. A sign of its restlessness was the appearance of a great spy mania. Suddenly it came to be believed that the country was not only full of spies but full of traitors. It was even said that when an American force, after its failure to invade Canada, was floating down the St. Lawrence River, an American judge named Ford, who lived within sight of the stream, had burned a light in the upper story of his house, as the signal for the British who then opened fire on the Americans. Poor Judge Ford had done nothing of the kind, but that did not matter. The President's supporters in the house, plagued perhaps by the way the war was going, decided to make war upon such of their own countrymen as might be accused of aiding the enemy. They actually introduced a resolution providing that the army might try, by drumhead court martial, citizens accused of treason and, if they were found guilty, put them to death.

Of course the whole thing was ridiculous—war-mania. It was in plain violation of the Constitution, which declares that civil courts shall deal with treason charges. This was an opportunity for Webster, who even at thirty knew the purposes and the spirit of the Constitution better than did many of those who made it. He quickly got into action. The proposition, he said, was monstrous. He was shocked at the arguments of some of those who favored it. What an astounding thing to advocate a drumhead court martial for the trial of citizens accused of treason—merely to avoid the necessity of producing witnesses! Let the army accuse, try, convict, and kill upon suspicion and "belief"! No government that even pretended to be free had ever done such a thing.

Webster's speech finished the resolution. It was referred to a committee and never reported out.

By this time Webster was bearing the full brunt of the criticism of those who, having declared war when they were not ready to wage it, sought to blame the administration's critics for taking a course that discouraged enlistments. The introduction of a bill to stimulate enlistments by offering high bounties gave Webster an opportunity to smash back at his adversaries.

It was not true, he said, that the opposition of men like himself had divided the country in its attitude toward the war.

"The more I perceive a disposition to check the freedom of inquiry by extravagant and unconstitutional pretenses," he said, "the firmer shall be the tone in which I shall assert, and the freer the manner in which I shall exercise it.

"It is the ancient and undoubted prerogative of this people to canvass public measures and the merits of public men.

"It has ever been enjoyed in every house, cottage, and cabin in the nation.

"It is not to be drawn into controversy.

"It is as undoubted as the right of breathing the air or walking on the earth.

"Belonging to private life as a right, it belongs to public life as a duty; and it is the last duty which those whose representative I am shall find me to abandon.

"Aiming at all times to be courteous and temperate

['814] Webster delivered a strong address in Congress in opposition to the conduct of the war offering the enforcement of a draft which included minors. He claimed the government should give up the idea of invasion and if the war must be continued, it should be defensive of maritime rights.

in its use, except when the right itself shall be questioned, I shall then carry it to its extent.

"I shall then place myself upon the extreme boundary of my right, and bid defiance to any arm that would move me from my ground.

"This high constitutional privilege I shall defend and exercise within this house, and without this house, and in all places, in time of war, in time of peace, and at all times."

Nobody thereafter tried to gag Webster or anybody else.

A number of other incidents that occurred about this time, are interesting now because they show how government has changed and how the American people have been compelled to change since the War of 1812. The Madison administration, pressed for money with which to carry on the war, had laid a tax upon land. The tax had produced, in 1813, three million dollars. The Madison administration sought to double it, and introduced legislation to bring it about. Webster voted against it. He did not doubt that the bill would be passed, as indeed it was; but believing that Madison had neither the ability to wage war nor make peace he did not choose to take whatever responsibility might be attached to him by supporting the administration even to this extent. Webster voted against all of the war-taxes, declaring they were more than the people could pay.

Webster fought and helped defeat national conscription. He fought it on the ground that conscription was a state right and not a national one. The state had the right to conscript men for service in the militia, and the national government, he held, had the right to call the militia of the several states to the service of the nation. It would not seem to make much difference to a conscripted citizen whether he was put into the army by his state or by the nation, but it made a great deal of difference to Webster. If there were to be conscription he wanted it brought about in the manner provided by the Constitution and not otherwise. The people backed him up in his fight and, as he wrote to his brother Ezekiel, "so terrified the vehement senators" that the matter was dropped and there was no conscription during the War of 1812 except by the several states for the purposes of their respective militias.

Webster was so great a stickler for the observance of both the letter and the spirit of the Constitution that he refused to help bring relief, by what he considered a questionable method, to seven thousand marooned citizens of Massachusetts who, during a particularly cold winter, were freezing and almost starving. Madison's embargo of 1813 had, among other interdictions, prohibited American commerce between American ports. Webster regarded this as unconstitutional. The effect of the embargo upon the people of the little island of Nantucket—fifteen miles long, three miles wide, and thirty miles at sea—was to cut them off from supplies of fuel and food. Webster refused to vote to let the islanders trade with the mainland, because he said they had the right under the Constitution so to trade, and to give them congressional permission to do so would seem to admit that they had no such constitutional right. A little later, Webster had the satisfaction of seeing Madison make an about-face with regard to the whole embargo project and abandon it.

Webster's political foes tried to catch him by seeking to connect him with the notorious "Hartford Convention," which was called by opponents of the war to take— if they dared—New England out of the Union. Gouverneur Morris, whose hand actually wrote the Constitution of the United States, was there and took part in its proceedings. Daniel Webster was not there.

If we look for the chief reason that Webster, opposing war in war-time and voting against taxes with which to wage it, was not destroyed by his enemies, we shall probably find it in the lack of organized propaganda machinery. The lie about Webster's alleged connection with the Hartford Convention could be orally told a few times each day, but it could not be told many millions of times each day, in every city in the country, in cartoons and big headlines. It is also true, of course, that Webster's great urbanity served him well. He had an oratorical trick of always preceding hard words with soft ones. By the time he had got down to what he really wanted to say he had all but maneuvered the minds of his opponents into a willingness to like whatever he might offer. If they continued to differ from him, they nevertheless both liked and respected him. Webster had tact.

Aug 24, 1814 Capital at Washington burned by British.
In 1814 Webster was re-elected to congress.

IX

A SESSION of congress, however, is not all a matter of fierce forays in the forum. In Washington, then as now, there were nights as well as days—long hours in which each member might seek happiness in the manner best suited to his tastes. Webster liked good company and plenty of pleasant conversation. Serious talk, light talk, stories, reminiscences, and whatever anybody had to offer for the entertainment of his companions.

Such company Webster had in Crawford's hotel, in Georgetown, where he boarded. At the head of the table sat old Christopher Gore, under whom Webster had studied law and who—having been defeated for reelection as governor of Massachusetts because the common people did not like to see him ride to and from the capitol in a coach-and-four—had been elected to the senate and brought the coach-and-four and servants in livery to Washington. There was Jeremiah Mason, with whom Webster had fought in most of the courts in southern New Hampshire and who was now a senator. There was Rufus King, senator from New York, who had been a member of the convention that framed the Federal Constitution, who had been tendered by George Washington the post of secretary of state and had declined it, and who had later been appointed by Washington minister to England. And, as if this company were not enough to burst the walls of the little inn, there was later added John Marshall, Chief Justice of the Supreme Court of the United States.

When Webster was an old man he pointed out to Peter Harvey, a Boston friend, the old hotel at which he had boarded, and mournfully commented upon the fact that all of those who had lived with him at the Crawford House were dead. "They were great men," he said. "We have no men like them now and shall never see their like again." Yet John Marshall was the only one mentioned by Webster whose name has gathered luster with years, and the others are scarcely remembered at all. Webster apparently shared the human tendency to believe that the great men are all dead, and their equals will never be born. Yet, even as Webster spoke, Lincoln was not far away, either in time or space.

While Webster was enjoying himself at the Crawford House, his wife and two children, up in Portsmouth, had their house burned over their heads. When Webster heard of it, he wanted to hurry home, but before he could start word came from Mrs. Webster that she had got her little brood under Mrs. Jeremiah Mason's roof and he could do them no good by leaving his post. So he remained in Washington. Webster had just bought the house for six thousand dollars, carried no insurance, lost all his furniture and also his library.

Mrs. Webster derived small comfort from her husband's first years in congress. While the wives of other members made merry at the Crawford House, it was her lot to remain in Portsmouth, doing the housework and caring for her children. She was cheerful about it, yet she wanted to see the national capital, take part in its life, and get a little of the sweet with which her husband's cup seemed to be overflowing. As the autumn of 1816 drew near its end it was agreed that the time had come when Mrs. Webster could leave the children for a few months. Grace was six years old, Daniel Fletcher, three. The mother needed a rest. In December she accompanied her husband to Washington.

? In 1816 the Webster family moved to Boston

They had been there but a few days when they were hastily summoned back to Portsmouth. Grace was very ill. The parents hurried home. Grace was suffering from what her father said was "a consumption." In January she died. In January, 1818, a year later, Julia Webster was born. She was the only daughter of Daniel Webster who grew to womanhood.

? (1817)

X

DURING these years in congress, Webster, whenever he could get a case, appeared as an attorney before the United States Supreme Court. Such opportunities did not come often, but one of them led to an encounter that culminated in a highly dramatic incident. What the case was, Webster, in his old age, could not remember, but he recalled perfectly the gentleman with whom he came in collision.

It was William Pinkney, of Maryland. He was eighteen years older than Webster, and at the time they met was regarded as the greatest lawyer in the United States. Behind him was a brilliant record. He had been a member of the Maryland convention called to ratify the Federal Constitution. He had commanded a regiment of riflemen in the War of 1812, and been wounded at Bladensburg. He had been minister to England, minister to Russia, and a special envoy to other countries upon numerous occasions. He had been attorney-general under James Madison. He had been a member of the house of representatives, and was destined, four years later, to become a United States senator. He was a big man, a very great lawyer—and knew it. And Webster? Mr. Pinkney, in court, could barely perceive him.

Mr. Pinkney came to court that morning in his usual fashion. He rode from his house attended by a servant, also on horseback, whose duty it was, at the end of the journey, to take the overalls in which his master always clad himself when about to bestride a horse. Once in the courtroom he carelessly tossed his hat and cloak upon a table, carefully removed the white gloves that he had put on fresh that morning, never to be worn again, and stood forth in all his splendor—dressed almost like a dandy, Webster said.

Such a man naturally would have difficulty in seeing Daniel Webster, unrenowned as a lawyer, as he was at that time, beyond the confines of his own state. Indeed, Pinkney did not like Webster. Webster said Pinkney's dislike for him arose from the fact that he refused to follow the custom of other small lawyers who hired Pinkney to draw their briefs, and outline their arguments, giving him therefor the bulk of their fees. Webster did not want to practice law by proxy, and he felt, moreover, that if his clients hired him they were entitled to his services and the best he could give them at that. So, even before the case began, there was a little coolness between the two.

The case had not gone far before Pinkney's manner toward Webster became what it had oftentimes been before, "very aggravating and annoying," to use Webster's words. Soon the note of contempt was sounded. "He pooh-poohed, as much as to say that it was not worth while to argue a point that I did not know anything about; that I was no lawyer. I think he spoke of 'the gentleman from New Hampshire.'"

Chief Justice Marshall, boarding where Webster did at the Crawford House, knew him well and liked him; he noted that Pinkney was "riding" his young friend "and was pained by it." Webster had difficulty in restraining his indignation but nevertheless did so, "knowing in what presence I stood." Pinkney construed Webster's silence as proof of lack of spirit and had more contempt for him than ever. Court adjourned for the day with matters at that stand.

Mr. Pinkney was again the dandy, about to go upon parade. He picked up and put on his gloves, picked up his whip, threw his cloak over his arm "and began to saunter away." Webster went up to him "very calmly" and said:

"Can I see you alone in one of the lobbies?"

"Certainly," replied Pinkney, apparently believing, Webster said, that he was about to ask his pardon.

Silently they strode along through the capital. Webster peered into a vacant grand-jury room, remote from the main courtroom; it seemed to suit his purpose. They entered. Webster locked the door behind them and put the key in his pocket, an act that Pinkney did not observe.

Once in the room, Webster advanced toward Pinkney until they were only inches apart.

"Mr. Pinkney," he began, "you grossly insulted me this morning in the courtroom; and not for the first time, either. In deference to your position and to the respect in which I held the court, I did not answer you as I was tempted to do on the spot."

There was fire in Webster's eyes, and Pinkney, beginning to realize that a storm was brewing, started to parley.

"You know you did," shouted Webster. "Don't add another sin to that. Don't deny it. You know you did it and you know it was premeditated, and if you deny it, you state an untruth. I am here to say to you, once for all, that you must ask my pardon and go into court tomorrow morning and repeat the apology, or either you or I will go out of this room in a different condition from that in which we entered it."

Pinkney "trembled like an aspen leaf." Again he tried to explain. Again Webster shut him off.

"There is no other course," said Webster. "I have in my pocket the key to this room and you must apologize or take what I give you."

Pinkney crumbled. "You are right," he said. "I am sorry. I did try to bluff you. I regret it and ask your pardon."

"Enough," said Webster, interrupting again. "Now one more promise before I open the door. You must promise that tomorrow morning you will state to the court that you have said things that wounded my feelings and that you regret it."

Pinkney promised, and Webster let him out. The

apology was duly made, and the two were ever afterward close friends.

Four years later, they were arguing a case before the same court when Pinkney, complaining of sudden illness, asked that the court adjourn, as he did not feel able to remain for Webster's reply, which he much wished to hear. The court granted the request. Webster hastened to the side of his friend to make inquiries and remained to help him adjust his cloak. Pinkney never heard Webster's argument. In forty-eight hours he was dead.

Daniel Webster, when he was an old man, told this story, as it is set down here, to his friend Peter Harvey of Boston.

XI

THE war, by this time, was drawing to a close. British troops had raided Washington, burned the Capitol, *Aug 24, 1814* the President's house and other public buildings. Madison had tried to convince the country that these depredations were not to be attributed to the miliary weakness of the government but to the "barbarity" of the British, who had violated civilized usage by attacking public "monuments."

The war that Webster said had been begun so rashly was coming to an end, slowly and painfully from sheer lack of public interest in it. Perry's victory on Lake Erie and some other naval victories were the sole events of which any American could be really proud. Madison himself had no will to go on, and was awaiting only a favorable opportunity to bring the miserable proceeding to an honorable end.

The Czar of Russia offered mediation, and Madison snapped at it, at once appointing commissioners to go to Europe and negotiate. England turned a cold shoulder to the proposal. She would negotiate only with the United States. Madison knuckled under and appointed new commissioners to treat directly with England. These commissioners, in collaboration with those appointed by England, eventually agreed upon a treaty that was acceptable to both sides. The treaty contained no reference to the grievance that had been put forward as the cause of the war. So far as the treaty was concerned, England was free to continue to halt American ships on the high seas and, if British subjects were found among their crews, take them off. This matter was left to Webster to settle, years later, when he was secretary of state, not by going to war, but by backing England into a corner in an argument from which she could not escape.

But the treaty, at least on paper, ended the war, though it did not immediately end it in fact. Before news of what had happened could cross the ocean on a sailing ship, Andrew Jackson had fought and won the battle of New Orleans, which not only ended the war but saved the reputation of the American army.

Webster continued to live at the Crawford House. Daily he saw old Christopher Gore and Rufus King sally forth in their coaches-and-four, with liveried servants, drive down Pennsylvania Avenue, and halt before the shabby little building in which the senate, following the fire, had found temporary quarters. It may not be exactly correct to say that Webster was tiring of congressional life, but at any rate he had determined to give it up. He took a vigorous part in such measures as arose, but no thought of future greatness seemed yet to have come to him.

Moreover, his finances troubled him. His New Hampshire law practice, when he was there to attend to it, brought him only two thousand dollars a year. He was receiving fifteen hundred dollars a year as a member of congress, but what he earned in Washington was mostly offset by reduced income from his Portsmouth law office because of his prolonged absence. The thing to do, it seemed to him, was to quit congress and remove his law office to a city in which he could earn more.

Most of the things that Webster did during what he believed were to be his last days in congress have no interest now. Some of them will always be interesting. Fulton having invented steam navigation, and the United States having no navy to speak of, it occurred to the naval committee of the house of representatives to introduce steam power into the navy. They wished to erect "steam batteries" to be stationed at the mouth of the Mississippi, at the entrance of Chesapeake Bay, and at the lower end of New York harbor. Most of the committee thought these "batteries" could not cruise at all, but a few hoped they might be able to navigate as far as from New York to Philadelphia. Webster was more optimistic. He believed such batteries would be able to go wherever there was enough water to float them and should be therefore, as a part of the navy, under the control of the President. His view, which prevailed, was of importance, inasmuch as the point under debate was whether it should be left to the President or to congress to determine where the batteries should be placed. Webster succeeded in giving this power to the President.

There is a tradition that when, a few years later, steam railroads were proposed, Webster opposed them on two grounds: first, that the speed of twenty miles an hour would kill the passengers by making it impossible for them to breathe, and, second, that if their breath should not be taken away, they would inevitably be killed at the end of the line by reason of the engineer's inability to stop the train. This story has been told since Webster's day, but there is no mention of it in any of his early biographies. Even if Webster so believed, he misjudged the locomotive no more than did Napoleon the steamboat, which, when Fulton proposed it to him, he would not even investigate.

Webster's life at this time was also enlivened by a challenge to a duel from John Randolph, of Virginia, then forty-three years old, who at the age of fifty-two was to fight a duel with Henry Clay. Randolph believed that he was a descendant of the Indian princess Pocahontas, and was properly proud, not only of that, but of everything about himself. He had a slashing tongue and a withering sarcasm, but like most men thus equipped, a very sensitive skin. During a debate in the house, Webster said something to which Randolph chose to take offense and the challenge followed. Webster wrote to Randolph:

Sir:

For having declined to comply with your demand yesterday in the house for an explanation of words of a general nature, used in debate, you now "demand of me that satisfaction which your insulted feelings require" and refer me to your friend, Mr. ——, I presume, as he is the bearer of your note, for such arrangements as are usual.

This demand for explanation, you, in my judgment, as a matter of right, were not entitled to make of me; nor were the temper and style of your own reply to my objection to the sugar tax of a character to induce me to accord as a matter of courtesy.

Neither can I, under the circumstances of the case, recognize in you a right to call me to the field to answer what you may please to consider an insult to your feelings.

It is unnecessary for me to state other and obvious

considerations growing out of this case. It is enough that I do not feel myself bound, at all times and under any circumstances, to accept from any man, who shall choose to risk his own life, an invitation of this sort; although I shall always be prepared to repel in a suitable manner the aggression of any man who may presume upon such a refusal.

Your Obedient Servant,
DANIEL WEBSTER.

Nothing more was heard of Randolph.

A month after the duel blew over, Webster received word from his brother Ezekiel that their mother was dying.

"I have hardly a hope that she can still be living," replied Webster, "but if she should be, tell her I pray for her everlasting peace and happiness, and give her a son's blessing for all her parental goodness. May God bless her, living or dying. If she does not survive, let her rest beside her husband and our father."

This was one of the very few letters written by Webster in which he mentioned his mother. She died on April 26, 1816, at the age of seventy years, and was buried on the old farm at Franklin, beside Judge Webster and two of their children.

Webster retired from congress when the session closed on March 3, 1817. It had been a great experience, such as comes to few men of thirty-four years, but he must hurry on. Success was awaiting him elsewhere. Just where, he could not at once say. Perhaps in Albany. Perhaps in New York. "Our New England prosperity and importance," he wrote his brother Ezekiel, "are passing away. . . . If any great scenes are to be acted in this country within the next twenty years, New York is the place in which those scenes are to be viewed."

Notwithstanding this reasoning he moved to Boston. The fact that he quitted the state that had sent him to congress indicates that he expected never to return.

A definite change was taking place in Webster—a change destined to leave a mark upon him. Far gone were the days when Daniel, Ezekiel, and their father, each heavily in debt and dunned at the same time, pitifully wrote to each other for help—days when Daniel was happy notwithstanding his poverty. Since then, Webster had tasted the flesh-pots and found that they were good. Two or three thousand dollars a year, in the Washington of his day, was a very comfortable sum upon which to live, but it was not enough for Webster. He wanted to go where he could earn more money, not because he cared about money as such, but because he wanted to indulge himself. He wanted to eat well, drink well, dress well, and, as soon as he could make the arrangements, live on a great estate in truly baronial style. Nobody in his day knew better than he did how to array himself in striking fashion—blue coat with brass buttons, yellow waistcoat, big white tie, silk stockings and shining shoes. When at last he acquired his baronial acres, he knew by instinct how to play his part as the proprietor of a great landed estate. What he did not know, nor ever learned, was the value of a dollar, and, like Jefferson, death found him at the door of the poorhouse.

At thirty-four, however, Webster was full of illusions about the power of money to bring happiness, and removed to Boston to realize his dreams.

PART TWO

IT is remarkable that involuntarily we all read as superior beings. Universal history, the poets, the romancers do not . . . anywhere make us feel that we intrude . . . All that Shakespeare says of the king, yonder slip of a boy . . . feels to be true of himself. We sympathize in the great moments of history . . . because there law was enacted, the sea was searched, the land was found, or the blow struck for us, as we ourselves in that place would have done.

      —RALPH WALDO EMERSON. ESSAYS, "HISTORY."

I

DANIEL WEBSTER practiced law in Boston six
years. These years, from thirty-four to forty, were
to him what the month of June is to the rose. What a
flowering there was! Everything that his past had promised was fulfilled in profusion. Everything that he was
capable of becoming was clearly indicated. For the first
time, he stood revealed.

What was revealed was a very complex personality,
which so far as his main talents were concerned was
wonderfully harmonious. It was so complex that even to
this day it easily escapes understanding. Some persons
speak of him as a great statesman, some as a great orator,
some as a great diplomatist, some as a great lawyer, and
Jeremiah Mason said that he had qualities that would
have made him a great actor. Webster was all of these,
and yet, in another sense, he was but one of them.

First, foremost and all the time, Daniel Webster was
a great lawyer, and, even more, a great advocate. All
that he was and all that he could be proceeded from his
ability to take facts and apply to them his reasoning powers. Everything else about him was either a product of
this ability or a means that he had adopted to make
it more effective. He was a greater lawyer than he would
have been if he had not also been a great orator. Having
wrapped about his ample shoulders the robe of reason,
Webster pinned upon his breast the blazing jewel of
oratory. The jewel was, of course, to be admired for its
own sake, but most of all it was intended to bring out in
sharper relief the mantle. Webster knew the power of

oratory, if used sparingly and at the right moments, to influence not only juries but high courts. Nor was he unaware of the actor's power, which he employed at appropriate moments throughout his life, and upon one occasion at least, before the United States Supreme Court.

No one can understand Webster who does not get these facts clearly in mind: Webster was the great expounder and defender of the Constitution, because he had to a high degree that passion for orderly procedure which finds its expression in the law. He was a great secretary of state because the same abilities were required to outmaneuver and outreason a foreign diplomatist that were necessary to the winning of a lawsuit in the United States. He was a great orator, not because he was a lawyer at all, but because there had been born in him an emotional nature as sensitive to the breezes and blasts of eloquence as are the strings of an instrument that tremble at the touch of a zephyr. Webster not only had this emotional nature, but within himself he possessed the power to gratify it. No one was more touched by his own words than he was himself. Years after he delivered the eulogy of Adams and Jefferson he tried to read it, but could not do so because, as he said, he "choked up."

Webster's part in bringing about judicial interpretations of the Constitution was a work of the highest statesmanship. He had in some degree vision—the capacity to look ahead—that alone makes great statesmanship possible. He was not, however, a great constructive thinker. Also, he had more reverence for the old than for the new and lacked daring. He was at first against a protective tariff and then for it. The idea of converting this country into a manufacturing nation made him recoil, smacking, as it did, too much of change.

But as a lawyer, Webster was magnificent. He would not have made a good judge. He said so himself. As an advocate of causes, however, this country has never produced his superior if it has, indeed, his equal. First, he had an uncanny capacity for seizing upon that aspect of his case which could best be developed, and having grasped it, he proceeded to build up his case so simply, so logically, and so powerfully that his verdict was half won by the time he had finished the presentation. Usually he won the other half when the time came to deal with his adversary. He was a terror to those who came to court against him. He was as shrewd in choosing the weakest point in his opponent's case as he was in selecting the strongest point of his own. And having spotted the weakest point in his foe's defenses, he put everything he had into the work of expanding the spot into a breach in the wall through which he and his client might drive in a coach-and-four. Under and into the wall he was trying to overturn, he sapped, he mined, he drilled, he dug. No one who met him in the cross-examination of a lying witness cared ever to meet him thus again. And, when the time came for argument, he was nearly irresistible! At first, his speech flowed as clearly and as limpidly as a mountain brook suddenly turned between the green banks of a meadow. So obviously intent upon being perfectly fair was he that one unfamiliar with the case he was pleading might have had difficulty, if he had stepped into court at such a moment, to determine upon which side Webster was arguing. But when all of the preliminaries had been completed, and the time arrived to close in upon his opponent, Webster closed in as Wellington did at Waterloo. Oratory came to reenforce reason, the walls of his adversary came crashing down, and the coach-and-four drove through.

Webster never shone more brilliantly as a lawyer than he did in the Dartmouth College case, the arguments upon which began before the United States Supreme Court March 10, 1818, when he was in his thirty-sixth year. What was to be decided was whether the legislature of New Hampshire had the right, without the consent of the college, to alter its charter and diminish its rights.

The supreme court of New Hampshire had decided in favor of the legislature. Dartmouth took the case to Washington for review, and the importance of the court's decision, whatever it might be, lay in the fact that, once given, it would apply to every legislature and to every franchise that had been or might be given. It was destined to be, in fact, the most important decision with regard to property rights that the court has ever handed down, having been cited by the court, in subsequent decisions, more than a thousand times. Webster contended that the charter, or franchise, given to Dartmouth was a contract and, as such, could not be altered or amended by either party to it without the consent of the other party.

A hundred years and more have gone since the Dartmouth College case passed into history, and today, in the minds of most Americans, it is as dead as the bones along a caravan trail in the Arabian desert. Yet it was never merely a suit at law—of vast importance, perhaps, but of interest only to lawyers and deadly as an opiate to everyone else. It was a thrilling drama based upon some of the strongest emotions that move humankind. Religion is in itself a sufficient theme upon which to base a play, but the Dartmouth case had not merely one sect but two, and they were fighting. Bigotry, Intolerance and Selfishness did not content themselves with stalking across the stage—they stopped to shake their fists. Politics, the Constitution, and Hatred completed the cast, and some said that Hatred occasionally appeared arrayed in the silken robes of a judge.

In the middle of the eighteenth century, the Reverend Eleazar Wheelock established a charity school at his own expense upon his farm, which occupied the present site of Dartmouth College in New Hampshire. Desiring to do good, he went out into the forests to get Indian boys to come and partake of food, clothing, and education, afterward sending them out among their tribes as missionaries.

Others having joined in the work with gifts of money and tracts of land, Wheelock applied for a charter which, in 1769, was granted by the legislature of New Hampshire in the name of the British king. The charter, which was declared to be perpetual, provided: that the governing body should be twelve trustees and a president; that Wheelock should be the first president, with power to name his successor; and that the twelve trustees should have power to appoint their successors. Wheelock died in 1779, after having named as his successor, his son John.

John Wheelock's appointment did not sit well with some of the trustees, who objected to what they called a "family dynasty." Others opposed him because he, like his father, was a Presbyterian and a liberal, while they were Congregationalists and Federalists. The combined opposition on the board of trustees constituted but a minority of the whole, but from the first it was troublesome and potentially dangerous. It was troublesome because it constituted a sore spot; it was dangerous because the minority were Federalists and Congregationalists, and New Hampshire, at that time, was under the control of Federalists, and Congregationalism was the state religion. People were taxed to support the Congregational Church. Congregational ministers and most of their parishioners were Federalists. Not a nice environment for Presbyterians inclined to political liberalism.

For thirty years the work of undermining John Wheelock went on, and by 1809 it had been completed. Changes had occurred in the personnel of the board of trustees, and he had lost control of it.

After six years more, the fires that had been smoldering underground for more than a generation burst into the open. The Wheelock faction took their grievances to the public in a series of pamphlets. Their opponents answered with more pamphlets. The newspapers printed the news. The people soon became deeply interested.

John Wheelock determined to take the matter to court. What lawyer should he employ? He could not get Jeremiah Mason, because Mason was allied with the faction of the Dartmouth trustees who were fighting him; nor, for the same reason, could he get Judge Smith. Perhaps Daniel Webster would do. Wheelock consulted Webster, paid him a fee, and according to Henry Cabot Lodge obtained from Webster a "promise of his future services." Wheelock also sent a memorial to the legislature asking for the appointment of a committee of investigation. The committee was appointed.

When Wheelock learned that the committee was about to hold a hearing he wrote to Webster, reminding him of their conversation, enclosing a fee of twenty dollars and asking him to appear before the committee. Webster did not appear. Webster, after making what Lodge declared to be a "very unsatisfactory explanation of his conduct," abandoned Wheelock and went over to the other side. Webster's closest personal and political friends were Federalists. Apparently they had put pressure upon him to get him out of the Wheelock camp.

The new majority in the board of trustees forthwith

It may be said that Webster's arguments in the celebrated "Dartmouth College case" placed him, at the age of 36, in the foremost rank of the constitutional lawyers of the country. For the main points of the reasoning was sustained, he was probably indebted to Mr. Mason who was what lawyers call a "cause-getting man", who had previously argued the case before the Supreme Court of New Hampshire, but his superiority to Mason was shown in the eloquence, the moral power, he infused into his reasoning, so as to make the dullest and citations of legal authority tell on the minds he addressed.

There is one incident connected with this speech which proves what immense

WEBSTER AT THE AGE OF THIRTY-EIGHT

When he made the greatest formal oration of his life at Plymouth, Massachusetts. From a miniature by Miss Goodrich, in the possession of the Massachusetts Historical Society

price is given to simple words when a great man — great in his emotional nature as well as great in logical powers — is behind the words. "It is, sir, as I have said, a small college. And yet there are those who love it." At this point the orator's lips quivered, his voice choked, his eyes filled with tears, — all the memories of sacrifice endured by his father and mother, his brothers and sisters, in order that he might enjoy its rather scanty advantages of a liberal education, and by means of which he was there to plead its cause before the supreme tribunal of the nation, rushed suddenly upon his mind in an overwhelming flood. The justices of the Supreme Court- great lawyers, tried and toughened by experience into a certain obdurate sense of justice, and insensible to any common appeal to their hearts, melted into unwonted tenderness, as, in broken words, the advocate proceeded to state his own indebtedness to the "small college", whose rights and privileges he was there to defend. Chief Justice Marshall's eyes were filled with tears; and the eyes of the other justices were suffused with moisture. As the orator gradually recovered his accustomed stern composure of manner, he turned to the counsel on the other side — one of whom, at least, was a graduate of Dartmouth,— and in his deepest and most thrilling tones, thus couched his argument: "Sir, I know not how others may feel; but for myself when I see my Alma Mater surrounded, like Caesar in the senate-house by those who are reiterating stab after stab, I would not, for this right hand, have her turn to me an say, Et tu quoque, mi fili! - And thou too, my son." The effect was overwhelming; yet by what simple means was it produced, and with what simple expenditure of words! The eloquence was plainly "in the man, in the subject, and in the occasion," but most emphatically was it in the man.

proceeded to remove Wheelock from office and appoint in his place the Reverend Francis Brown, a Congregationalist and a Federalist. Wheelock, realizing that he was in a fight for his life, determined to carry it into politics, which he did by deserting the Federalist party, in the campaign then proceeding for the election of state officials, and joining the Democrats. To the consternation of the Federalists, Wheelock aroused so much sympathy that the Democrats elected their candidate for governor and a majority of the members of the state legislature.

Webster, seeing that his friends were in a tight pinch, advised them to try to soothe the Democrats and also to scare them a little by circulating rumors that a new college might be established. But the Democrats were neither to be soothed nor intimidated. The legislature proceeded at once to pass an act amending the charter of Dartmouth by increasing the number of trustees from twelve to twenty-one, and creating a board of twenty-five overseers to be appointed by the president and the board of trustees. The additional trustees and other officers were duly appointed by the governor, and their first act was to expel from the office of president the Reverend Francis Brown and appoint in his place John Wheelock. Brown refused to get out and the new board refused to give up the college seal and other property. The old board soon afterward brought suit to recover its property, which it could do, of course, only by upsetting the law under which it had been taken.

The Dartmouth College board was first represented in court by Mason and Judge Smith. Webster joined them when they appeared before the state supreme court. The opposition was represented by Ichabod Bartlett and George Sullivan, shrewd, hard-headed gentlemen, upon whom nobody could impose, who knew the law and knew their case. Sullivan, in open court, so severely criticized Webster for deserting Wheelock that Webster asked that his remarks be stricken from the record.

We shall not understand what is immediately to follow if we take as gospel truth all that Webster's early biographers said about him. Nor shall we understand him if we follow later biographers, like Lodge, who, compelled to yield to Webster their tribute of praise for the manner in which he handled himself in the Dartmouth College case, nevertheless do so grudgingly. Lodge said that the constitutional point upon which Webster won in the United States Supreme Court was first suggested by John Wheelock, a layman, and moreover "was not a very remarkable idea in itself." This view does not fit the facts. If Webster, in the Dartmouth College case, had won mostly because of tricks and stratagems, the lawyers of America would not immediately thereafter have placed him, as they did, at the head of the American bar. Lawyers cannot be fooled with regard to the performances of another lawyer.

We shall understand Webster, now and later, if we keep always in mind the fact that, first, foremost, and all the time, he was a great lawyer and a great advocate. This view harmonizes everything that otherwise is discordant. Webster was a great lawyer and, as such, when he undertook a cause, he was soon consumed with a desire to win. A little later we shall see him, because of this desire, hanging two men who were legally innocent and morally guilty of murder. The law, to Webster, was a great game of chess, to be played, of course, according to the rules. If by the movement of one piece, he could checkmate his adversary, well and good, but if the movement of several pieces were required, he moved as many pieces as were necessary. Webster did not play the game of law, as some men play chess, mostly for the pleasure of playing—he played to win.

The Supreme Court of New Hampshire is now ready to hear the case on appeal. Mason and Smith speak first and make the principal arguments. Webster, still regarded as a second-rate lawyer, follows with a shorter address. The three of them do what all lawyers try to do. They fire as many shots as they can, hoping that at least one will hit the mark. The facts and the law were such that good judges might decide either one way or the other. Who could tell which argument would bring down a judge? The only safe way to do was to "buckshot" their Honors with several arguments. Mr. Mason therefore devoted twenty-three printed pages to the elaboration of what all three believed to be their principal point—that the legislature had exceeded its powers—eight pages to the contention that the constitution of New Hampshire had been violated, six pages in seeking to make it appear that the Constitution of the United States had been set at naught—the paragraph prohibiting the enactment of any law impairing the obligation of contracts. Smith and Webster apportioned their space in about the same manner. A little less than one-sixth of their time devoted to the point that eventually brought down four of the seven justices of the United States Supreme Court.

How many of the New Hampshire judges did all three of the points bring down? Not one. The court decided unanimously in favor of Webster's opponents. When the case went to the United States Supreme Court, Webster regretted that it had been appealed upon the single constitutional point with regard to contracts. Webster, always the lawyer and, above everything else, the advocate, sought to remedy this difficulty in his argument by going far outside the legal limits of the case and subtly and powerfully appealing to the passions, the prejudices, and the sympathies of the court in every way that his great mind could command.

Nor let it be doubted that the members of the court had their passions and their prejudices. Chief Justice Marshall, in particular, was a Federalist of the Federalists, a hater of Jefferson and of everything for which Jefferson stood. Webster, in his fierce desire to win, mustered his every artful resource to revive in Marshall his hatred of Jefferson by making it appear that Jefferson's freethinking, atheistic followers were seeking to lay unholy hands upon an institution founded in the fear of God. Such words were entirely out of place in a courtroom. Webster, after expounding the law and arguing upon it, which he did beautifully, should have stopped. He didn't stop. He knew his man. He had lived at the same hotel and spent long evenings with him.

While the appeal was pending in Washington and before the arguments were made, Webster had tried hard to get out of the case altogether. Smith and Mason did not want to go and, in the end, did not go, but they were most anxious that Webster should try to do in Washington what all three of them had failed to accomplish in New Hampshire. The outlook was not encouraging, and perhaps they would have been glad to let the odium of defeat fall upon their young associate rather than upon themselves. To their repeated entreaties Webster at first replied that he did not know what more he could say in Washington than he had said in New Hampshire.

His letters of hesitation, written at this time, are of interest to common men and women who assume that a great mind, working at a great moment, always functions perfectly and at high speed. In this matter, Webster's mind at first functioned very poorly. Opportunity was knocking at his door as it has seldom knocked at the door of any man, yet he seemed to perceive neither the importance of the case nor what it offered for his own advancement. No man could have hesitated who knew what was impending. But Webster did not know, and so we find him writing to a number of others, as he wrote to Jeremiah Mason, that he "had not thought of the subject, nor made the least preparation"; that he "could do no good," and that Mason and Smith should follow up, in their own manner, "the blows which have already been so well struck."

It was only after much argument that Webster permitted himself to be drawn back into the case, and when he consented he seemed to do so almost with regret. He wanted Mason and Smith to dump all of their materials into his lap—arguments, citations of authorities, and what not—to the end that he might have to work no more than necessary. Not only was Webster slow to realize the importance of the case, but it is doubtful whether he realized it the day he argued it in Washington. He seemed still to believe that the question chiefly concerned Dartmouth and other colleges, while the fact was that it was later to concern the corporations of the United States a thousand times more.

Webster was no exception to the rule that no man will work so hard as a lazy man, once he has become really interested and is lost in his dream of achievement. But he still had to a degree the meager opinion of his own abilities brought with him from his youth. The day was to come when he could and would say to a close friend: "I am not unaware of the importance in this country and in this world of Daniel Webster." But that time had not yet arrived.

When the great day for the argument in Washington came, however, Webster was ready. We see him going into the shabby little brick building near the foot of Pennsylvania Avenue in which the court, after the British had burned the Capitol, held its sessions. What was in his mind? The determination to win, we may be sure. He was entering that little room a lawyer practically unknown outside the state of New Hampshire. In that room he was to speak five hours, set in motion forces that were to affect the lives of hundreds of millons of human beings yet unborn—forces that are still in operation today—and to win the leadership of the bar of the United States. Did he think of one or both of these things? We may be sure that he never even dreamed of either of them. He was to argue, primarily, the cause of a small college and, secondarily, the causes of all other colleges and charitable organizations. So he believed, and what great glory was there in doing that?

The room is small but crowded. Who are these people? A good many are Washington lawyers. Some are minor public officials. Some are visitors who just happened in off the street. Some are women of the official class of the sort that, to this day, are always eager to see a good show in a public forum. Perhaps, in all, a hundred. The room would hold no more.

A back door opens, and the chief justice steps through. The court crier calls out: "The honorable, the Supreme Court of the United States is now in session." The other members of the court, arrayed in their black silk robes, come trooping along behind the chief justice. "God save the United States and this honorable court," continues the crier. Tall, gaunt John Marshall seats himself in the center. Bushrod Washington, nephew of the country's father and appointed to the court in 1798 by the elder

Adams, takes the place at Marshall's right. A mite of an emaciated man, with a face as white as marble, he looks, as he sits beside the great Marshall, almost like a doll. To the right and left of these two are Associate Justices Story, Livingston, Duval, and Todd.

The chief justice reads aloud from a paper that he holds in his hand, something about the case of the Dartmouth College Trustees *vs.* Woodward, which is up for hearing before the court on a writ of error. He utters only a sentence or two, but what he says is the signal for the great case to begin.

Webster rises from his chair and draws a step or two nearer the judges.

"May it please the court—"

The ladies present must at first have felt that while Webster, who always fascinated women, was good to look at, he was not much to hear. Such a diffident manner of speaking—no fight, no fire. Such prosy stuff, too. Lord Mansfield, on a certain occasion, had said this, but on the other hand, the learned Bishop Stillingfleet, speaking before the House of Lords, had said that. For that matter, what lady cared what either of them had said? The lawyers present, however, and the judges on the bench, realized as Webster went on that he was making a wonderfully clear and powerful presentation of his case. If it were proper to speak of a brick wall running like a river, one might say that Webster laid down, one after another, bricks from Roman law, English law, and American law, and so cemented them with argument made of common sense that his limpid discourses flowed on like a majestic stream of water headed for the sea.

On and on went the flow of words. Three hours had elapsed. John Marshall, chief justice, sharp-featured but with kindly eyes, sat as men sit when they know not where they are, oblivious of everything except the edifice of law, precedent, and reason that the speaker was rearing. The mite of a man, Mr. Justice Washington, demonstrated that a thin, white face which looks like death can be brought to life by eyes revealing the mind's rapt attention. Mr. Justice Story, who had sat for three hours with a quill pen poised to take down such of the speaker's points as he might afterward wish to recall, laid down the pen without having written a word. The argument was so clear that his mind could hold it without the aid of ink. Associate Justices Livingston, Duval, and Todd were not less attentive than their brothers on the bench.

Three hours and a half! The ladies in the court-room who had come out for a free afternoon show were having it, without being able to say, perhaps, exactly in what it consisted. Neither they nor men unlearned in the law could appreciate anything of the speaker's argument except that intangible part that permeates the air and defies definition. Before two hours had passed they knew they were beholding, not the usual performance, but something mysteriously splendid. The significance of what they were seeing flashed from the speaker's eyes and the eyes of the black-robed men upon the bench. If Webster had been speaking Chinese, the ladies and the other uninitiated persons would have known from his manner that he was doing something far removed from the ordinary and doing it magnificently.

Webster—having finished the presentation of the issue upon which the case had been taken to the United States Supreme Court—was now arguing the points upon which the Supreme Court of New Hampshire had decided against him. The purely New Hampshire matters had no place in the argument at Washington, as Webster frankly admitted, yet he continued to argue them, and no justice tried to stop him. Webster did not know what argument or what stray bit of reasoning might bring down a judge and therefore gave them buckshot and fired off both barrels.

How determined Webster was to win became apparent during the fifth and last hour of his argument. Gradually there had come over the musical flow of his words a subtle change. No more were there references to what Lord Mansfield, the learned Bishop Stillingfleet, or anybody else had said. What he was discussing now could be perfectly understood by everyone in the room. The hardships and the heartaches of the pioneer poor! Their pitiful attempts to make a living! Their deep desire to spare their children from these woes by giving them an education! The good Dr. Wheelock, now forty years in his grave, what a man was he! How his heart had gone out to all the poor, even to the Indian boys in the forest! How magnificent of him to conceive the idea of establishing a college in which poor young men (women did not yet count) might receive an education and thus be in the way of realizing the hopes of parents who, for themselves, had never dared to hope. And, at the death of this good man, how loyally had his son John assumed his father's burden!

Words that, as here set down, are but the dead leaves and dust of language, leaped from the mind of Webster like living things. The ladies began to dab their eyes with their handkerchiefs, and we have it from Dr. Chauncey A. Goodrich, a Yale professor who was there, that tears glistened in the eyes even of old John Marshall. Gone were all thoughts of Roman law, English law, American law, and the sayings of ancient lawyers and judges. What the court and the audience were now considering was the awful thing it is to be poor and the meritorious thing it is to set up a college in which poor boys can develop the capacity to avoid hard work and poor pay.

Four hours and a half, and the wringing of hearts went on. Women began to sob. Bushrod Washington leaned forward with an eager, troubled look. John Marshall bent toward the speaker that he might not miss a word. Webster's voice rose and fell like a flail beating upon those who had become his helpless victims. What were in his eyes? Tears. What at times gripped him until it seemed as if he could not continue speaking? His own thoughts were choking him.

Would the man never stop? Had he no mercy? It seemed that he would not stop and that he had no mercy. As he went on, the deep furrows in Marshall's cheeks, we are told, expanded with emotion. A strained look came upon every person in the court-room. What the ladies and some of the men had expected to be a pleasant afternoon pastime had become a painful and distressing thing. "It was a relief," said Justice Story, "to gain in his momentary pauses some short interval of repose." Webster himself got no relief nor apparently wanted any. "There was in his whole air and manner," said Justice Story, who heard him from the bench, "in the fiery flashings of his eye, the darkness of his contracted brow, the sudden and flying flushes of his cheeks, the quivering and scarcely manageable movements of his lips, in the deep, guttural tones of his voice, in the struggle to control his own emotions, in the almost convulsive clenchings of his hands without a seeming consciousness of the act—there were in these things what gave to his oratory almost a superhuman influence."

The poor pioneer people! The good Dr. Wheelock!

Washington April 24. 1830

Dear Sir,

I thank you for your kind letter of the 2? April. If my speech has done, or shall do, the slightest good, I shall be sufficiently gratified. It was, in the thickest dense, unexpected, & occasional; yet I am willing to confess, that having the occasion thus forced upon me I did the best I could, under its pressure. The subject & the times have given it a degree of circulation, & which its own merits could not have entitled it. Connected with this subject, one good thing – excellent, & most important – will one day be made known. At present, it is locked up in confidence. All I can say is, & I wz? not have that repeated,
except

FACSIMILE OF A LETTER WRITTEN BY DANIEL WEBSTER
Reproduced by permission of the Boston Public Library

perhaps, his father, that the world will one day - perhaps not a distant one - know Mr Madison's sentiments on these constitutional questions, fully & precisely; together with his understanding of the V.a Resolutions of 1799-8 It will be an important paper.

You are thought, that pains are taking to sound the Senate, with a view of ascertaining the expediency of a renomination of Isaac Hill. No doubt, a great effort will be made. I hope, not with success. — I never shall believe he can either get thro' the Senate, or get into it, till I see it.

It is difficult to get copies of the Executive Journal. I have obtained one, this session, for Ch. Kent. — If possible, I will hunt up another yet for you; but if not this year, hereafter
                                    shall I

condo it next. If I can get it, we'll see it sent, in a safe manner. —

It seems now to be understood that the actual incumbent of the Presidency intends to stand for reelection. This disappoints more than one.

If that should not happen, I hesitate not to say I think Mr Clay's chance much the best. He is evidently gaining, in the west, I mean, among the political men here. What will be advisable, if Genl. J. should be again candidate, cannot now be decided. —

I shall be happy to hear from you, as often as you will confer that favor. Have the goodness to present my regards to your father, & believe me, with much sincere respect,

Yrs
Danl Webster

Hon Wm Plumer jr
Epping N. H.

Ah, but there was a bad man too, and as a last grand smash at the prejudices and passions of John Marshall he was to be brought in, not in person, nor even by name, yet in a manner so clear that neither John Marshall nor anybody else could fail to recognize him.

A bad man. An infidel. Some said a free-lover. Thomas Jefferson. Jefferson, the political leader of the forces that were trying to wrest Dartmouth from the hands of John Wheelock in which it had been placed by his father.

Webster hastily painted again the picture of Dartmouth, "founded by the piety of our ancestors to alleviate human misery," told how small, weak, and helpless it was. It was now in the court's hands. The court, if it wished to do so, could destroy it. But if it were to do so, it would logically have to set about the destruction of every other college in the land. It was a small college, he repeated; "yet there are those who love it."

Webster himself, choked by his own emotions, had to stop. "For two or three minutes," said Doctor Goodrich, "the court-room presented an extraordinary spectacle." "The whole audience," said Justice Story, "had been wrought up to the highest excitement. Many were dissolved in tears. Many displayed the most agitating mental struggles. Many were sinking under the exhausting efforts to conceal their own emotion."

Had the man no heart? Would he never stop? The man had no heart, but he would soon stop. One more shot at Jefferson and he would be through. This was the shot:

"Sir," said Webster, addressing the chief justice, "I know not how others may feel [glancing at the opponents of the college before him] but for myself, when I see my Alma Mater surrounded like Cæsar in the senate-house, by those who are reiterating stab after stab, I would not, for this right hand have her turn to me and say, '*Et tu quoque mi fili* (*And thou too, my son?*)'"

At last! The thing was over! Webster sat down. Nobody spoke. Nobody moved. Just silence. The ticking clock seemed to be the only live thing in the room. Some minutes thus passed, said Justice Story, who added that "the whole seemed but an agonizing dream from which the audience was slowly and almost unconsciously awakening."

An agonizing dream perhaps, but now ended. The ladies, going out the door to Pennsylvania Avenue, were in time to get a cheering bit of warmth from the spring sun as it settled low over the Virginia hills. The judges formed in line and passed back through the door they had entered, to their chambers. The janitor came into the empty room and, while the clerk was picking up his papers, began to sweep. The clock tick-tocked. Nobody but the judges and the lawyers realized that anything very remarkable had happened and even their conception of the occasion's importance fell far short of the facts.

II

WEBSTER had warmed himself up a bit and done his best to win, but in a few hours he cooled off. The next day we find him writing about the arguments in the case to Judge Smith, up in New Hampshire, as he might have written about a small damage suit. Indeed, before many more days had elapsed we read from his own pen that in an abstract he had made of his argument he had "left out all the nonsense," meaning thereby all the oratory, all the pathos, all the flubdub about poverty and piety, and also his thinly veiled attack upon Jefferson. We know that he meant these things because they are all left out of the report of his address which he prepared several months later for inclusion in his published works. Webster's address as he made it was not taken down stenographically and therefore ceased to live, except in the memories of those who heard it, the moment he ceased to speak. The address that he himself prepared for publication in his book contains the argument, the citations of authorities, and the reasoning, but is otherwise as dead as a door-nail and closes with a hundred words or so of Latin which, of course, he never uttered in court. All we know is that the speech he really made all but convulsed those who were in the court-room, and revived in the breast of Marshall a hatred of Jefferson that not unlikely determined the decision of the court.

This court-room scene, so extraordinary that, if many reliable persons had not borne witness to it, we might well suspect never occurred as stated, provokes both speculation and comparison. Were the Americans of that day much more emotional than Americans are now? Webster, during the first half of his life, was always telling about this one or that one "bursting into tears" over almost nothing at all. Certain it is that neither Daniel Webster nor ten like him rolled into one could go into the United States Supreme Court today and so argue about anything as to fill the room with sobbing women and bring floods of tears to the eyes of the chief justice and his associates upon the bench. The thing, in these days, simply is not done. Men and women do not "burst into tears" very easily, and in public practically never. Webster and those who heard him wept over the matter of which of two groups should control a small college. The destinies of Muscle Shoals, Boulder Dam, Porto Rico, the Philippines, the Hawaiian Islands, and the Panama Canal could be discussed in the United States Supreme Court today without bringing a tear to the eye of anybody. And, as for oratory, if a lawyer today were to begin an oration before the supreme court, the chief justice would soon give him a hard look which, if he did not heed, would likely be followed by the suggestion that he lower his voice and confine himself strictly to the business of stating and arguing his case. But Webster lived in another day and used other methods, including oratory. Like every orator, he had to hypnotize himself first before he could hypnotize others, and this he was able to do to a most astounding degree. In the moment of frenzy he believed everything he said—even his stabs at Jefferson, in whose home he was within a few years to spend several happy days as the guest of the Sage of Monticello.

Webster was not only a great lawyer and a great orator—he was, as Jeremiah Mason once said he had the power to be, a great actor. Such a combination of qualities makes a formidable man as those who opposed Webster soon learned. In the Dartmouth College case he was acting, not a little but a great deal. When he was arguing law points he was a lawyer and a very great one, but all the pathos about the pious poor, the "choking up" about the "little college" that was not without lovers was, to use his own word, "nonsense." So was his pretended fear of Jefferson. It would be unkind as well as unjust to say that, while he was thus acting, he did not for the moment believe every word he uttered. An orator, while he is speaking, has to believe every word he utters or he could make no one else believe him. The orator, however, has the advantage, in that he can recover from his frenzy and regain his sanity, while his words sometimes long continue to reverberate in the minds of those who lack the mental power to throw them off.

Webster wept in court when he thought of the small college. He wept because he was acting. He was not acting and he did not weep when at first he refused to argue the case in Washington after it had been lost in New Hampshire. Dartmouth College was just as small then as it was a few months later, but he was not acting nor did he weep when he told Jeremiah Mason and Judge Smith that he had not thought much about the case, one way or the other, and that the best thing for them to do would be to go to Washington without him and follow the lines that had failed in New Hampshire.

As we follow Webster along, we shall find that it was for him the rule, rather than the exception, to do as he did in the Dartmouth College argument, which he began cold as a clam, and finished at such a heat that both himself and his auditors were melted to tears. If we seek an explanation of this peculiar characteristic, we shall probably find it in a faculty that all good craftsmen have, and which he, as a master craftsman, had to a very extraordinary degree. A good craftsman of any sort always has the ability to generate an interest in what he is doing, quite irrespective of whether, when he began, he was interested or not. The problem that at first does not appeal grows interesting with the handling until, for at least a time, it fills the mind. So it was with Webster, only in his case, when his soul began to sing with the joy of his work, his tongue transmuted his ecstasy into words that communicated to others both his ecstasy and his frenzy.

The arguments having been made, the attorneys on both sides were naturally anxious to know when a decision might be expected. Nowadays, no lawyer would

79980

EMORY AND HENRY LIBRARY

presume to ask a justice of the United States Supreme Court such a question, but perhaps the tribunal a hundred years ago was not held in so much awe. Or perhaps it was because the leading counsel for the side opposed to Webster was Mr. William Wirt, Attorney-General of the United States—who, by the way, being overworked and, as he himself admitted, unprepared, had made a very bad showing in the case. The story is that Wirt inspired his associate, a Mr. Holmes of New Hampshire, to ask Chief Justice Marshall the question. "The chief justice said," according to a letter written by Webster, "that the court would not treat lightly an act of the legislature of a state and the decision of a state court, and that the court probably would not render any judgment at this term." Webster construed Marshall's reply to mean that the chief justice, at any rate, was on his side, inasmuch as Marshall and his associates, if they should desire to do so, could with propriety go promptly about it to sustain a state legislature and a state court. Which was perfectly true, as later we shall see.

March 14, the day after the closing of the arguments, which had lasted three days, Webster wrote:

"I have no accurate knowledge of the manner in which the judges are divided. The chief and Washington, I have no doubt, are with us. Duval and Todd perhaps against us; the other three holding up. I cannot much doubt that Story will be with us in the end, and I think we have more than an even chance for one of the others. I think we shall finally succeed."

Another bulletin written the same day by Webster:

". . . yesterday the chief justice told us that the court had conferred; that there were three different opinions, and that some judges had not formed opinions; consequently the cause must be continued."

A month and more has passed with no news from the court. Doubts are beginning to arise. There is talk of rearguing the case, or possibly of taking it to the supreme court again, not on different grounds, but in a little different way. On April 23, Webster writes a very illuminating letter to his old friend Jeremiah Mason, with whom he had been associated when the case was lost in New Hampshire.

"As to the college case," he began, "I cannot argue it any more, I believe. All that I said in Washington was but those two arguments [Smith's and Mason's] clumsily put together by me." (Too modest by far. In an earlier letter to Chief Justice Smith he had admitted that he had departed "a little" from Smith's and Mason's arguments; that he had "labored the point that Dartmouth was a private corporation," which was the basis of the pivot upon which the decision eventually swung.)

"They are hastily written off, with much abbreviation and contain little else than quotation from the cases. All the nonsense is left out." (Webster is writing of the notes from which he spoke in making the Dartmouth College argument, and the "nonsense" that he left out was the oratory and the pathos about the "small college" threatened with corruption by the Jeffersonian atheists. As one lawyer writing to another and reverencing only reason, he apparently felt moved to admit that he had put some "nonsense" into his argument.)

We now see Webster himself doing a little gumshoe work around the chambers of the United States Supreme Court. Evidently he has heard that Associate Justice Story either from the first has been on his side or has come over to it, because on September 9 we find him writing as follows directly to this member of the court:

"I send you five copies of our argument. If you send

one of them to each of such judges as you think proper, you will of course do it in the manner least likely to lead to the feeling that any indecorum has been committed by the plaintiffs."

Webster, cautious as he usually was in his letters, has opened the shutters a little here, and now we shall throw them open. A great campaign was in progress, led by John Marshall himself, to get three justices to join him in favor of a decision for the Dartmouth trustees and against the Jeffersonian attackers.

Four justices were necessary to render a decision. Webster's side had three—Marshall, Washington and Story. Another must be brought over. Marshall adjourned court until the following February, not to give time to get another man—such a statement could not be proved— but during the recess, the fourth man was obtained. He was Mr. Justice Brockholst Livingston of New York who, during the Revolutionary War, was on the staff of Benedict Arnold in the operations against Burgoyne. Chancellor Kent, a great New York Federalist, is generally given credit for bringing him into camp.

Nor is this expression carelessly used. There was a dragnet out for justices. A change of any one of the four votes against them would do. All in all, the drive for the additional vote constituted such a spectacle as never before had been attached to the court, nor has been since. Most of the work was done under cover, but much of it came to the surface. Newspapers took part in the task of influencing public opinion. It was like a polite, modified Presidential campaign. Public opinion is supposed to have nothing at all to do with the formulation of supreme-court decisions, but in that day the forces behind Webster and Marshall proceeded as if they believed otherwise. Social, political and personal influences were called into play. The appeals to passion that Webster had made in court were publicly printed that they might inflame that part of public opinion which was created by the Federalists.

As this campaign for a fourth vote proceeded, the adversaries of Webster at Dartmouth became uneasy. Belatedly they seem to have become aware that Wirt and Holmes had made a poor showing at Washington and that it might be well to employ abler counsel and see if the whole matter could not be reopened. On November 17, we find Mr. Joseph Hopkinson, Webster's associate in the case, writing to him as follows:

"In my passage through Baltimore, I fell in with Pinkney [the man whom Webster once locked in a room and threatened to whip] who told me that he was engaged on the other side in this matter and that he is desirous to argue it if the court will let him. I suppose he expects to do something very extraordinary in it as he says, 'Mr. Wirt was not strong enough for it; has not back enough.'"

A disquieting note. Webster agreed with Hopkinson that they should not be expected to reargue the case merely to give Pinkney an opportunity to make a speech. But when the time came, Chief Justice Marshall himself took care of Pinkney, and this is how he did it.

The time was the opening of court for the term beginning in February. Bright and early Pinkney was there. He arose to speak, but Marshall either did not hear him or pretended not to do so. At any rate, Marshall proceeded forthwith to announce that the court had come to an agreement in the case and that the decision was in favor of the college. Pinkney, as soon as he could, tried to mix matters by proposing a number of things that would have meant delay, but Webster was on his feet instantly, opposed each of them, and the court decided against them all. The case had indeed come to a close.

The same day, February 2, 1819, Webster wrote to Judge Smith of New Hampshire:

"I have the pleasure to tell you that the college cause has been decided in our favor. The chief justice, Washington, Livingston and Story, *concurrentibus,* Duval, *dissentiente; absente,* Todd."

On the same day Webster's associate, Hopkinson, wrote to a friend:

"Our triumph in the college cause has been complete . . . The court goes all lengths with us."

Webster had indeed wrung victory from the very jaws of defeat. It had long been the custom to regard certain grants made by states to citizens, and agreements made among individuals, as contracts. The Dartmouth College decision declared that charters and franchises were also contracts, and, as such, could not be canceled or modified without the consent of both parties. This would have been of slight importance if only the charters and franchises of "little colleges" had been concerned. But as the country developed, legislative bodies were called upon to grant and did grant franchises to many different kinds of corporations—railway, telephone, electric light, and many others. Some of these franchises were too hastily given—valuable property belonging to the public was handed over for little or nothing; sometimes franchises were obtained by the bribery of legislators. The Dartmouth College decision protected the first kind, while a little later the second were protected by a decision handed down by the court in the case of Fletcher *vs.* Peck, which declared that the fact that a legislative body has been bribed to grant a franchise is not sufficient reason for declaring the franchise void.

Most of the bad practices to which the Dartmouth decision led have been stopped. In many cases, the power of legislators to act in such matters has been restricted. Franchises are more carefully drawn, usually with certain limitations. Compensation for valuable rights given away or sold for too little is obtained by taxing franchises. There is still no remedy for the decision that holds a franchise valid, even if obtained by bribery, except to exercise more care in the choice of public officials. On the whole, the Dartmouth College decision has probably worked for the public good. At a time when the country needed development it at least contributed to the stability of the economic structure. There must be contracts that will stand before men will go ahead with any great enterprise calling for the expenditure of large sums of money.

III

ONE summer day in 1820, the advance agents of the Civil War, though neither of them was yet so recognized, rode through Boston, bowing right and left to the cheering crowds. The man seated at the right was John C. Calhoun, whose later rôle in history it was to take the first steps toward steeling the nerves of the South to strike. The man at his left was Daniel Webster, who, in looking back at him as we may now do, seems almost to have been born for no other purpose than to breathe into the North such a love of the Union that, when the time of trial came, it was ready for anything and everything that might follow.

But the Civil War is yet far away, and on this summer day no shadow of it falls athwart the pathway of these two great men. Webster, by this time, is widely recognized as a man of parts, but he is out of office and not yet of Calhoun's stature. Calhoun is the secretary of war, visiting Boston to inspect its forts and arsenals and— strange as it may now seem—the favorite of many New Englanders for the Presidency. Webster spends the day with him, going with him to the arsenal and the forts, and in the evening has him at dinner at his home, where a number of prominent citizens are invited to meet him. Some of those who attend the dinner speculate as to why Webster is so attentive to the secretary of war. One guess is that it is because he hopes Mr. Calhoun will yet become President. Another is more suspicious—something political may be brewing. "They have been driving together all day and they understand each other." How well, indeed, did these two men understand each other! Though later they were, from opposite sides, to juggle with fire and swords, each continued to his death to have the most profound respect for the abilities of the other. Webster always said that Calhoun was the greatest man he met in the senate.

This colorful summer day spent with Calhoun was a pleasant break in what had already become the hard, grinding life of Webster. He had quit congress to go to Boston to make money, and, according to the standards of his day and station, he was making it. His cash book, kept in his own hands, shows that during the fiscal year that ended August 12, 1819, his law business brought to him $15,181. The Dartmouth College argument, which first gave him a reputation as a great lawyer, had not taken place until almost the close of this year, and therefore had not had time much to increase the importance of the causes committed to him nor the size of his fees. The largest of these fees was two thousand dollars, paid by "Messrs. A. and A.," whoever they were—the nature of the services rendered not mentioned. The next in size was a balance of fifteen hundred for arguing the case of the United States Bank before the supreme court in Washington. The rest of the fees were five hundred dollars each or less, a great many as low as twenty dollars. John Jacob Astor was able to retain the services of Webster by a payment of fifty dollars, adding ninety dollars when the work was done. After the Dartmouth College argument the small cases and the small fees came to an end, though Webster never received such fees as are now paid to lawyers of reputation. A few months before he died the Goodyear Rubber interests offered him a fee of fifteen thousand dollars—ten thousand as a retainer and five thousand more if he should win—which was so large that Webster made inquiries to ascertain if they could afford it. Having satisfied himself upon this point, old and worn as he was, he dropped for a few days his work as secretary of state, went up to Trenton, and won the case.

By 1820, Webster's law business was booming. In comparison with all the standards he had ever known, money was rolling in. Prosperity was getting a grip upon him. But something else was also trying to take charge of his life. Political ambition, the thing he thought he had killed when he quit congress, again began to stir within him. There was to be a lifelong battle to see which of these forces would win.

So, in the autumn of 1820, we see the busy lawyer immersed in two labors that, having nothing to do with the law, were of a nature that would inevitably call him to the favorable attention of voters. The first of these tasks began in November, and the second—of historic importance—came in December before the first task was finished.

The first task was imposed upon him by his election as

a delegate to a convention called to revise the constitution of Massachusetts. What can be more deadly than such an assemblage? It all depends upon who is there. Webster's part in this one still makes good reading. Except in his attitude toward the proposal that the constitution of the state should continue to require state officials to subscribe to the Christian religion, Webster took what in our day would be regarded as an extremely conservative position. Indeed, many of his views were even then so regarded by a majority of the convention, which again and again voted against him. He carried with him, in his plea for religious freedom for state officials, most of the five hundred delegates, but failed in his attempts to make the senate a body mostly based upon property, and the judiciary an institution that only with the greatest difficulty could be touched by impeachment proceedings.

A brilliant man, however, can be quite as interesting in defeat as in victory. "Our friend Webster," wrote Justice Story, "has gained a noble reputation. It was a glorious field for him . . . On the whole, I was never more proud of any display than his in my life."

Webster was always interesting, even in those matters as to which the majority differed from him, because he brought to each subject so many well-arranged historical facts and related them so admirably. We see this capacity even more adequately displayed in the oration that, a few days later, he made to commemorate the two-hundredth anniversary of the landing of the Pilgrims. The date was December 22, 1820.

Old John Adams wrote to Webster:

"This oration will be read five hundred years hence with as much rapture as it was heard. It ought to be read at the end of every century, and indeed, at the end of every year, forever and ever."

WEBSTER IN HIS PRIME

*When he was practicing law in Boston.   Reproduced by
courtesy of Lincoln Hall, the present owner of Marshfield*

At the home of the Websters the morning of December 21, a number of people gathered. The oration was not to be delivered until the next day, but they were to start early to drive what we should now call the short distance from Boston to Plymouth. The journey, it seems, was to be a sort of holiday, and five friends were to make the trip with them. Is it not strange how a great event holds everybody who was in it just as a cake of ice holds everything that was in the water when it froze? We see in this group Mr. and Mrs. I. P. Davis, whose names are now preserved for no other reason than that they were there—and their names are all we know about them. Mr. F. C. Gray and Miss Mary Mason were likewise of the party. Miss Mason was the daughter of Jeremiah and therefore does not seem a stranger. And in the group at the door was also Miss Stockton, whose importance is derived from the fact that her father was one of the signers of the Declaration of Independence.

Two carriages were out in front, in each of which were numerous woolen blankets to protect the travelers from the keen December frost. The women were carefully tucked in.

Mrs. Webster, for whom this was an unusual occasion, was in her happiest mood, talking and laughing almost continuously. Her husband had from the beginning but little to say, and soon lapsed into complete silence. Some of the others may have thought that his work at the constitutional convention had tired him, while Miss Mason and Miss Stockton suspected that he was pondering over his forthcoming oration. The truth was that Webster was only indulging himself in a pastime of which he always had been and always would be fond— the pastime of getting out into the country and letting his mind loose to wander where it would.

At the half-way house they stopped for luncheon. Inside were sixty persons, most of whom Webster knew and many of whom were his close personal friends, all bound, as he was, for Plymouth. There was plenty of good talk, plenty of laughter and, for the gentlemen at least, a nip now and then of strong waters.

Man and beast having been fed, the cavalcade moved on. All the afternoon was spent on the road. When Plymouth was reached, they found the little place dressed for a holiday. Flags were flying and lights were burning at every window. A band, followed by a crowd of boys and men, appeared in front of the place where Webster was stopping, and serenaded him. After supper, some of the leading citizens came to call. Among them was old Mr. Samuel Davis, a descendant of the Pilgrims, who knew ancestors whose memories had run back almost to the occasion that was to be commemorated upon the morrow.

The first thing Webster did the next morning after breakfast was to visit the old First Church in which he was to speak. He ascended to the pulpit, and decided that it was not the place for him to stand when he spoke. Below the pulpit, however, was the deacon's seat and, after two or three experiments, he chose this place. A table was extemporized, and over it was spread a green baize cloth. These arrangements made, Webster returned to his hotel.

A great crowd filled the streets, not half of whom could get into the little church, which held but two or three hundred. What did it matter to those who could not get in? Not much. The holiday spirit was the thing, and they were getting it. What was a speech, more or less, anyway? Nobody knew what John Adams was going to say of it a day or two later, and much less did anybody realize that it was destined to be written about, read, and discussed, perhaps for centuries.

Webster spoke an hour and a half, but his speech was not printed for a year. The newspapers printed articles of praise about it, but none of them seemed to think it worth while to print the speech itself. But when we read Webster's Plymouth oration today, we see that what John Adams said about it is true. It is as interesting now as ever it was, and a thousand years hence it will be no less so.

Webster began with pictures, using words instead of paint. The embarkation of the Pilgrims from England for Holland has been told perhaps ten thousand times, but never before nor since as Webster told it two hundred years after it took place. One can feel the darkness of the night, the chill of the air, and the dumb terror in the hearts of the women, as they awaited the boat that was a day late in coming to take them away from England forever. We see them later, after they have sailed from Holland for America, at the height of a storm in the middle of the ocean; the little craft sturdily climbing one side of the great waves and sliding down the other; most of the women seasick; many of the children crying; the men standing stolidly about the deck silently speculating as to whether the voyage is soon to end, not in America, but at the bottom of the sea. And then, at last, the sighting of land! As Webster tells it, it is a great story, as vivid and moving today as ever it was.

There is always a small pleasure, when watching a great craftsman at work, in speculating as to why he does this or that. Why did Webster begin his Plymouth address with a series of pictures? A single quotation reveals the pith of his reasoning:

"It is a noble faculty of our nature which enables

us to connect our thoughts, our sympathies and our happiness with what is distant in place or time; and looking before and after, to hold communion at once with our ancestors and our posterity."

Webster tried to get the little crowd huddled in the church at Plymouth to reach out with their minds, forward and backward. It is doubtful if he changed the course of a single person present. It seems that either one is born with a peering mind or he isn't, and that's the end of it. Apparently all that can be done is to give good minds something upon which to feed, and this is what Webster did in his Plymouth oration.

What he said about the relationship of property and government went to the very heart of a vital subject that is of no less interest now than it was then. He believed that government should be based upon property, because interest in government is necessary and the way most likely to produce this interest in those who have property is to base government upon it. Well and good. But he did not stop there. He went on to say that the chief reason the Pilgrim Fathers soon became so attached to the land of their adoption was that each had an opportunity to become a property-owner.

In France, too, a policy had been adopted which had brought about a wide distribution of the land among the people. Webster, flying in the face of all European opinion, predicted that if the French government, within fifty years, did not change the laws, the laws would change the government. What he predicted came to pass. The monarchy fell. The people did not love it, because it did not protect their property interests.

Webster predicted that England, if she did not transfer the ownership of her land from the few to the many, would have trouble. Before what were known as the

Corn Laws were enacted, a few years later, England very nearly had a revolution, and to this day she is having trouble that a widely diffused ownership of land would decrease if not destroy.

Webster, in his Plymouth address, thundered at the slavery problem. What were the clanging sounds that came from Boston, and why were certain pillars of smoke rising to the sky? The smoke arose from furnaces owned by thrifty New England gentlemen who were engaged in the manufacture of manacles and fetters to put around black legs and arms. The clanging sounds came from the blows struck by workmen hammering into shape things with which to bind slaves. "It is not fit," he said, "that the land of the Pilgrims should bear the shame longer."

We hurry along through the oration to its conclusion in which he says that "when from the long distance of a hundred years [that's now] they [you and I] shall look back at us, they shall know at least that we possessed affections which, running backward and warming with gratitude for what our ancestors have done for our happiness, ran forward also to our posterity, and met them with cordial salutation, ere yet they have arrived on the shore of being."

"Advance then, ye future generations!" said Webster, in closing. "We would hail you, as you rise in your long succession, to fill the places which we now fill, and to taste the blessings of existence where we are passing and soon shall have passed, our own human duration. [Mr. Ticknor tells us that as Webster spoke he stretched out his arms as if to welcome the future generations, pitched his voice in a tone of most attractive sweetness and spread over his face "that peculiar smile which in him was always so charming."]

"We bid you welcome to this pleasant land of the fathers. We bid you welcome to the healthful skies and the verdant fields of New England. We greet your accession to the great inheritance which we have enjoyed. We welcome you to the blessings of good government and religious liberty. We welcome you to the treasures of science and the delights of learning. We welcome you to the transcendent sweets of domestic life, to the happiness of kindred, parents and children. We welcome you to the immeasurable blessings of rational existence, the immortal hope of Christianity, and the light of everlasting truth!"

Mr. Ticknor said:

"The effect of the whole was very great. As soon as we got home to our lodgings, all of the principal people then in Plymouth crowded about him. He was full of animation and radiant with happiness. But there was something about him very grand and imposing at the same time. He seemed as if he were like the mount that might not be touched, and that burned with fire."

Henry Cabot Lodge, in his Life of Webster, speaks of the Plymouth oration as if it had been but a sweet wind that tinkled musical little bells in the ears of each listener. In doing so, Lodge "missed a figure," as Webster used to say. Sweet wind there was in spots, but it was the least important ingredient of the Plymouth oration which, as old John Adams pointed out, has real substance.

During the long drive back to Boston, Mrs. Webster, who the day before had been so gay, was rather quiet. Perhaps the excitement had worn upon her, but her husband's great effort, which had cast a spell over everybody, had affected her most of all. At such times, she looked up to him almost as if he had been a god. Webster, however, was still thinking about the Pilgrim Fathers and chose the occasion to tell his little audience more interesting things about them than he had discussed in Plymouth. Did they realize, for instance, that creeds in religious matters had something to do with the outbreak of revolution? Such, in his opinion, was the fact. The Pilgrim Fathers had laid down the doctrine in their moral teachings that there should be no compromise with wrong-doing. As it was said in those old days, they "stood on points." This practice was soon carried over from religion into politics. Lord North came along with his tax upon tea. It was a small tax that everybody could afford to pay, but it might lead to a larger one, not only upon tea but upon other things. What did they do? Just what, in religious matters, they had always done. They stood on points. They refused to pay the tax.

As the horses briskly trotted along, Webster warmed to his story. What a wonderful people the Pilgrims were! "Our excellent ancestors." In each of them, he said, were all the Christian virtues except charity, yet none of them doubted that he had that too. One vice they had, however, though they never suspected it. A certain amount of religious hypocrisy had got into them. Paying too much attention, as they did, to external conduct, they made rules to govern too many acts, and soon began to exalt themselves because they observed the rules so well. Was it wrong to covet another's wife? Indeed it was, and the brethren of Connecticut forthwith made it a crime for a man, when going to church, to walk nearer than ten feet to his own wife. Gentlemen thus stalking along the country roads with their wives knew they were overdoing the thing, but they were also filled with self-approbation that they were able to do it at all.

[1822] Nominated for congress by people of Boston & Dec. of following year took his seat this time representing Mass.

116   WEBSTER'S GREAT LAW CASES

IV

DURING this period of Webster's life, the United States Supreme Court, under Chief Justice John Marshall, was making certain fundamental interpretations of the Constitution of the United States. These interpretations were destined to chart the course of important events, perhaps for centuries. It was the great good fortune of Webster that he helped to make these interpretations. The proof that he helped make them is that he won all of his cases, and the decisions of the courts followed closely his arguments. The Dartmouth College case was one; another was that of the United States Bank, or, as lawyers call it, McCulloch *vs.* Maryland.

Congress, in 1816, had, for the second time founded a Bank of the United States, to which it gave the right to establish branches throughout the states. Such a branch was in Baltimore. The Maryland state banks did not like its competition. The Maryland legislature accordingly placed a tax upon it. The United States Bank refused to pay the tax, and its cashier, McCulloch, was arrested by the Maryland authorities, indicted and convicted. The Maryland Supreme Court sustained the conviction. An appeal to the United States Supreme Court followed. Webster, Wirt and Pinkney appeared for the bank. Hopkinson (Webster's old associate in the Dartmouth College case), Holmes and Martin for the state. An imposing battery of lawyers on each side.

The importance of this case arises from the fact that Webster put into three lines a truth that Marshall, in his decision, shortened into one: "The power to tax is the power to destroy." The Maryland law could not be constitutional because it gave the state power to destroy what congress had the right to create. Such a law, for instance, would make it possible for the states to tax post offices and federal buildings of every sort, thus breaking down the services they were meant to render.

A much more interesting case involved the question of whether anybody except Livingston and Fulton, or those licensed by them, should have the right to navigate steamships on the waters of the state of New York. The New York law gave these two a monopoly, which was inconvenient for Cornelius Vanderbilt, who in 1817 had built a steamship, of which he was the captain, to ply between New York and New Brunswick, New Jersey. The story goes that he often let a young woman steer his craft into New York harbor, while he secreted himself in the ship's hold, his idea being that if anybody were to be arrested, the ship could spare the young woman better than it could him, so he took no part in testing the law.

The origin of the law is, in itself, an interesting story, illustrating, as it does, how men's ideas change. When human beings, more than a hundred years later, were about to fly, nobody thought of applying to any legislative body for the exclusive privilege of navigating the air. But in 1787, the legislature of the state of New York quite willingly gave for fourteen years to John Fitch the sole right to navigate steamships upon all waters under the state's jurisdiction. The legislature did this notwithstanding the fact that Fitch, at this time, had no steamship that could go anywhere. All he had was a small toy steamship with which he used to amuse bystanders who came to what was known as the "Collect Pond," which occupied the present site of the New York City prison. Fitch had the idea, but no money and perhaps not enough inventive ability to develop his ship. At any rate, his craft never progressed beyond the toy stage.

We now see how a good idea sometimes gets away and runs about from place to place. Perhaps Fulton got the idea of a steamship from Fitch; at any rate, we soon see Fulton outside the great Napoleon's door begging permission to exhibit his plans for a steamship which, if it is what its inventor believes, is just what Bonaparte needs to invade England. But Napoleon is too busy to talk with cranks, and Fulton goes away. Robert R. Livingston, American minister to France, gets wind of what has brought Fulton there and, having less on his mind than Napoleon has, sees that it is a good thing. Livingston quietly proceeds to induce the New York legislature to repeal the monopoly given to Fitch and give it to him for twenty years. Meeting Fulton soon afterward, Livingston, an inventor interested in creating a steamship, convinces Fulton, an inventor interested in the same thing, that their mutual welfare would best be promoted by cooperation. Fulton agrees and, at the request of these two, the New York legislature, in 1803, gives to them jointly, and to those licensed by them, for a period of twenty years, the exclusive right to navigate New York waters with steam. After the Clermont, in 1807, actually steams up and down the Hudson, the legislature passes a supplementary act extending the monopoly for five years for each of the next two steamships that Fulton and Livingston may build.

The law was now on the books, but the next thing was to enforce it. Some obeyed it by paying for and receiving licenses from the monopolists, while others ignored it, as did the founder of the Vanderbilt fortune. Nor was opposition to the law confined to New York. The Fulton-Livingston monopoly was interfering with the commerce of adjoining states. The legislature of Connecticut retaliated by enacting a law forbidding ships licensed by the monopolists to enter Connecticut waters at all. The legislature of New Jersey passed an act providing that if citizens of the state should be restrained from plying New York waters with steamships they should be entitled to begin damage suits, in the Jersey courts, against the New York monopolists and recover treble costs.

Thomas Gibbons of New York, one of the wealthiest men engaged in the shipping trade, determined not only to ignore the law but, if challenged, to fight it. He was soon challenged by a competitor named Ogden, who having paid the monopolists for a license to operate did not relish Gibbons's bootleg competition. Ogden began proceedings before the great Chancellor Kent to restrain Gibbons from using his steamships. Chancellor Kent looked into the New York law, said it was good, and issued the restraining order. Gibbons took an appeal to the highest state court and was beaten again. Having no mind to quit, he employed Daniel Webster and William Wirt to take the case to the Federal Supreme Court.

Here were a problem and a case that were exactly to Webster's liking. The problem was to take what appeared to be the short end of an argument and yet succeed; to make his views prevail over those of Chancellor Kent and some of the other great legal minds of the state of New York and to upset an act of the New York legislature. The case itself was suited to him because it gave him ample opportunity to exercise his great power of disentangling a complicated proposition, resolving it into its elements, and making it stand forth almost as if it were a simple thing. After the lapse of more than a hundred years, it now seems strange that anyone should ever have questioned the right of a ship having a license from the United States Government to engage in the coasting trade to enter New York waters; but until Webster spoke, this right was denied by Chancellor Kent, by the justices of the highest court of the state and by the New York legislature. It was important to the future welfare of all the states that this monopolistic interference with commerce should be destroyed, yet years after the decision Associate Justice Wayne—who as a member of the United States Supreme Court heard Webster's argument and helped decide the case—said that if it had not been for Webster the decision, quite likely, would have gone the other way. Webster, near the close of his life, said that he believed this case was the most important one he ever argued. Justice Wayne said the court's decision "released every creek, harbor, river, and bay in our country from the interference of monopolies."

Mr. William Wirt, the distinguished attorney who, as Webster's opponent, made so poor a showing in the Dartmouth College case, appears to have done no better in what Webster always called the "steamboat case." Webster himself years afterward told the whole story, as it is here related, to his old friend Peter Harvey of Boston. Wirt and Webster having met for consultation in Washington where they had gone to argue the case, Wirt asked his associate upon what constitutional grounds he intended to rest his case. Webster replied that he intended to rest it upon the clause that gives congress the right to regulate commerce. Wirt replied that he did not believe such a plea would give them a ghost of a chance to win. Webster asked Wirt how he would argue it. What Wirt replied Webster, at the time he was telling this story, had forgotten, but whatever his reply was, Webster said:

"Mr. Wirt, I will be as frank with you as you have been with me and say that I do not see the slightest ground to rest our case upon, in your view of it."

"Very well," said Wirt, "let us each argue it in his own way, and we will find out which, if either, is right." Peter Harvey, quoting Webster, continues:

"The case came on for argument. Mr. Wirt made one of his brilliant arguments before the court. I followed with my view. I can see the chief justice as he looked at that moment. Chief Justice Marshall always wrote with a quill. He never adopted the barbarous invention of steel pens. That abomination had not been introduced. And, always before counsel began to argue, the chief justice would nib his pen; and then, when everything was ready, pulling up the sleeves of his gown, he would nod to the counsel who was to address him, as much as to say, 'I am ready; now you may go on.'

"I think I never experienced more intellectual pleasure than in arguing that question to a man who could appreciate it and take it in; . . . the opinion of the court, as rendered by the chief justice, was little else than a recital of my argument. The chief justice told me that he had little to do but to repeat that argument, as it covered the whole ground. And what was a little curious, he never referred to the fact that Mr. Wirt had made an argument. . . . That was very singular. It was an accident, I think. Mr. Wirt was a great lawyer and a great man. But sometimes a man gets a kink and does not hit right. That was one of the occasions. But that was nothing against Mr. Wirt."

V

WEBSTER, in December, 1823, returns to congress, having been elected to the house of representatives the year before from the Boston district. Mr. Clay, the speaker, appoints him chairman of the judiciary committee and Webster votes against Clay's protective tariff bill. As chairman of the judiciary committee he thwarts the attempt of western and southern congressmen to revamp the supreme court in such a manner that it cannot declare unconstitutional the act of a state legislature without a majority of the whole court—instead of a mere quorum—concurring. Webster accomplishes this feat by himself proposing a revamping measure that fails of passage, and the situation is left unchanged. He makes an impassioned speech in favor of the Greek revolutionists who are trying to gain independence from Turkey, which nobody a century later will remember, though he likes it better than any other address he has ever made in congress. But he lacks interest in much of the dull routine of the house, and cultivates the art of sitting at his desk, perhaps writing, without hearing a word of what is going on about him. "This is an admirable improvement," he says, "upon the old maxim, 'Hear with both ears.' I hear with neither."

A presidential election is coming on. The candidates are John Quincy Adams, Andrew Jackson, Clay, Crawford, Clinton. Webster has not much interest in any of them, though he would prefer Calhoun if Calhoun had a chance, which Webster believes he has not. Calhoun, then, for the Vice-Presidency, and he so advises his friends in New England, who take his advice and carry their states for Calhoun for second place. Webster believes the election will be thrown into the house of representatives; this proves to be the fact. Webster votes for Adams, who is elected on the first ballot. Calhoun is chosen Vice-President by the electoral college.

Webster visits the White House, after the inauguration of Adams, and notes with pleasure that the drawing-room is now warm enough for one to be comfortable in it without an overcoat; he remains to dinner and reports that the food is good and well-served. Mrs. Webster, too, is glad that the White House is warmer. Writing to a friend in Boston she says: "Instead of shivering and shaking in that immense cold saloon, we were shown into a good warm parlor, with a nice little white damsel to take care of our coats, etc."

The White House itself, she calls the "palace."

"The furniture in the palace below stairs," she writes, "is precisely as it was. . . . I wish I could send you an inventory of the furniture as it was up-stairs when Mrs. Adams came into possession—it's a curiosity."

Nothing escapes her woman's eyes.

"Mrs. Adams looks well in her new station . . . The President now and then sheds a tear which looks benign." (Mr. Adams has a lachrymal duct that occasionally closes and at such times gives him the appearance of weeping.)

Pleasant days. Pleasanter still, about this time when Webster hears that it may be possible to accompany his friend Ticknor upon a visit to Jefferson. Ticknor fishes for an invitation for Webster and gets it. Jefferson writes that Webster's "talents and principles entitle him to the favor and respect of all his fellow citizens and have long ago possessed him of mine." Webster will indeed be welcome.

George Ticknor, his wife, Anna, and Webster are to make the trip. Mrs. Webster is not going because she spends most of her time back in Boston with the children and is there now. The party of three begin their journey in mid-December by boat to Fredericksburg Landing, which they reach at night. Next morning they start off with a carriage and four horses over very bad Virginia roads with mud often up to the hubs. At noon they stop for dinner at a tavern, and the landlord drops his knife

and fork with astonishment when he learns that the man
for whom he is carving turkey is Daniel Webster. Push-
ing on through the mud, they plan to spend the night at
Dr. Tyrrel's tavern; on account of the bad roads they do
not reach there until after dark. What a tavern, at that!
The least said about it the better. But Webster's spirits
are high, and so are those of the others. He tells stories,
sings scraps of old songs and—why, here is an idea! Why
not go a little out of the way and call upon James Madison? George Ticknor and his wife agree. Before going
to bed, Ticknor writes a polite note to the former President, which it is planned to dispatch at daybreak the next
morning by special rider, informing him of what is in
the wind and intimating that, if to do so would be agreeable to him, they would like to call upon him. The next
morning, when only five miles from Dr. Tyrrel's, the
returning messenger meets them with word from Mr.
Madison that he will be glad to see them. The warmth
of the response is heightened by the fact that the former
President sends his coachman to pilot the party over the
obscure roads.

Montpelier is reached late in the afternoon. It has
been the home of Madison all his life. He is now seventy-
four years old, but good for another dozen years and not
too old to enjoy good company. He knows Webster well
and warmly welcomes all three of them. Dinner is announced soon after nightfall, and lasts two hours. Rising
to go to the drawing-room, Webster, who is on edge with
a desire to get all he can of a reminiscent nature out of
Madison, whispers to Ticknor to say nothing about leaving the next morning. Once in the drawing-room, Webster sets about it to extract real information from the
man who is even now known as the "Father of the Constitution." How did it happen that the convention four

times voted against placing in the Constitution a specific authorization for the supreme court to declare acts of congress unconstitutional? Big questions and little ones. How did the various notables impress Mr. Madison? Was it true that Gouverneur Morris, to win a wager, once approached Washington as he was walking about the grounds during the noon-hour, slapped him upon the back and called him "George"? Mr. Madison did not see Morris do this, but he understands that the story is true. As to the supreme court, some light, but not much, will come out when Mr. Madison's journal of the convention is published, but it will not appear until after he is dead.

The travelers are tired; Mr. Madison's habit is to retire early, so the party is interrupted by the necessity of sleeping. The next morning, the head of the house is not visible. It is his custom, when guests are present, to let them entertain themselves until the evening meal, while he does the same. It is Sunday morning and the guests are asked if they would like to mount horses and visit various parts of the estate. Webster is not much of a rider and would prefer to spend the day with Mr. Madison, but there is nothing to do but go galloping, and he goes. In a little while they are off the Madison estate and in about as cheerless a country as ever they have seen. Woods, brush-fields, hard footing for horses and bad traveling for their riders. Still Webster is light-hearted, laughing and joking as they go along. Surveying the forbidding landscape, which includes not a single house, it occurs to him that he is now in the congressional district of the Honorable Philip Barbour. He laughs as he says, "I wonder where Phil Barbour's constituents are." Mrs. Phil herself lives only a few miles away, so why not canter over to see her? They canter.

Mrs. Phil is at home. Webster satisfactorily answers all of her questions as to the state of her husband's health when he saw him a few days ago, and with appropriate adieux, the party ride away.

After the return to Montpelier for dinner, another delightful two hours is spent at the table, followed by an hour or two in the drawing-room. Mr. Madison is obviously trying his best to make Webster's visit pleasant, and Webster is just as obviously trying to keep the conversation away from subjects that might be embarrassing to both of them. The War of 1812, for instance. The bond between them is not politics but patriotism, and Webster rejoices in the opportunity to listen to a man who not only knew but knew well all of the great characters who made up the Philadelphia convention of 1787. "Madison is the wisest of our Presidents except Washington," Webster says the next morning as they jog along toward the home of Jefferson. The distance is only thirty-two miles, but more than a day is required to cover it.

At Charlottesville, before going up to Monticello, they stop at a tavern for the night. Webster receives a letter. In a moment, his whole appearance changes. His little son Charles, almost two years old, is quite ill. Charles is the third son and the fifth child; two years younger than his brother Edward. The father's mind goes back to little Grace, his first-born, now no more. He is worried, but his common sense tells him he is making a mountain out of a molehill. Anyway, he is days and days away from Boston, the baby will undoubtedly soon be better, and Mr. Jefferson is expecting him.

The next morning they go up to Monticello. Jefferson, now eighty-one years of age, greets them at the door. The greeting is all that one might expect of a Virginia gentleman, long resident at the court of France. Webster and Jefferson are going to get along famously, as each instinctively feels from the first.

How does Jefferson look? Webster, who has never before seen him, does not fail to eye narrowly the man who wrote the Declaration of Independence. It is the work of but a few seconds to note most of the host's chief physical characteristics: height more than six feet; frame large and bony; head habitually carried well forward on a long neck; hair once red but now turning white and of an indistinct sandy color; eyes small, light blue, and neither brilliant nor striking; chin rather long but not sharp; nose small but well formed, with the nostrils a little elevated; good mouth and good teeth, the latter generally pressed tightly together creating an impression of contentment and benevolence; skin, once light and freckled, now marked by age and cutaneous affections; legs uncommonly long; hands, feet, and wrists unusually large; walks in an easy, swinging manner; when sitting, slides down in his chair; wears in the house a dark gray coat, a yellow waistcoat, and beneath that another one of dingy red; loose, long gray trousers; gray stockings, heavy shoes; a round hat; not a slovenly dresser, but obviously not much concerned as to how he looks; health apparently fine, though death is awaiting him but two Fourths of July away; sight good, needing glasses only in the evening; hearing good provided too many persons are not speaking at the same time, in which case he becomes confused.

Jefferson is indeed glad to welcome his guest from Massachusetts. Would the guest care to accompany him on a horseback ride that he is about to take here and there around the estate? Webster will be glad to go, and they set off, Jefferson wearing a long gray overcoat fastened with large pearl buttons. Jefferson tells him that it is his daily custom to ride horseback at least seven miles and perhaps twice that much. As Jefferson goes on with the story of how he lives, Webster marvels that so old a man can be so active. He rises as early in the morning as he can see the hands of his clock; goes to the thermometer, observes the temperature and makes a note of it, as he has done for many years; writes until he breakfasts at nine on tea, coffee, and two or three kinds of Virginia bread, some of which are served hot; goes for his ride, then works in his library until four when dinner is served; eats a moderate dinner composed mostly of vegetables, with no wine until after the meal is finished, then the best wine that France affords, but not much of it; afterwards to the drawing-room, where between seven and eight tea and coffee are served; and at nine o'clock to bed. Jefferson tells him that he has so long been accustomed to retiring early that it is essential to his health.

This program suits Webster and his party so well that they remain five days. Webster finds Jefferson to be exactly the kind of conversationalist that he likes best. He knows the American Revolution, he knows France, he knows the learned world; and how delightfully he goes, when led by Webster's interest, from one of these subjects to another! Webster, who later in life is to say that if he had three lives to live he would devote one to the study of geology, another to the study of astronomy, and the third to literature, is probably amazed to learn that the tastes of Jefferson are practically identical with his own. Moreover, they are both intensely interested in the great characters of the American Revolution. Patrick Henry? Jefferson knew him well and, since Webster is interested, warms to the story that he is about to tell.

Patrick Henry in his youth was a bartender. He was married before he was twenty and changed to some other

business at which, within a year, he failed. He next began
to read law, and after a few weeks' study applied to the
four examiners at Williamsburg for a license to practice.
Two of the examiners voted to reject his application for
a license. Henry prevailed upon the other two to favor
him. One of the two who at first opposed him was later
induced to give his consent, provided Henry, before
hanging out his shingle, would study some more. Henry
made this promise, but did not keep it. He never then or
afterward knew much about law, but he had so great a
gift at speaking that the first two cases he tried brought
about his election to the legislature. He seldom spoke
more than half an hour upon any subject and usually
but fifteen minutes. His pronunciation was "vulgar and
vicious," but his effects were tremendous.

Jefferson could never quite understand how he obtained these effects. Many a time, after Henry had spoken
in opposition to Jefferson with so much fire that even
Jefferson himself was moved, the latter would ask himself, "What the devil has he said?" but never could answer his own inquiry. Henry was like that. While he
was on his feet he seemed always to be speaking to the
point, but after he had finished it was difficult if not
impossible to tell what he had said. But no man was ever
better suited to his time and without him it would have
been more difficult to carry along the Revolution. Nobody equaled him in maintaining the spirit of rebellion.
He carried the rank and file along with him, and their
votes served as a warning to the timid to keep still. His
temper in debate was usually excellent, but his anger,
when provoked, was terrible. Among his friends he was
agreeable and facetious, in polite society all that he
should have been; "but in his heart he preferred low
society and sought it as often as possible." He went hunt-

ing in the pine woods with overseers and remained two weeks at a time without changing his clothing!

How Henry ever achieved his command of proper language was something that nobody could answer. "He was a man of very little knowledge of any sort, had read nothing and had no books." 'He wrote almost nothing; "he *could* not write." One autumn, Henry borrowed from Jefferson two volumes of Hume's Essays with which to while away winter evenings. In the spring he brought them back, saying that he had not been able to go farther than the first twenty or thirty pages of the first volume. Wirt, in his biography of Henry, said that Henry "read Plutarch every year." Jefferson doubted if he ever read a volume of it in his life. Henry's unlettered condition was a fact that made only more remarkable his powers. The Revolution did not exactly depend upon him, because there were several others of nearly equal abilities, but Henry was better in his line than any one of them.

Webster listens with the rapt attention of a child. For the moment he seems to be living with Henry in the days of the Revolution.

Day after day, beginning with dinner at four and lasting until nine, this exchange of experience, recollections, and ideas goes on. Webster, more eager to listen than to speak, encourages Jefferson to do most of the talking, which Jefferson does, in deference to the plain wishes of his guest, but does so with great modesty. This evening Jefferson makes a remark that causes Webster to tell a story that amuses Jefferson very much. Jefferson expresses the opinion that men often obtain undeserved credit both for the amount of their knowledge and for the readiness with which they command it. Webster agrees with him and says that this is especially true of lawyers. An event that occurred to himself is a case in point.

When he was a struggling young lawyer in Portsmouth, New Hampshire, a blacksmith came to him to get his opinion as to a small bequest that had been left to him in a will. The point at issue was somewhat obscure, and Webster asked the blacksmith to give him a few days in which to look up the law. He read through his own small collection of books without getting any light, then borrowed from Jeremiah Mason and another lawyer such books as they had that bore on the subject. The blacksmith called for the opinion, but was again sent away. Webster went to Boston, bought fifty dollars' worth of books and spent a month in studying them. He became convinced that his client had a case, so advised him, won it in court and received a fee of fifteen dollars.

A number of years later, Webster, while in New York on his way to Washington, received from Aaron Burr a note saying that he wished to consult him upon an important legal matter. The appointment was made, Burr called and began to tell his story. He had not been talking long before the thought came to Webster's mind, "Why, this is the old Portsmouth blacksmith's case all over again!" Webster remained silent while Burr went on. When Burr ceased speaking, Webster, with his brief in the blacksmith's case clearly in his mind, proceeded to state the law. What the courts had decided, clear back to the time of Charles II, was stated with no more hesitation than if they had made the decisions the day before. Burr, astonished at Webster's familiarity with the subject, interrupted to ask him if he had already been consulted by the other side. Webster did not like the question but showed no resentment, assured Burr that he had never before heard of the case, and went on with his statement. Webster later gave Burr a written opinion for which he charged him not only enough to cover the blacksmith's case of years ago, but something extra as compensation for Burr's suspicion that Webster had previously been consulted by the other side. Burr undoubtedly believed that Webster was a much more learned lawyer than he actually was, and, in the circumstances, Webster did not think it worth while to enlighten him as to the exact extent of his knowledge.

The next morning, Webster rises at daylight to catch Jefferson as he is looking at his thermometer. Jefferson, refreshed by his night's rest and with a clear sky heralding a fine Virginia winter day is willing to be caught. They have a little light conversation, followed by breakfast together, but Webster is too wise to remain long with his host. On horseback he spends the day with George Ticknor and his wife, riding about the country. When they return at four they are more than ready for their dinner, because they are not accustomed to two meals a day with dinner seven hours removed from breakfast.

After dinner, Jefferson, quite by chance, tells a story about the Revolution that interests Webster exceedingly. It has to do with the manner in which the fires of revolt were lighted in the Old Dominion. Webster had always understood that Virginia burst into flame almost as if there had been spontaneous combustion. It appears that such was not the fact. "About the time of the Boston port bill," Jefferson tells him, "the patriotic feeling in Virginia had, from some cause or other, become languid and worn out. It was thought by some of us to be absolutely necessary to excite the people. At length it occurred to us to make grave faces and have a fast."

Some of the younger members of the assembly, including Jefferson, went about it to put this resolution into effect. They drew up resolutions "after the most pious and praiseworthy examples"—so pious in fact that it would have seemed absurd for them to introduce them. So the duty of sponsoring the resolutions was assigned to Mr. Nichols, "a grave and religious man," while some of the young fellows solemnly seconded them, and they were adopted unanimously.

"Our fast produced very considerable effects. We all agreed to go home and see that preachers were provided in our counties, and notice given to the people. I came to this county and notified the people, who wondered what it meant, and came together in multitudes. I took care to provide a preacher for the occasion."

Webster, who knows history as it is written, is very keen in his appreciation of this important bit of history as truthfully related by a man who helped make it. A fast engineered by legislators and conducted by preachers to stir up people and make them either volunteer or submit to the draft when it comes. Oh, well, it is news to him that in Virginia the Revolution was begun in this way! But it is only what has happened many a time before and what will probably happen many a time in the future.

What about General Jackson—what does Mr. Jefferson think of him?

Jefferson does not think at all well of General Jackson and is "alarmed" at the prospect that he may become President. "He is one of the most unfit men I know of for such a place. He has had very little respect for laws and constitutions and is, in fact, merely an able military chief. His passions are terrible. When I was president of the senate he was a senator, and he could never speak, from the rashness of his feelings. I have seen him attempt it repeatedly and choke up with rage. His passions are, no doubt, cooler now; he has been much tried since I knew him, but he is a dangerous man."

Anna Ticknor has been waiting for some time to ask a question and now a momentary pause gives her an opportunity to do so. She is curious to know whether Mr. Jefferson, when he was the American Minister to France, met Madame Necker, mother of Madame de Staël, and, if so, how she impressed him.

Mr. Jefferson remembers Madame Necker well. A very sincere and excellent woman, but not a pleasant person with whom to converse. She was subject to "what we call, here in Virginia, the 'budge,'" meaning thereby that she was exceedingly nervous and fidgety. Jefferson had known her to rise from the dinner table five or six times during the course of a single meal and walk up and down the room to compose herself.

George Ticknor inquires about Monsieur Buffon, the great French naturalist and philosopher. The inquiry quickly brings a smile to the face of Jefferson, as his mind flits back forty years to Paris. He recalls the first time he ever saw Buffon. It was at his country place, outside Paris. A sort of show place. Big grounds, open gates, walks, drives, shrubs, flowers. Everybody welcome to come in, but nobody at liberty to speak to him if he should happen to meet him. Jefferson, who had been taken to the place by a French marquis, ran across Buffon, but obeyed the rule as to silence. The idea was that the great man's time must be his own until the dinner hour. On the other hand, anybody who came to the place to visit the grounds might remain to dinner, regardless of whether he knew the host or not.

Jefferson and his friend remained to dine. Jefferson was introduced by the marquis as a gentleman from Virginia who had written certain things in the field of natural history that were in conflict with some of the published statements of Monsieur Buffon. "When Mr. Jefferson shall have read this," said Buffon, handing his latest book to Jefferson, "he will be perfectly satisfied that I am right." But Jefferson was not satisfied. Buffon had said things about some of the animals of North America that Jefferson knew were not so. Jefferson had made the written statement that American deer had horns two feet long. Buffon told him that if he could produce a single specimen with horns one foot long he (Buffon) would acknowledge himself beaten. Jefferson sent to America and had forwarded to Buffon a set of horns four feet long. Buffon scouted the suggestion that American reindeer could walk under the belly of an American moose. Jefferson paid two hundred dollars to have a stuffed moose sent to Buffon, who, at sight of it, acknowledged his error, promised to correct it in the next edition of his book, but died before he could do so.

After much more talk about Paris, Webster switches conversation back to his favorite subject—the American Revolution and its great characters. "John Adams," says Jefferson, "was our Colossus on the floor; not graceful, elegant, nor remarkably fluent, but with a power of thought and expression that sometimes moved us from our seats."

Sam Adams was another remarkable man. He had a hesitating, grunting manner, but in originating and sustaining revolutionary measures perhaps no man in congress equaled him and certainly none excelled him.

Jefferson, at this point, makes a statement that is of unusual interest to Webster, the New Englander. Jefferson says that Virginia, and the four New England states *made* the Revolution. Acting together throughout the conflict, they possessed five votes always to be counted upon. "They had to pick up the remaining two for a majority when and where they could."

Thus the time passes. Webster wishes the rain would cease, so he and the Ticknors could start back to Washington. He is anxious for news about his little boy, and he would also like to know what is going on in congress. Jefferson takes no newspapers except the Richmond Enquirer, and that comes but once a week. After five days, the sun comes out, and Jefferson's guests depart.

When the party reached the Rivanna River, which they had to cross by boat, they found the stream much swollen by recent rains.

"You find your work hard enough this morning, I think," said Webster to the ferryman.

"Yes, sir," he replied. "It puts a man up to all he knows, I assure you."

This expression much amused Webster, with the result that he frequently used it, causing it to spread all over the country.

At the tavern where they spent the night, they drew up and agreed upon a statement as to what Jefferson had said upon a number of interesting subjects. Future generations might be interested in seeing this great man as they saw him.

Back in Washington. A letter from Mrs. Webster— two letters. Bad news. The first letter says little Charles is dead, and the second says he has been placed in the tomb under St. Paul's Church in Boston beside his little sister Grace. Webster goes to his room after supper, bowed with grief, and writes five stanzas of verse, addressed to the memory of the baby.

> Thou rear'st to me no filial stone,
> No parent's grave with tears beholdest;
> Thou art my ancestor—my son!
> And stand'st in Heaven's accounts the oldest.

But the world must go on, government must go on, and a statesman, even if he cannot forget his private griefs, must continue at his work. Webster resumes his duties and continues to write letters. Less than a month after the receipt of the bad news from home we find him writing to the Ticknors, who have returned to Boston, in the same old strain—what congress was doing, what was occupying his time, both in and out of congress, and asking when he might expect to see them again. Two months after the child's death Mrs. Webster, with tears still swimming in her eyes, writes to him urging him not to let his afflictions weigh too heavily upon him. "Those dear children, who had such strong holds upon us while here, now allure us to heaven." She adds a bit of verse of her own and concludes:

"Farewell, my beloved husband. I have not time to write more, only to say I regret you have lost the pleasure of Mr. and Mrs. Ticknor's society which you need so much."

VI

NOBODY who saw Daniel Webster sitting at his desk in the house of representatives writing letters to friends while the house was in session would have considered him either an industrious or a hard-working man. It was his custom, when the proceedings in the house were dull and he felt the need of mental refreshment, to employ the time in writing to old friends in New England, particularly to the Ticknors, both of whom remained devoted to him until the end of his life. This, for instance, to Mrs. Ticknor:

"I write this in the house while Mr. Clay is speaking. I wish you were here to hear him. The highest enjoyment, almost, which I have in life, is in hearing an able argument or speech. The development of *mind* in those modes is delightful. In books we see the result of thought and of fancy. In the living speaker, we see the thought itself, as it rises in the speaker's own mind. And his countenance often indicates a *perception* before it gets upon his tongue. I have been charmed by observing this operation of minds which are truly great and vigorous; so that I am sometimes as much moved, as in reading a part of Milton and Shakespeare, by a striking and able argument, although on the dryest subject."

Webster is in the clutch of circumstances—in the whirl of events—that pull him in diverse directions. Politics pulls him with a peculiar tug. Having begun political life as a Federalist he sees his party die, and the second time he is elected to the house from the Boston district he is backed by the wing of the Democratic party that is opposed to Andrew Jackson. Oratory, having first diverted him at Plymouth, is about to call him out again at Bunker Hill. But above and beyond everything, it would seem, is the law. He is a member of the house of representatives, but big clients follow him to Washington with big cases that they wish argued before the United States Supreme Court. He is in court as much as he is in the house. In one winter he has fifteen cases before the court, and one case upon which he is employed intermittently for a number of years yields him seventy thousand dollars. Webster is earning money—big money.

But Webster is never too busy to remember one thing which when necessary he forcibly brings to the attention of others—that the United States of America is a nation, not a collection of states. Always his point of view is that of an American; not merely that of a citizen of Massachusetts. Never is his orderly mind more admirable than it is when we see this idea of nationality threading its way through every .appropriate subject that comes to hand. An appropriation bill is under consideration to extend the Cumberland Road to Zanesville, Ohio. A representative from South Carolina opposes it on the ground that it is sectional, and that no appropriation should be made until the government is ready to build roads everywhere and give each locality an appropriation based upon relative population. Webster opposes the South Carolinian and gives as his reason that it is his business, as an American sitting in congress, to see where immediate improvements are most needed and make them, quite regardless of where the localities concerned may be.

Webster is also in favor of making American money worth one hundred cents upon the dollar everywhere. Irredeemable paper currency issued by banks, fluctuating in price almost from hour to hour, and never worth its face value does not appeal to him. He gives an instance of one of the numerous tricks that such currency invited. "Let me tell you a short story," he writes to a friend:

A year or two ago, a client of mine, a trader, came to my rooms to pay me for a legal opinion. The sum was fifty dollars. He handed me ten five-dollar notes on a country bank in good credit, but a hundred miles from Boston. He was a good-natured man, and I addressed him thus:

"You give me this fee in country notes; now I wish to tell you what I suspect. I suspect that when you left your counting-house, you filled up a check on a Boston bank for fifty dollars; you put it in your pocket and, on your way hither, you called at a broker's, sold your check for these country notes, and received a premium of one or one and a half per cent—say fifty or seventy-five cents, with which it is your intention to buy a leg of mutton for dinner.

Now, sir, that mutton is mine. You shall not dine at my expense in your own house. The legal opinion that I gave you was not below par. I will not be paid in anything that is. Sit down and draw me a check for fifty dollars."

He at once admitted that the process had been as I stated, very nearly.

Webster worked hard, earned much, but often took time to play and spend some of his money. One such occasion marked a memorable period in his life. It was the time he bought Marshfield, a country place along the ocean shore, thirty or forty miles south of Boston.

On a beautiful day in summer, Webster and his wife were out riding. They were talking, as they had talked a thousand times before, about the country place that sometime they would buy. He was eager for it, and so was she. He had been away from the country long enough to want to get back, and perhaps he was also the victim of the obsession that to this day overcomes so many successful lawyers—that they would be equally successful as gentlemen farmers—a "superstition," as Mark Twain would say, that has cost some of them a lot of money. Webster wanted to get back to the soil, and his wife even knew precisely the kind of place she wished he would buy. She was describing it as she had described it many times, when, coming to the top of a hill, she saw the place of which she had so long dreamed nestled at the foot, next to the sea! The spectacle seemed almost to take away her breath.

"Oh, Daniel, let us stop and see this place! Let us drive in," she said.

They drove in. But not until a little later did Mrs. Webster know that her husband had played a small trick upon her. He had not come upon the place by accident.

He had heard that perhaps it might be bought, and the day's drive was for the purpose of seeing it.

Webster's knock at the door was answered by a very old man—John Thompson, who had been a captain during the Revolutionary War. When he learned the identity of his visitors, his head seemed to go around a bit. Although he had never before seen Mrs. Webster, he kissed her on the cheek, then called loudly to his wife and two sons to come—Daniel Webster was at the door!

The place was indeed what both Webster and his wife wanted. It had beauty—before the door was a spreading elm, and two miles away was the sea, plainly within sight. It had a history— the farm had been the home of Peregrine White, the first white child born in America. At the outbreak of the Revolution, the Thompsons owned it; but the Thompsons were royalists, and the colonists confiscated it. All of the Thompsons were royalists but one— and that one, now an old man, stood before them. Because he had taken the part of the colonists, the government after the war returned to him a third of the estate, representing his mother's dower interest. The place was heavily mortgaged, and Thompson was willing to sell.

Webster was willing to buy—on one condition. Captain Thompson and his wife must continue to live in the house, rent-free.

On these terms, title to the property changed hands, and the old couple, to the end of their lives, lived in their favorite room.

Marshfield, as Webster ever afterward called the place, and as it is still called, was just such a farm as a man like Webster would naturally buy. It consisted of one hundred and sixty acres of sand. The only signs of vegetation were bushes and a kind of matted grass, dry as shavings and tough as wire. But the sea, the sea! Webster,

to the end of his days, never, when at home, could take his
eyes from it. Oh, of course, there was sand! But what did
that matter to a gentleman farmer? He had great plans
for agriculture, but his esthetic nature must be fed first
and next his sporting proclivities. What a place to fish
and shoot!

The house was not much, but it could be made more.
It was a substantial, square old mansion, built in 1765.
It consisted of four or five good rooms down-stairs and as
many above. As years passed, Webster added to the house
until it bore no resemblance to the original structure.
Also, he bought adjoining land until his one hundred
and sixty acres became eighteen hundred. After the death
of Ezekiel Webster, Daniel took over the old homestead
at Franklin, New Hampshire, and thus became the proprietor of two farms. At each place Webster had an over-
seer with whom during all of his years in Washington—
that is, until the end of his life—he conducted a brisk
correspondence. By letter, Webster directed everything
in detail—what crops should be sown and how much
land devoted to each, what kind and how much fertilizer
should be used, which oxen should be kept and which
sold—even to the killing of the turkeys. Nothing escaped
his attention.

Webster's interest in Marshfield increased with his
years. All of his summers were spent there, and whenever
he could get away from Washington for a few days of
fishing or hunting he packed his bag and turned his eyes
northward. Often he wrote in advance to invite friends
in New York or Boston to be his guests.

Webster's particular specialties were fat cattle and
fat sheep. Neither cattle nor sheep can subsist upon sand,
so the immediate task was to enrich the soil. Webster
bought guano by the ton, but guano, even in those days,

WEBSTER'S HOME AT MARSHFIELD

The pre-Revolutionary mansion which was burned in 1879

cost a good deal of money. He finally solved the problem
by taking a leaf from the Indians. He fertilized with
fish. The land was full of sand, the sea was full of fish—
put the fish into the land and see things grow. Fortunately there came along the coast every summer great
schools of "hardheads," a fish ten or fifteen inches long,
weighing about a pound. They arrived in such numbers
that the fishermen employed by Webster often caught
with their nets five hundred barrels a day. Webster mixed
the fish with muck or decayed vegetable matter, let them
stand until they were thoroughly "ripe," then applied
ten or twelve loads of the mixture to the acre. It was a
very good mixture—a single fish was said to be the equiv-
alent in fertilizing value of a shovelful of manure; and
the nutriment, once in the soil, remained a long while to
do good—but its most striking characteristic, at least
from the point of view of the neighbors, was the smell
and the enormous number of murderous flies that it attracted. Old General Lyman said that once when he was
in Pembroke he told a man that he was about to go to
Marshfield.

"Well," said the man, "you will of course see the
squire's farm." (The neighbors always called Webster
"the squire.")

"Quite likely," Lyman replied.

"Well," said the man, "you will see something worth
seeing. I did not know, two months ago, but that he would
drive us all out of Pembroke. I believe the squire spreads
on his land, in summer, about all the fish he can find in
the sea. These breed a pestilential quality of flies; not
our house-flies, but black, glossy fellows, that come about
two hundred times as thick as you ever saw house-flies
about a plate of molasses. When the wind is in the east
it brings them here, and they remind us of Scripture times

and the plagues of Egypt. These insects are known in the neighborhood as 'Webster flies.' "

Webster learned that kelp, or rockweed, which storms pile upon the shore in great quantities, was worth three times as much for fertilizing purposes as ordinary manure. Year after year kelp was therefore plowed into the land. Kelp, fish, and guano at last brought the sand to life, but at an awful cost to Webster's pocketbook. Webster's letters to his farm overseers were seldom without a check for fifty or a hundred dollars. Labor, even then, cost money, as did also fancy bulls, blooded rams, swine, horses, and farm implements. Webster plowed in dollars and took out dimes; but many seasons had not passed before he had the satisfaction of owning a real farm. There was none, anywhere near him, like it. His live stock took the blue ribbons at the fairs, and his guests ate from his table every good thing that could be produced in his latitude, all of his own raising. Guests complimented him upon his "grounds." Webster corrected them. "I haven't got grounds," he said. "I've got a farm."

To an audience in Rochester he once said: "Why, gentlemen, I live on the sandy seashore of Marshfield and get along as well as I can. I am a poor farmer upon a great quantity of poor land; but my neighbors and I, by very great care—I hardly know how—contrive to live on."

One reason that Webster's neighbors were able to "live on" as well as they did was that he helped them, both by example and with gifts of whatever he had that was particularly good—improved seed-corn, better potatoes, and the like. Whatever he did, his neighbors, to the extent of their abilities, copied. Having seen him fertilize with fish, they began to do likewise. This imitative tendency once brought the master of Marshfield a cash reward. Webster happening to meet a farmer on the road with a load of fish, the farmer explained that Webster's fishermen, having made an unusually large catch, had permitted him to draw away all he could pile into his wagon-box. The farmer, of course, intended to pay for them, and here was fifty cents which he forthwith handed over. Webster took the money, fearful that by refusing, he might hurt his neighbor's feelings, but felt that something very strange had happened.

"It was the only money I ever received from Marshfield," he afterward said. Of course this was not strictly true—his overseers received money for him—but it had in it enough truth to remind him of the ghastly fact that his farming was a costly venture.

Webster's attempts to practice the art of agriculture brought him, when he could forget their cost, great contentment. He liked to break an ear of corn in two and put the halves into the open mouths of two fat steers. "I like to be out here, feeding the stock," he once said to his son Fletcher. "I would rather be here than in the senate." Then smiling a little, he added, "I think it is better company."

Webster liked to get close to the soil again and feel that he was making things grow. He liked Marshfield because it was a glorious retreat. Most of all he cared for it because it was ever in sight of the sea. "I can see, in two days," said he, "all there is at my father's old home at Franklin, but the sea is ever changing and ever new." Webster had no more appreciation of small lakes than he had of small fields of grain. What most appealed to him must be big—the ocean; eighteen hundred acres of land instead of one hundred and sixty; big fields of grain, big sheep, big cattle.

Marshfield, from the time he bought it to the end

of his days, played so important a part in Webster's life that nobody can understand him who does not also know what he did there and why he cared so much about it. As he built on to the old house addition after addition it soon assumed dimensions that made it possible for him to entertain, for so long a time as he pleased, as many guests as he wanted; nor did anything in the world please Webster so much as congenial company. Nobody ever valued friends more; few ever did so much to entertain them. He could entertain well, because he could both talk and listen. He could give pleasure by speaking, because he had so great a capacity for throwing a little useful light upon almost any subject that might come up during a natural, drifting conversation. No man of his time had so great a fund of stories, anecdotes, and recollections. No man of any time ever had a greater capacity for the enjoyment of the discourse of others—the grave, the gay, the weighty, or the ridiculous. Webster liked nothing better than to laugh, and whatever appealed to him as witty, humorous or delightfully absurd quickly traveled from his ears to his tongue. So stored was his mind with humorous anecdotes that the slightest touch was enough to set it off. Was the day particularly hot? Then this was one of Dr. Danforth's days. What, a guest would ask, is a Dr. Danforth day? Webster would explain that there once lived in the vicinity of Marshfield a very irascible old doctor named Danforth who, happening to be at a funeral, bent down to the ear of an old gentleman and whispered:

"It is a warm day, Mr. Jones."

Mr. Jones being more than a trifle deaf, whispered back: "What did you remark?"

"It is a warm day," was the reply.

"I am very deaf and did not understand you," whispered the old gentleman.

"I said it was as hot as hell; do you hear that?"

At ten o'clock at night, lights were out, but between three and four in the morning, in summertime, Webster was up, dressed, and out feeding ears of corn to his favorite cattle. Webster had a passion for the morning, and particularly for that early hour when first the stars begin to pale and the stillness of the night is broken by the introductory chirping of the birds. Fond as he always was of occasional periods of solitude, he liked to be up and about alone to see, by himself, the gorgeous panorama associated with the coming of the new day. Once while the grass was still wet with dew he went into his library and wrote to his brother-in-law's wife, Mrs. Page:

It is morning—and a morning sweet, fresh and delightful. . . . Among all our good people of Boston, not one in a thousand sees the sun rise once a year. Their idea of it is that it is that part of the day which comes along after a cup of coffee and a beefsteak or a piece of toast. With them, morning is not a new issuing of light, a new bursting forth of the sun, a new waking-up of all that has life, from a sort of temporary death, to behold again the works of God, the heavens and the earth; it is only a part of the domestic day, belonging to breakfast, to reading the newspapers, answering notes, sending the children to school and giving orders for dinner. The first faint streak of light, the earliest purpling of the east which the lark springs up to greet, and the deeper and deeper coloring from orange into red . . . this they never enjoy for they never see. . . .

I never thought that Adam had much advantage of us from having seen the world while it was new. The manifestations of the power of God, like his mercies, are "new every morning" and "fresh every evening." We see as fine risings of the sun as Adam ever saw, and its risings are as much a miracle now as they were in his day, and I think a good deal more, because it is now a part of the miracle that for thousands and thousands of years he has come at his appointed time, without the variation of a millionth part of a second. Adam could not tell how this might be.

This is interesting, not alone because it shows that Webster thought about the morning, but also because it indicates what he believed about the origin of man and the age of the earth. Webster shared the common opinion of his time that the earth was a few thousands of years old, never dreaming that within a century, science would increase his estimate by a billion years.

It was Webster's custom, after absorbing the morning, to go to his library and work until nine, when he had breakfast. Often, by ten o'clock, he would say, "I have finished my day's work, written all my letters, and now I have nothing to do but enjoy myself." Ordinarily, his first form of enjoyment was to put on old clothes and go out into the fields where the men were at work. It was pleasure for him, for a while, to get behind a six-ox team and hold the plow-handles. Dinner came at four, after which he drove out or went down to the beach to meet returning fishing craft and hear the stories of the day's adventures. Whist or conversation in the evening, and then to bed.

Such was the routine of ordinary days. On extraordinary days there was fishing or hunting. Webster kept his boats and all of his fishing apparatus at the mouth of Green Harbor River, two miles from his house. Every boat and every pail had "D. W." painted upon it; everything in its place, everything in order—the salt beef, brown bread, cheese, mustard, knives, forks, and whatever else might be considered necessary for a day's cruise. He had a sailboat and took with him a man to sail it;

and often, before it was fairly light in the morning, Webster's boat could be seen far from shore, slowly tacking its way, back and forth, toward the horizon and the rising sun. Often too at evening, when the light had faded almost to twilight, Webster's boat could be seen laboriously making its way toward the harbor at the mouth of the river. Dinner and perhaps some interesting guests had been missed, but what a day! "The sea, the sea, the sea!" The sunshine, the sky, the water, the air, and the day's catch of fish—what, in comparison with such compensations, was a missed dinner?

Afloat or ashore, Webster liked to fish, and nobody ever whipped a trout stream with more enjoyment or more patience than did he. Also, until he learned better, he liked to shoot birds on the wing, a "sport" that later in life he abandoned. Once when he heard a musket shot on his farm he said to one of his men:

"Drive that fellow from my premises. I don't want these birds disturbed. I watch them with delight and protect them; their nests have my constant care and oversight, and I never permit anybody to disturb them."

Fish, however, had no rights, and Webster was ever after them. A report of good fishing in a new place was always enough to attract him. His son Fletcher often told a story of a report that thus lured his father. The stream was eight or ten miles distant from Marshfield and was owned by a man named Baker upon whom they called. Fletcher's report of the conversation between Baker and his father, and his own comments, follows:

Webster: Well, Mr. Baker, with your leave we would like to try to take a trout from your brook.

Baker: Oh yes, sir, very welcome to.

Webster: I have heard that there was very good fishing in it, Mr. Baker.

Baker: Well, a good many folks have been here and taken a good many trout out, sometimes.

Webster: We must try and see what we can do this morning. Where do they usually begin to fish?

Baker: Oh, I'll show you.

The old man accompanied my father to the brook and pointed out the spot. It was where the brook was thickly overhung with alders and the ground was very miry. Father sank into the mud half-way up his leg.

Webster: Rather miry here, Mr. Baker.

Baker: Yes, that's the worst on't.

After throwing his line several times and catching his hook in the alders:

Webster: These alders are rather in the way, Mr. Baker.

Baker: I know it; that's the worst on't.

The mosquitoes now began to bite most annoyingly; one hand was busy all the time, slapping them off the face and the other hand.

Webster: These mosquitoes are pretty thick and very hungry, Mr. Baker.

Baker: I know it; that's the worst on't.

Now the heat in the low ground, without a breath of air, had become intense. My father wiped his forehead and rested a moment.

Webster: It is very hot down here in these bushes, Mr. Baker.

Baker: I know it; that's the worst on't.

My father resumed his fishing, and after an hour's struggle with the heat, the bushes, the mire and the mosquitoes:

Webster: There seem to be no fish here, Mr. Baker.

Baker: I know it; that's the worst on't.

There was no resisting this. My father put up his rod and departed, but he laughed all the way home at the "worst on't" and always took pleasure in recalling the occurrence to mind.

A story that Webster frequently told to his guests at Marshfield had its origin in rather a hideous picture of himself that was in a friend's house in Boston—an engraving showing him with a big white cravat; cheap and badly done. Some of his friends told him they did not like it, asked his opinion of it, and he told them this story:

The last time I went up to New Hampshire, before the railroad was built above Concord, I rode in a stage with but one other passenger, an old gentleman. I asked him where he was from and he said "Salisbury." Then I was interested and tried to find out his name.

"Did you know Mr. Webster?" I said.

"Old Captain Eb Webster? I guess I did! I knew him and all his family. They were my neighbors and friends, and a nice old man he was."

"Did you know him intimately?"

"Very intimately. He had a son who was a very extraordinary man. Ezekiel Webster was a son of Captain Webster, and was the greatest man New Hampshire ever raised. I was in the Concord courtroom, where I was a juryman at the trial, when he fell dead. He was arguing a case very eloquently when he suddenly fell to the floor. It made much excitement among the people. We were all proud of Ezekiel Webster. We should have sent him to congress if he had lived."

"Had Captain Webster any other children?"

"There were one or two girls, but they died young, I believe; and there were one or two other sons."

"Do you remember anything about any of Ezekiel's brothers?"

"He had a brother, I think—a younger brother."

"What was his name?"

"Let me see; oh yes, I think his name was Daniel."

"Did you ever see him?"

"I used to see him when he was a boy."

"Did you know him at all?"

"Oh yes, very well."

"Well, is he still living?"

"I guess he is. I never heard of his dying. I never thought anything about it, but I believe he is a lawyer down about Boston somewhere."

"Do you remember what kind of looking man he was?"

"Well, so far as I can remember, he was rather a *starn*-looking young man."

And (said Webster) that was rather a *starn*-looking portrait. Such is fame.

Such was life at Marshfield. It was a great life that Webster thoroughly enjoyed because, keeping no account of receipts or expenditures at either farm, he was able, most of the time, to forget how much it was all costing him.

The house in which Webster lived and died was burned in 1879. The second Mrs. Webster in 1880 built a much more pretentious house, which is still standing. In 1929 the only buildings at Marshfield that Webster ever saw were a stable and a small structure that he built to serve as a law office. The house and eight hundred acres of land were owned in 1929 by Mr. Lincoln Hall, whose father, an admirer of Webster, bought the place in 1884. The land is under even better cultivation than it was in Webster's day.

PART THREE

A POWER which has dotted over the surface of the whole globe with her possessions and military posts; whose morning drumbeat, following the sun, and keeping company with the hours, circles the earth with one continuous and unbroken strain of the martial airs of England."

—THE MOST BRILLIANT SINGLE JEWEL IN WEBSTER'S ORATORICAL CROWN. (See page 229.)

*An interesting description of Mrs Webster is given in (Two Centuries of Costume in America, by Alice Morse Earle Vol II. page 804) when she attended the commemoration of Bunker Hill.

"She wore a pearl-gray silk hat & gown. Her costume was not only rich, but thoroughly elegant, and in the full heighth not only of the best American, but the best French fashions which succeeded the empire modes. The hat was of the shape known as the "Restauration". No elegante of the Champs Élysées wore a more distinctive hat than this of Mrs Webster's. A younger woman might have added an ostrich plume to the row of ribbons, but it would be in no better style.

[1825] John Quincy Adams
Elected President.

[1824] Delivered in House of Rep. a
speech on "The Greek Revolution"
[1825] Address in connection with laying
of cornerstone of Bunker Hill monument.
[1826] Oration on lives and service of
John Adams and Thomas Jefferson in
Feneuil Hall, Aug 2.
[1826] Elected U.S. Senator

I

DURING a fourteen-month period in the years 1825-26, Daniel Webster delivered two orations, either of which, if he had done nothing else in his life, would have entitled him to substantial fame. One of these orations, delivered in the very presence of Lafayette and a small, grizzled group of Revolutionary veterans on June 17, 1825, commemorated the laying of the cornerstone of the monument at Bunker Hill. The other, delivered on August 2, 1826, was a eulogy of Adams and Jefferson, who had died less than a month before, on the fiftieth anniversary of the adoption of the Declaration of Independence. Regarded merely as an oratorical effort, neither of these addresses soared to the height attained at Plymouth, which is generally considered to register Webster's highest achievement as an orator. The Bunker Hill address comes second, and the Jefferson-Adams eulogy, third.

But there is, in this matter, a higher court than that which professionally passes upon the quality of oratory. That higher court is the opinion of the people. The decisions of this higher court are made known by the avidity with which it absorbs certain utterances and the tenacity with which memory holds them. Measured by these standards, the two orations that we are now about to consider stand unapproached, to this day, in American oratory. Extended excerpts from each of them soon found their way into our school readers where, fifty years after the events commemorated, they were still thrilling children who, as men and women, remember them yet. Cold print must contain something to be vividly held in mind half a century.

The hurrying, full-pulsed life of our time is apparently unaware, for the most part, that these addresses were ever made. The old school readers are gone, and the books that have taken their places are devoted to other matters. This is an oversight of which the twentieth century needs to be reminded. So long as the government of the United States continues to rest upon the Constitution framed in 1789, these addresses of Webster cannot die. So long as the present Constitution endures, there must be interest, both in the struggle from which it sprang, and in the men who set the government going under the Constitution. These addresses by Webster are flying leaps back into the past. One reads them and, as if by magic, goes back to the eighteenth century, and sits among that great company, listening to every word that is uttered, sharing the hopes and the fears of the fathers.

It is perhaps a quality peculiar to greatness that, at critical moments, it sometimes doubts its own powers. Webster did not want to make the address at Bunker Hill, believed he was not the man to make it, and, after he had written it, was firmly of the opinion that it was very bad. Writing to his friend Ticknor, he said:

"I did the deed this morning; that is, I finished my speech, and I am pretty well persuaded that it is a speech that will *finish* me, as far as reputation is concerned. There is no more tone in it than in the weather in which it was written."

Webster meant just that. Apparently he had chiefly in mind the form and structure of the address, which are not particularly good. He had put together a number of interesting fragments rather than do as he did at Plymouth, when he began at the bottom and, with a sure touch, carefully developed his theme along harmonious, majestic lines. What Webster overlooked, in condemning his work, was his own marvelous power to transport audiences—and future generations—through space and time. What he saw he was always able to make others see, and what he saw that day was not men talking at Bunker Hill, but men fighting there.

The address contained two very great moments; one when he spoke directly to the Revolutionary veterans, who were assembled immediately in front of the speaker's platform, and the other when he turned and addressed Lafayette, who was seated upon the platform. When Webster spoke to the old men, who as young men had fought under Washington, his whole heart went with his words. He was tremendously moved, as were those who heard him. This part of his address, which most "fifth readers" five decades ago contained, follows:

Venerable men! You have come down to us from a former generation. Heaven has bounteously lengthened out your lives that you might behold this joyous day. You are now where you stood fifty years ago this very hour, with your brothers and your neighbors, shoulder to shoulder, in the strife for your country.

Behold, how altered! The same heavens are indeed over your heads; the same ocean rolls at your feet, but all else, how changed! You hear now no roar of hostile cannon, you see no mixed volumes of smoke and flame rising from burning Charlestown. The ground strewn with the dead and the dying, the impetuous charge; the steady and successful repulse; the loud call to repeated assault; the summoning of all that is manly to repeated resistance; a thousand bosoms freely and fearlessly bared in an instant to whatever of terror there may be in war and death;

all these you have witnessed, but you witness them no more. All is peace.

The heights of yonder metropolis, its towers and roofs, which you then saw filled with wives and children and countrymen in distress and terror, and looking with unutterable emotions for the issue of the combat, have presented you today with the sight of its whole happy population, come out to welcome and greet you with a universal jubilee . . . All is peace; and God has granted you this sight of your country's happiness, ere you slumber in the grave. He has allowed you to behold and to partake the reward of your patriotic toils; and he has allowed us, your sons and countrymen, to meet you here, and in the name of the present generation, in the name of your country, in the name of liberty, to thank you. . . .

Veterans, you are the remnant of many a well-fought field. You bring with you marks of honor from Trenton and Monmouth, from Yorktown, Camden, Bennington and Saratoga. Veterans of half a century, when in your youthful days you put everything at hazard in your country's cause, good as that cause was and sanguine as youth is, still your fondest hopes did not stretch onward to an hour like this! . . .

But your agitated countenances and your heaving breasts inform me that even this is not an unmixed joy. I perceive that a tumult of contending feelings rushes upon you. The images of the dead, as well as the persons of the living, present themselves before you. The scene overwhelms you, and I turn from it.

May the Father of all mercies smile upon your declining years and bless them; And when you shall here have exchanged your embraces, when you shall once more have pressed the hands which have so often been extended to give succor in adversity, or grasped in the exultation of victory, then look abroad upon this lovely land which your young valor defended and mark the happiness with which it is filled; yea, look abroad upon the whole earth and see what a name you have contributed to give to your country, and what a praise you have added to freedom, and then rejoice in the sympathy and gratitude which beam upon your last days from the improved condition of mankind!

Picture the scene that day in June. Twenty thousand persons, from far and near, closely packed around the speaker's platform upon rising tiers of temporary seats. Every seat occupied, and the hillside, to the rear, covered with those who are compelled to stand. Every eye on Webster, and his voice the only voice that is heard. A paragraph follows that wrought up the emotions of the audience to the highest pitch and soon reverberated throughout the country:

We come as Americans to mark a spot which must forever be dear to us and our posterity. We wish that whosoever, in all coming time, shall turn his eye hither, may behold that the place is not undistinguished where the first great battle of the Revolution was fought. We wish that this structure may proclaim the magnitude and importance of that event to every class and every age. We wish that infancy may learn the purpose of its erection from maternal lips, and that weary and withered age may behold it, and be solaced by the recollections it suggests. We wish that labor may look up here and be proud in the midst of its toil. We wish that in those days of disaster, which, as they come upon all nations, must be expected to come upon us also, desponding patriotism may turn its eyes hitherward, and be assured that the foundations of our national power are still strong. We wish that this column, rising toward heaven among the pointed spires of so many temples dedicated to God, may contribute also to produce in all minds a pious feeling of dependence and gratitude. We wish finally that the last object to the sight of him who leaves his native shore, and the first to gladden his who revisits it, may be something which shall remind him of the liberty and the glory of his country. Let it rise, let it rise till it meet the sun in his coming! Let the earliest light of the morning gild it, and parting day linger and play on its summit.

Sitting upon the platform all of this time, listening to every word that is said, is an old man who, in his youth, helped to make America—Lafayette. Webster suddenly turns and addresses him:

Sir, we are assembled to commemorate the establishment of great principles of liberty, and to do honor to the distinguished dead. The occasion is too severe for eulogy of the living. But, sir, your interesting relation to this country, the peculiar circumstances which surround you and surround us, call on me to express the happiness which we derive from your presence and aid in this solemn commemoration. Fortunate, fortunate man! With what measure of devotion will you not thank God for the circumstances of your extraordinary life. You are connected with both hemispheres and with two generations. Heaven saw fit to ordain that the electric spark of liberty should be conducted, through you, from the new world to the old; and we who are now here to perform this duty of patriotism have all of us, long ago, received it in charge from our fathers to cherish your name and your virtues. You will account it an instance of good fortune, sir, that you crossed the ocean at a time which enables you to be present at this solemnity. You now behold the field, the renown of which reached you in the heart of France, and caused a thrill in your ardent bosom. You see the lines of the little redoubt thrown up by the incredible diligence of Prescott; defended to the last extremity by his lion-hearted valor, and within which the cornerstone of our monument has now taken its position. You see where Warren fell, and where Parker, Gardner, McCleary, Moore, and other early patriots fell with him. Those who survived that day, and whose lives have been prolonged to the present hour, are now around you. Some of them you have known in the trying scenes of the war. Behold! They now stretch forth their feeble arms to embrace you. Behold! They raise their trembling voices to invoke the blessing of God on you and yours forever. . . . Illustrious as are your merits, yet far, oh, very distant be the day, when any inscription shall bear your name, or any tongue pronounce its eulogy.

Within a few days the country was ringing with the Bunker Hill oration. Lafayette, after he returned to France, wrote to Webster: "Your Bunker Hill has been translated into French and other languages, to the very great profit of European readers."

Fletcher Webster afterward said that most of the Bunker Hill address was composed while his father was standing up to his waist in water, fishing for trout. The son, who was fishing some distance away, noticed after a while, that his father seemed preoccupied. "He would let his line run carelessly down the stream, or hold his rod still while his hook was not even touching the water." Two or three times Fletcher called his father's attention to the fact that his hook was hanging on a twig, or was caught in long grass; but each time Webster's attention quickly drifted away from his fishing. This interested Fletcher so much that he quietly crept up to his father and watched. Webster seemed to be gazing at the overhanging trees, then he advanced one foot, extended his right hand, and began to speak: "Venerable men! You have come down to us from a former generation."

II

ON the seventeenth of June, 1826—a year from the day Webster spoke at Bunker Hill—he stopped in Quincy to make a respectful call upon John Adams—"the President," as Webster always called him. It was a hot day, and the old man, much fatigued and weakened, was lying on a couch while two women were fanning him.

"I hope the President is well today," said Webster as he approached the sofa and reached out for the extended hand.

"No," replied Adams, "I have lived in this old and frail tenement a great many years, it is very dilapidated, and, from all I can hear, my landlord doesn't intend to repair it."

Seventeen days later Adams died. Twenty-nine days after his death, Webster delivered a eulogy of Adams and Jefferson that contained one feature so remarkable that not only was it put into schoolbooks but it was for years a subject of controversy throughout the nation. Webster did a daring thing to accomplish this. He went back fifty years in time, passed through the locked doors of the Continental Congress—doors that were always locked when the congress was in session—and gave what appeared to be an exact report of an argument on the floor of the house between an unnamed member, who was opposed to declaring American independence, and John Adams.

There was no attempt to deceive, yet the art with which Webster did the thing *did* deceive. It was both great oratory and great acting. Adams, who had just died, seemed alive again; not only alive but young and flaming with the ardor that he had when Jefferson said: "He was our Colossus on the floor."

The ideas attributed to Adams and his unnamed opponent were known to be correctly stated. This knowledge was what made the supposed speeches so persistently deceptive. Webster had been so artful in weaving what was known to everybody into what appeared to be a running report of a debate that some of the people of his day did not live long enough to get the facts straight in their minds. To this day, one occasionally sees references to Adams's "speech" with nothing to indicate that the writers knew that Webster, and not Adams, made it. Yet nothing was attributed to Adams that he himself had not often said.

It is worth while to examine in detail this celebrated fragment of a notable address that furnished reading matter for two generations of American school children. Webster speaks:

> Let us then bring before us the assembly which was about to decide a question thus big with the fate of empire. Let us open the doors and look in upon their deliberations. Let us survey the anxious and care-worn countenances. Let us hear the firm-toned voices of this band of patriots.
>
> Hancock presides over the solemn sitting, and one of those not yet prepared to pronounce for absolute independence is on the floor, and is urging his reasons for dissenting from the declaration.
>
> "Let us pause! This step, once taken, cannot be retraced. This resolution, once passed, will cut off all hope of reconciliation. If success attends the arms of England we shall then be no longer colonies with charters and with privileges; these will all be forfeited by the act, and we shall be in the condition of other conquered people, at the mercy of the conquerors.

"For ourselves, we may be ready to run the hazard, but are we ready to carry the country to that length? Is success so probable as to justify it? Where is the military, where the naval power by which we are to resist the whole strength of the arm of England, for she will exert that strength to the utmost? Can we rely on the constancy and perseverance of the people, or will they not act as the people of other countries have acted and, wearied with a long war, submit in the end to a worse oppression?

"While we stand on our old ground and insist on redress of grievances we are right and are not answerable for consequences. Nothing then can be imputed to us. But if we change our object, carry our pretensions further and set up for absolute independence we shall lose the sympathy of mankind. We shall no longer be defending what we possess, but struggling for something which we never did possess, and which we have solemnly and uniformly disclaimed all intention of pursuing, from the very outset of the troubles.

"Abandoning thus our old ground of resistance only to arbitrary acts of oppression, the nations will believe the whole to have been mere pretense, and they will look on us, not as injured but as ambitious subjects. I shudder before this responsibility. It will be on us if, relinquishing the ground on which we have stood so long and stood so safely, we now proclaim independence and carry on the war for that object while these cities burn, these pleasant fields whiten and bleach with the bones of their owners, and these streams run blood. It will be upon us if, failing to maintain this unseasonable and ill-judged declaration, a sterner despotism maintained by military power shall be established over our posterity, when we ourselves, given up by an exhausted, a harassed, a misled people, shall have expiated our rashness and atoned for our presumption on the scaffold."

It was for Mr. Adams to reply to arguments like

these. We know his opinions and we know his character. He would commence with his accustomed directness and earnestness.

"Sink or swim, live or die, survive or perish, I give my hand and my heart to this vote. It is true indeed that, in the beginning, we aimed not at independence. But there's a Divinity which shapes our ends. The injustice of England has driven us to arms, and, blinded to her own interest for our good, she has obstinately persisted till independence is now within our grasp. We have but to reach forth to it and it is ours.

"Why then should we defer the declaration? Is any man so weak as now to hope for a reconciliation with England which shall leave us either safety to the country and its liberties or safety to his own life and his own honor? Are not you, sir, who sit in that chair, is not he, our venerable colleague near you— are you not both already the proscribed and predestined objects of punishment and vengeance? Cut off from all hope of royal clemency, what are you, what can you be, while the power of England remains, but outlaws?

"If we postpone independence, do we mean to carry on or to give up the war? Do we mean to submit to the measures of Parliament, Boston Port Bill and all? Do we mean to submit and consent that we, ourselves, shall be ground to powder, and our country and its rights trodden down into dust?

"I know we do not mean to submit. We never shall submit. Do we intend to violate that most solemn obligation ever entered into by men, that plighting before God of our sacred honor to Washington when, putting him forth to incur the dangers of war, as well as the political hazards of the times, we promised to adhere to him, in every extremity, with our fortunes and our lives? I know there is not a man here who would not rather see a general conflagration sweep over the land, or an earthquake sink it, than one jot or tittle of that plighted faith fall to the ground. For myself, having twelve months ago, in this place, moved you that George Washington be appointed commander of the forces raised, or to be raised, in defense of American liberty, may my right hand forget her cunning and my tongue cleave to the roof of my mouth if I hesitate or waver in the support I give him.

"The war then must go on. We must fight it through. And, if the war must go on, why put off longer the Declaration of Independence? That measure will strengthen us. It will give us character abroad. The nations will then treat with us, which they will never do while we acknowledge ourselves subjects, in arms against our sovereign. Nay, I maintain that England herself will sooner treat for peace with us on the footing of independence than consent, by repealing her acts, to acknowledge that her whole conduct towards us has been a course of injustice and oppression. . . .

"If we fail, it will be no worse for us. But we shall not fail. The cause will raise up armies. The cause will create navies. The people, if we are true to them, will carry us and carry themselves gloriously through this struggle . . . Sir, the Declaration will inspire the people with increased courage. . . . Read this Declaration at the head of the army; every sword will be drawn from its scabbard and the solemn vow uttered to maintain it, or to perish on the bed of honor. . . .

"Sir, I know the uncertainty of human affairs, but I see—I see clearly—through this day's business. You and I, indeed, may rue it. We may not live to the time when this Declaration shall be made good. We may die; die colonists, die slaves; die, it may be, ignominiously and on the scaffold. Be it so. Be it so. If it be the pleasure of Heaven that my country shall require the poor offering of my life, the victim shall be ready at the appointed hour of sacrifice, come when that hour may. But while I do live, let me have a country or at least the hope of a country, and that a free country.

"But whatever may be our fate, be assured—be assured—that this Declaration will stand. It may cost treasure and it may cost blood, but it will stand and it will richly compensate for both. Through the thick gloom of the present I see the brightness of the future, as the sun in heaven. We shall make this a glorious, an immortal day. When we are in our graves our children will honor it. They will celebrate it with thanksgiving, with festivity, with bonfires, and illuminations. On its annual return they will shed tears, copious gushing tears, not of subjection and slavery, not of agony and distress, but of exultation, of gratitude and of joy.

"Sir, before God I believe the hour is come. My judgment approves this measure and my whole heart is in it. All that I have and all that I am and all that I hope in this life I am now ready to stake upon it; and I leave off as I began, that live or die, survive or perish, I am for the Declaration. It is my living sentiment and, by the blessing of God, it shall be my dying sentiment, independence *now* and independence forever."

The faithful Ticknor was the first to hear the preceding speeches. The day before the meeting in Faneuil Hall, Webster sent for him and, upon his arrival, rather abruptly began to repeat the speeches. He had just written them and was uncertain whether they were the best or the worst of his oration. Ticknor told him to have no fears; that of the many fine things in the oration, nothing was better than the speeches. To the end of Webster's life he was compelled to answer letters from persons who, believing the speeches were actually made in congress, tried to prove it by him. Years later, President Fillmore asked

Webster about it. Webster explained and added: "I will tell you what is not generally known. I wrote that speech one morning before breakfast, in my library, and when it was finished, my paper was wet with my tears."

Ticknor enables us to behold the scene in Faneuil Hall. Every seat, on the floor and in the gallery, was filled. Webster "spoke in an orator's gown and wore small clothes. . . . He was in the perfection of his manly beauty and strength . . . When he came to the passage on eloquence and to the words, 'It is action, noble, sublime, godlike action' he stamped his foot repeatedly on the stage, his form seemed to dilate, and he stood, as that whole audience saw and felt, the personification of what he so perfectly described. I never saw him when his manner was so grand and appropriate."

Midsummer . . . dog-days . . . Marshfield.
Congress had expired of languor as it had a year or two before when a wag put an all-night session into verse:

> What guardian power my country's glory keeps,
> When senates doze, and e'en her Webster sleeps?
> When Clay, outwatched, forsakes his empty chair,
> And Warfield winks amidst the dusky air?
> Thro' the dim halls the wandering echoes stray,
> And yawning messengers look out for day.
> Cutt's laboring tongue can scarce pronounce the bills,
> And Cocke himself forgets his country's ills.
> Sigh answers sigh, and snore resounds to snore,
> Like billows bursting on some dreary shore.
> With lazy pace the long, long hours return,
> While worn-out Sibley cries, "Adjourn, adjourn."

III

THE last congress in which Daniel Webster was to sit as a member of the house of representatives assembled in Washington in December, 1826. It was a dull session, as second sessions usually are, concerned mostly with appropriation bills and other routine business. Only once was Webster aroused, and that was over a question involving state rights. Georgia threatened to use force to take over land within her borders that the Creek Indians said belonged to them. A rather truculent member from Mississippi said that his state, in dealing with its Indian lands, would do as it pleased, regardless of what the national government might think about it.

Webster called to account the gentlemen representing these states. He said that the government was bound by treaty with the Indians to preserve their rights in their lands. These treaties he meant to see fulfilled. He was ready immediately to vote money to buy the lands from the Indians, but it would be very risky for any state to use force to take lands that the Indians said belonged to them. He told his opponents very frankly that neither harsh words nor words loudly spoken would terrify him. But whatever was done must be done according to law, and that was the end of it.

Congress had not proceeded far into the new year before events in Massachusetts transferred Webster's attention from the national capital to his home state. A new senator was to be elected. The state senate, in February, voted for Levi Lincoln, the governor. Lincoln wrote a letter to the speaker of the house refusing to be a candidate. Webster wrote to Lincoln urging him to reconsider. Lincoln declined to do so.

Immediately forces were set into motion to elect Webster. He made it known that he preferred to remain in the house of representatives. Of course he knew that a senatorship was the higher station. But Webster felt that he could do more good in the house, where he was the leader of the administration forces. Webster, at this time, though never strictly a party man nor much of a believer in parties, acted with the faction of the Democratic party that backed Adams and opposed Jackson. Webster's membership in the house and his ability as a speaker gave to the Adams faction control of the house. The senate, on the other hand, was under the control of their opponents.

Opposing forces were pulling at Webster, some advising him to remain where he was and help his followers to retain control of the house, others urging him to go over to the senate and aid in swinging that body to their side. The Massachusetts legislature eventually took the situation into its own hands. Though Webster was not formally placed in nomination in either house, he was triumphantly elected senator for the term beginning March 4, 1827, and took his seat the following December.

IV

DANIEL WEBSTER'S wife never saw him sitting in the senate. Mrs. Webster throughout the preceding summer had been, by turns, sick and well; and as the time came for Webster to go to Washington it was apparent that perhaps more was the matter with her than anybody had suspected. Webster therefore, on his way to Washington, took her to New York to remain for a while in the home of his old friend Dr. Cyrus Perkins, who was to treat her and, if necessary, call in other physicians. It was soon definitely ascertained that she was suffering from an abdominal tumor for which nothing could be done and which must, of necessity, soon end her life.

Webster had gone on to Washington, little dreaming of what was to come. To this fact is due the receipt of mail from home that he treasured throughout life—communications upon the envelopes of which he wrote, "My dear Grace's two last letters."

? 1828 Buried his wife.

In the relations of Webster and his wife throughout their twenty years of married life, Mrs. Webster's attitude toward him had been perfectly clear. It was said in New England at the time by those who referred to Webster as "godlike" that such a term had never before been applied to any man during his lifetime; but Mrs. Webster looked up to him as if he had been indeed a god. As his fame ascended, she seemed to submerge her life in his. She was always solicitous about his health and his comfort. Were his rooms in Washington still cold? (He once wrote home that, except when he was in bed, he had not been warm for a week.) Had he recovered from the cough that he had when last he wrote? Her husband first, their children, well, perhaps not next, but almost second; and nothing else besides. She usually addressed him as "My Beloved Husband," and her letters were sprinkled with terms of endearment.

Webster was an honest soul, as good as gold to his wife, but sometimes, because of his honesty, a little club-footed. On one occasion, for instance, he sent her a diamond pin, with a little letter telling her all about it and expressing the hope that it would please her. That was all right, but he wrote too much. As she read on and on in the letter, she learned that Webster had sent to a jeweler for a diamond pin for his brother-in-law, that the jeweler, by mistake, had sent to the house not one pin but two, and that Webster, rather than make the jeweler trouble, had kept both and sent the extra pin to her. Upon the receipt of such a letter, many a woman would have thrown the pin in his face. Mrs. Webster kept it.

Webster usually addressed his wife as "My Love," but he was too busy with his politics, his law, his farming, his heavy correspondence, his hunting and fishing, and his friends in Washington, where he usually lived alone, to be always attentive to her. This statement comes to us, after the lapse of more than one hundred years, not in so many authoritative words, but as a matter of reasonable deduction and inference. Webster's love for his wife, which from the beginning was deep and strong, never faltered; but sometimes, in the press of business, he seemed for a moment to forget. The diamond pin incident certainly does not indicate a man whose wits were all about him, though it does prove that he was honest to the point of imbecility.

But if Webster, even for a moment, forgot his love for his wife, it was all brought home to him when he became aware of the nature and significance of her illness. Her last two letters follow:

Friday Morning, 11 o'clock, Dec. 1827
The first tribute of my heart is to the God who gives me strength to write, and the first of my pen to you, my best beloved. I need not say how much I rejoice to hear of your safe and rapid journey; but I do not trust myself to say one word further on the subject, so different has Providence ordered things from what I had promised myself. I am as comfortable since you left, but I fear I do not make much progress; but I beg you will not be too anxious about me, nor too much enhance the value of this poor life by your love for me.

Doctor Post is to be here this morning. I have

rather a dread of seeing him. I fear I am apt to be depressed more after a consultation. I can hardly tell why.

This is not such a letter as I would write you, my dearest husband, but such as it is, I know you will be glad to receive it from

Your devoted,
G. W.

Saturday Morning, 10 o'clock

I wrote you yesterday, my beloved husband, a very poor letter, but I flatter myself that a poor letter from me will be as acceptable as a good one from another.

I am sorry you do not get letters every day, but do not, my dear love, be too anxious about me. I felt in better spirits after Doctor Post was here, though I dreaded to see him. I would not have you, my dear husband, put yourself to the hardship of returning so soon as you talked of when you left, if I should continue as comfortable as I am now, though I sometimes feel the want of your cheering presence, and dear Daniel's kind and affectionate looks. . . . I feel persuaded that it is all for some wise purpose, but it is sometimes hard to say, "Not my will but Thine be done."

I fear you will hardly be able to read this, which I write lying on the sofa. I hope your health still continues good, and that we shall meet again under more favorable circumstances than we parted.

Farewell, dearest and best. May heaven bless and keep you, prays

Your Own Affectionate,
G. W.

P. S. Julia desires much love. Neddy is upstairs.

A day or two later Webster received word direct from the physicians that there was no hope. This news brought him to New York as rapidly as he could travel, which in those days was still by stage. Arrived at the Lyman house, he did nothing, day and night, but watch and serve. He employed a special cook to prepare her meals, with instructions never to offer her a second time anything that she had once refused. He ransacked the markets to find delicacies that might please her. Early in January, the weather having become colder and her strength less, she said she felt cold and wished she had a wood fire in the room. Webster, of course, did not own the house, but he went immediately to a mason, had the coal grate removed and a wood grate substituted. But nothing could help Mrs. Webster and, on January 21, 1828, five days after her forty-seventh birthday, she died.

"Poor Grace has gone to heaven; she has just now breathed her last," Daniel wrote to his brother Ezekiel under date of "Monday, quarter past two o'clock."

"All is over; my blessed wife has just expired," he wrote at the same hour to his friend Ticknor.

Her death dealt him a stunning blow from which he reeled for more than a year. He accompanied her body to Boston, where the funeral was held, and, though the day was stormy and he had on thin shoes, he insisted upon walking behind the hearse to the church. "My children and I," he said, "must follow their mother to the grave on foot." Holding Julia by one hand and Fletcher by the other, he plodded along through the cold slush. "He was excessively pale," says Ticknor.

It seems appropriate here to consider a letter, written by Webster about this time, which comes as near answering as anything in existence does, the question of whether he believed in religion, and, if so, what were his beliefs. James Parton, a biographer of some note, wrote a sketch of Webster, nineteen years after his death, in which he said that Webster had no religion—"not the least tincture of it"; that he went to church, talked piously, puffed the clergy and "patronized Providence" without believing anything.

What every man really believes as to such matters is hidden away in his own soul, into which he may or may not permit others to peer. No one can now say with certainty what Webster believed. But whoever studies his character, as it has come down to us, will have difficulty in agreeing with Parton. If Webster was not an intellectually honest man the search for such a one might as well be abandoned. No reason is apparent why he should have tried to deceive his nephew, to whom he disclosed part of his mind in a letter written two months after Mrs. Webster's letter. Incidentally, in this letter he paid the memory of Mrs. Webster a tribute that might well go down in company with the famous reply of Joseph H. Choate, who, when asked who he would prefer to be, if he could not be himself, said: "Mrs. Choate's second husband."

Webster said of his late wife: "Like an angel of God, indeed, I hope she is, in purity, in happiness, and in immortality; but I would fain hope that, in kind remembrance of those she has left, in a lingering human sympathy and human love, she may yet be, as God originally created her, 'a little lower than the angels'!"

As to immortality, Webster wrote to his nephew:

"It does not appear to me unreasonable to believe that the friendships of this life are perpetuated in heaven. . . . How can this world be rightly called a scene of probation and discipline if these affections, which we are commanded to cherish and cultivate here, are to leave us on the threshold of the other world? . . . Yet it must be confessed that there are some things in the New Testament which may possibly countenance a different conclusion. The words of our Saviour, especially in regard to the woman who had seven husbands, deserve deep reflection. I am free to confess that some descriptions of heavenly happiness are so ethereal and sublimated as to fill me with a strange terror."

Then he added the line that has been quoted about angels.

Webster distributed his three motherless children among relatives and friends in and near Boston, went back to his cold rooms in Washington, and resumed his duties as a senator. Justice Story, who had suffered a like bereavement, wrote him that work was the only thing that would save him—he must forget. Webster tried to do as he was advised, but on Washington's birthday we find him writing to Mr. Ticknor that he was "back in court where I have been so many winters," but that he had little zeal or spirit with regard to passing affairs and wished only to "sit down and sit still."

But he recovered. They usually do.

V

WEBSTER'S first achievement, after his return to the senate, was to step in at a moment when a bill for the relief of surviving Revolutionary officers seemed lost and, by making a speech, bring about its passage. The next occurrence of moment was a debate between himself and General Hayne of South Carolina, which proved to be the forerunner of the discussions in the senate with regard to nullification. During this debate, which had to do with a pending measure for the revision of the tariff, General Hayne for the first time made the statement that the interests of the South were being "shamelessly sacrificed" in the interest of other sections of the country and particularly of New England. Webster disputed this statement, declaring that New England had not sought the introduction of the pending bill and that in some respects it would, if enacted into law, be injurious to that section. Nevertheless, he was going to vote for it (as he later did) because he believed the revised schedules would be to the advantage of the country as a whole. And he was a whole American. He came from Massachusetts, but he legislated for the United States.

Webster seemed to feel more and more that something was brewing below the Mason and Dixon line—something that might eventually mean serious trouble. Speaking in Faneuil Hall, where a public dinner was given him the following June, he said:

"It is my opinion that the present government of the United States cannot be maintained but by administering it on principles as wide and as broad as the country over which it extends. . . . If there be any doubts whether so many republics, covering so vast a territory, can be long held together under this Constitution, there is no doubt, in my judgment, of the impossibility of so holding them together by any narrow, local or selfish system of legislation. To render the Constitution perpetual (which God grant it may be) it is necessary that its benefits should be practically felt by all parts of the country."

In other words, the South should learn and realize that whatever helped the nation as a whole was advisable, regardless of whether it helped a particular state or not.

Webster took no part in the bitter contest for the Presidency that was waged in 1828 between John Quincy Adams and Andrew Jackson. Classified as he was as a Democrat of the Adams stripe, he could not support Jackson, the candidate of the other Democratic faction, because he believed him to be "wholly unfit" for the office; honest and a good soldier, but no statesman. Toward Adams he perhaps felt a good deal as Ezekiel did when, after he had helped swing New England for Adams, he wrote to Daniel that New Englanders voted as they did from "a cold sense of duty, and not from any liking of the man." Perhaps Webster's low spirits also helped to keep him quiet throughout the campaign.

The fact that Webster had supported Adams in the house, and during the campaign did nothing for Jackson, caused much criticism in Massachusetts among Jackson's supporters. One of the critics—a gentleman of high social standing—went so far that Webster sued him for libel. What had happened was this: The Jackson papers had printed what purported to be a letter from Jefferson to William B. Giles in which he said that John Quincy Adams, in 1807 or 1808, had told him that a number of prominent New Englanders who were opposed to the embargo promulgated by Jefferson were planning to sever the New England States from the Union and join them to the British provinces. President Adams caused the National Intelligencer at Washington to print a denial that he had ever made such a statement to Jefferson. He admitted, however, that he had written to Giles that in his opinion the New England opposition to the embargo would ultimately have to be put down by force, in which event he believed the old Federalists in New England would try to form a confederacy under the protection of England, which he said he had long known to be their aim. The man whom Webster afterward sued went a step farther by publicly declaring that Webster was one of the treasonable Federalists whom Adams had named in his letter to Giles.

That was not true. Adams had never mentioned Webster. Webster had taken no part in the councils of those who were working under cover in New England to break up the Union. As already stated, he did not attend nor approve the notorious Hartford Convention. In this he differed sharply from some of his friends and from others who later became his friends. Webster's skirts were clean.

The man sued by Webster had not a legal leg upon which to stand. He himself had originated the charge of treason against Webster without having a particle of evidence to sustain it. But political feeling ran so high that the jury disagreed, ten jurors siding with Webster and two against him. The case was never tried again.

Jackson's victory was a surprise and a disappointment to both Webster and Clay, who had permitted themselves to believe that Adams would win. Clay wrote to Webster: "We are beaten. It is useless to dwell upon causes." Clay followed with the strategy that he believed he and Webster should adopt. His idea was to keep mum for a while, neither promising support to the new administration nor threatening it with opposition. He said threats would merely hold together the various discordant forces back of Jackson, which, if left to themselves, would soon fall apart.

Webster did not much care what Clay, himself, or anybody did. He was becoming increasingly tired of public life, which he felt injured him heavily financially without doing anyone any good. He wrote to Ezekiel's wife that, unless Ezekiel should be elected to congress (which he was not), he should retire at the expiration of his term. There was nothing of much importance to do in the senate, why should he remain? This, with the opportunity to reply to Hayne just around the corner!

It is plain now, a hundred years later, that Webster did not yet see the great picture of which he was so important a part. From his first days in congress, Webster had been doing necessary work of the very highest character. He had been trying to put a sense of nationality into men who, too often, thought in terms of states. The United States of America was a nation, not a group of nations! It was a nation, too, that was worth holding together and maintaining. A hundred years later it is difficult to realize that it was ever necessary to preach such doctrine. But when Webster first went to congress, the government, under the Constitution, was less than twenty-five years old. Nobody knew whether it was destined to last or not. Some hoped that it would not last. If the nation were to be preserved, such opinions must be changed. Webster helped change some of them. He did more than anybody else to stop secession talk in New England. He shot through the North the idea of nationality. This was not only a nation but a nation that must not be broken up. Webster made the North feel this as did no other man of his time.

But if Webster was not much interested in public life and saw only dimly his own importance in it, he could at least observe passing events and write to his relatives and friends about them. General Jackson was coming, and everybody was wondering what he would do.

"My opinion is," Webster wrote to a friend, "that when he comes he will bring a breeze with him." Which way it would blow he could not tell. If he had "real nerve" he would make friends and advisers of whom he pleased and be President "upon his own strength." But of this Webster had no hope.

"General Jackson has been here about ten days," he wrote to his sister-in-law on February 19, 1829. "A great multitude, too many to be fed without a miracle, are already in the city, hungry for office."

Webster also wrote to his sister-in-law that he was beginning to step out a little into social life. He had been to three "parties"—Mrs. Adams's last, Mrs. Clay's last, and Mrs. Porter's last. Mrs. Porter was the wife of the secretary of war. "Fine woman," Webster told Ezekiel's wife. If there should be a ball upon the twenty-second, he would go in honor of George Washington, he said, but otherwise his social season was at an end. It does not appear that there was a ball.

In a letter to Mrs. Ezekiel, dated "March 4, 1829, the first year of the administration of Andrew Jackson," Webster said:

"Today we have had the inauguration. A monstrous crowd of people is in the city. I never saw anything like it before. Persons have come five hundred miles to see General Jackson, and they really seem to think that the country is rescued from some dreadful danger."

Two weeks later, Webster wrote to Ezekiel that he expected the Supreme Court to adjourn within a few days and that his books were all packed in trunks so that, immediately upon adjournment, he could be off for Boston.

"Between us," he said, "my mind is settled. Under present circumstances, public and domestic, it is disagreeable being here, and to me there is no novelty to make compensation. It will be better for me and my children that I should be with them. . . . I can leave the court now as well as ever, and can earn my bread at home as well as here."

In a little more than a month from the date of this letter, Ezekiel was dead, and Webster was left the only survivor of a large family. By arrangement with the guardians of his brother's children, Webster took over the ownership of the old homestead at Franklin, which throughout life was to have a melancholy interest for him because his parents and several of his brothers and sisters were buried on the old farm. He spent most of the summer in Franklin, but in the autumn went to New York, "on professional business," so we are told, and remained several weeks. How his professional business fared we do not know, but we do know that in December, 1829, twenty-three months after the death of Mrs. Webster, he was married to Miss Caroline Le Roy, daughter of a wealthy merchant. The second Mrs. Webster was fifteen years younger than he was, and before Webster married her he made some sort of property settlement upon her—a fact that developed years later when he came to make his will.

On December 14, 1829, Webster wrote to his son Fletcher:

"My Dear Son: You have been informed that an important change in my domestic condition was expected to take place. It happened on Saturday. The lady who is now to bear the relation of mother to you and Julia and Edward I am sure will be found worthy of all your affection and regard; and I am equally certain that she will experience from all of you the utmost kindness and attachment."

In a letter to Mrs. Ezekiel he disclosed that his marriage had been a little sudden. When he went to New York in October he had not thought of such a thing. Webster assured his sister-in-law that she would find his new wife "amiable, affectionate, prudent, and agreeable." Certain it is that Webster was the last man in the world to live alone. He said he had a "multitude of acquaintances but few friends." Webster's second marriage saved him. He was all set to get out of congress when something happened that changed his mind. What was it? Does it seem a rash guess that the ambitions of a rich

CAROLINE LE ROY WEBSTER

Daniel Webster's second wife, who was fifteen years his junior and was in her thirty-third year when they were married. She died at the age of eighty-five. From a drawing by S. E. Dubourgal

young lady who had married an older man of great renown may have had something to do with it? At least
she cheered him up and enabled him to recover his interest in the world.

VI

THE first year of Andrew Jackson's administration
was destined to give Daniel Webster the greatest
opportunity of his life for public service and fame, but
in the beginning there was nothing to indicate it. On the
contrary, Jackson's administration began in such a manner as to disgust Webster. The President's action in raiding public offices in search of places for political friends
was not an inspiring spectacle. Washington business men
came to Webster, as they did to other influential members
of congress, and asked him if something could not be done
to stay the hand of the man in the White House. The real-
estate business, among other undertakings, was flat because
employees of the government were so uncertain as to
how long they might continue to draw salaries that they
dared not buy homes. Webster was urged to challenge the
power of the President to remove public officials without
the concurrence of the senate.

It is an interesting fact that the Supreme Court of the
United States did not, until almost a hundred years later,
finally settle this matter. Because Andrew Johnson removed a cabinet officer without the senate's consent he
came within a single vote of losing the Presidency. Webster, in the beginning, believed that Jackson had no constitutional power to remove without senatorial approval,
but when he studied the question more closely he changed
his opinion and sided with Jackson, whose use of such
power in the circumstances he nevertheless detested. A

hundred years later the United States Supreme Court said that the President had the power to remove presidential appointees without the consent of the senate.

Washington was puddling along with its sordid problems when suddenly a situation arose that both startled the country and marked a long step forward toward the Civil War. The stride was actually taken on January 26, 1830. That was the day that Webster replied to Hayne.

The discussion came about in the most unexpected manner. It all grew out of a relatively unimportant resolution that had been introduced by Senator Foote of Connecticut with regard to the sale of certain public lands in the West. The matter was debated back and forth without arousing particular interest until January 19, when General Hayne of South Carolina raked the resolution, fore and aft, in an exceedingly able speech that was intended to unite the West and the South against New England. He accused the New England States of deliberately going about, by curbing the distribution of public lands and in other ways, to retard the development of the West for the benefit of New England manufactures. How he thought manufactures anywhere could thrive better with jackrabbits on the prairies than with human beings, is beyond comprehension, but that, in his day, was the narrow way of looking at things. And Hayne went on to urge the West to join the South in exercising a peremptory veto upon such measures enacted by the national government—the tariff law, for instance—by refusing to obey them. Nullification! The importance of everything he said was increased by the fact that everybody knew he was speaking for John C. Calhoun, the Vice-President, who was the author of the nullification theory.

Webster, who was spending all the time he could in

the supreme court chamber where he had a heavy practice, happened to enter the senate chamber as Hayne
arose to speak. He listened throughout, and the next day
made a reply in which his chief interest seems to have
been to defend New England against the charge of self-
ishly sacrificing the West. Even yet he did not think the
matter of much importance; only some public lands.

The next day, Hayne replied to Webster. Webster
wanted the matter put over, as he had court business to
attend to, but Hayne insisted that the discussion proceed
immediately. He said he could see the gentleman from
Massachusetts in his seat and presumed he could make
arrangements to postpone his law business to another
day. Touching his breast, he said that Webster had said
things that rankle "here," and that since Webster had
discharged his fire in the speaker's face, he hoped he
would give him an opportunity to shoot back.

"I am ready to receive the gentleman's fire," said
Webster, rising. "So far as I am concerned, let the discussion proceed."

General Hayne proceeded and spoke the remainder
of the day. Again he assailed New England, in an effort
to drive a wedge between it and the West. The rest of his
speech consisted of an ingenious and acute exposition and
assertion of the nullification theory.

Webster took notes during Hayne's speech, and when
Hayne sat down was ready for him and immediately arose
to reply; but on account of the lateness of the hour, the
senate adjourned for the day.

That evening, Associate Justice Story called upon
Webster and, in view of what he said was the tremendous importance of meeting Hayne's argument and de-
stroying it, offered to help Webster in looking up materials for his reply.

"Give yourself no uneasiness, Judge Story," Webster said. "I will grind him as fine as a pinch of snuff."

During the evening, the report spread about Washington that, in the morning, Daniel Webster would reply to General Hayne. The result was that when the hour came for the senate to assemble, the chamber was filled to capacity, and the corridors leading to it were blocked. The speaker of the house remained in his chair, but most of the members deserted their posts to crowd into the senate chamber.

Webster began by recalling the fact that the resolution before the senate had to do with the disposal of the public lands, but that Hayne, in speaking to the resolution, had discussed almost everything except public lands. Hayne also had made some personal allusions, including a taunt, which Webster resented. Having squared away at his adversary, Webster proceeded to give Hayne such a hiding as no senator before or since has received at the hands of another senator. It is magnificent, even now, to see with what consummate skill Webster managed to avoid the slightest misstep that would have brought upon him rebuke from the presiding officer or perhaps from the senate itself, and yet to go the full limit allowed him by the senate rules in winding the lash around the body of his adversary.

The flow of his thoughts was no less admirable than the choice of his words. Everything was said as a gentleman would say it, but each word burnt. Webster never in his life was much given to the use of sarcasm and irony, but the first part of his reply to Hayne proved that when he chose, he could be a master in their use. If Webster had been less adroit, he would have made of Hayne a deadly enemy for life. It is a tribute to the essential decency of Hayne that he took his castigation like a man, his relations with Webster continuing to be as friendly as they had been before.

Webster's reply to Hayne would make about one hundred pages of this book. No summary can give more than the faintest suggestion either of its power or of its beauty. The manner in which he closed in upon Hayne, beating him down at point after point until he was driven behind his main defense, was superb. As to one matter after another Webster proved, to the satisfaction not only of the senate but of the entire North, that Hayne was wrong.

The question of transcendent importance of course—and it came last in Webster's speech—was whether Hayne was justified in asserting, as did Calhoun and many others in South Carolina, that each state had the right to decide for itself what laws enacted by congress, if any, were unconstitutional, and to disobey such as it did not approve. Webster disputed this claim and proceeded to show that if it were to be allowed there could not long be any national government. Twenty-four states, each with the power to decide which acts of congress it would obey and none with the power to bind any of the others—what could possibly come from such a situation except disaster?

Webster knew, all the while he was speaking, that the few hundreds within sound of his voice did not constitute his real audience. He realized that, throughout the length and breadth of the land there was more or less confusion in the minds of the people as to just how the Constitution had distributed the powers of government. Such matters had not, at that time, been threshed out as they have been since, and the people were waiting for light. Webster realized that the people wanted light, and in his reply to Hayne he gave it to them, always keeping his language down to the level of common comprehension. In this case it was one of his minor triumphs that he stated the legal aspects of the question in such a manner as to satisfy the requirement of lawyers for accuracy, while also satisfying the requirement of the people that it be simple and understandable.

This book never would have been written had it not been for an admiration for the character of Webster that was conceived by the author when, fifty years ago, he was a small boy in a country school in the Middle West. It seemed to the small boys of those days almost as if the school readers had been written by Daniel Webster. The readers of a later day and a more pre-occupied world may therefore pardon the inclusion of two excerpts from the "Reply to Hayne" that thrilled at least two generations of American school children. The first is Webster's response to the attack upon Massachusetts:

Mr. President, I shall enter on no encomium upon Massachusetts; she needs none. There she stands. Behold her and judge for yourself. There is her history; the world knows it by heart. The past, at least, is secure. There is Boston and Concord and Lexington and Bunker Hill; and there they will remain forever. The bones of her sons, falling in the great struggle for independence, now lie mingled with the soil of every state from New England to Georgia; and there they will lie forever.

And, sir, where American liberty raised its first voice, and where its youth was nurtured and sustained, there it still lives in the strength of its manhood and full of its original spirit. If discord and disunion shall wound it, if party strife and blind ambition shall hawk at and tear it, if folly and madness, if uneasiness under necessary and salutary restraint shall succeed in separating it from that union by which alone its existence is made sure, it will

stand, in the end, by the side of that cradle in which
its infancy was rocked; it will stretch forth its arm
with whatever vigor it may still retain, over the
friends who gather round it; and it will fall at last, if
fall it must, amidst the proudest monuments of its
own glory and on the very spot of its origin.

The peroration will be read for centuries as has De-
mosthenes's Oration on the Crown with which the "Reply" is often compared, and not to the disadvantage of
Webster:

> When my eyes shall have turned to behold for the
> last time the sun in heaven, may I not see him shin-
> ing on the broken and dishonored fragments of a
> once-glorious union; on states dissevered, discor-
> dant, belligerent; on a land rent with civil feuds, or
> drenched, it may be, in fraternal blood. Let their
> last feeble and lingering glance rather behold the
> gorgeous ensign of the republic, now known and
> honored throughout the earth, still full-high ad-
> vanced, its arms and trophies streaming in their orig-
> inal lustre, not a stripe erased or polluted, nor a
> single star obscured, bearing for its motto no such
> miserable interrogatory as "What is all this worth?"
> nor those other words of delusion and folly, "Liberty
> first and union afterwards"; but everywhere, spread
> all over in characters of living light, blazing on all
> its ample folds as they float over the sea and over the
> land, and in every wind under the whole heavens,
> that other sentiment, dear to every true American
> heart—Liberty *and* Union, now and forever, one and
> inseparable.

As Webster finished speaking and sat down, a southern senator passed over to him and said: "Mr. Webster,
I think you had better die now and rest your fame on
that speech." Hayne, who heard the remark, said to Web-

ster: "You ought not to die. A man who can make such speeches as that ought never to die."

At a White House reception the same evening Webster and Hayne met again.

"How are you this evening, General Hayne?" said Webster.

"None the better for you, sir," said Hayne, with a smile.

Webster's speech traveled over the country at what, in those days, was incredible speed. First, the eastern newspapers printed it in full, and as these newspapers traveled west the speech was reprinted in full by the local papers along the way. It was also printed, scores of times, in pamphlet form, with the result that its contents were soon known to everybody in the country.

And again there was a country-wide controversy as to how Webster had gone about it to prepare the "Reply." Some said he had done it overnight, while others said he had been working on it for weeks. A young preacher asked Webster whether the speech was extemporaneous.

"Young man," said Webster, "there is no such thing as extemporaneous acquisition."

A delicious use of the word "acquisition." The fact was, as Webster afterward explained, that the subject had been at his fingers' ends for a long time. "The materials of the speech," he said, "had been lying in my mind for eighteen months, though I had never committed my thoughts to paper nor arranged them in my memory."

The speech met with a reception throughout the country that apparently went beyond anything that Webster had expected. Webster took his honors with much modesty. "You are very civil in what you say about my speech," he wrote to one correspondent. "It has made much more noise than it deserved. The times favored its

Washington April 24. 1830

Dear Sir

I thank you for your kind letter of the
27 April. If my Speech has done, or shall do, the
slightest good, I shall be sufficiently gratified. It
was, in the strictest sense, unexpected, & occasional; yet
I am willing to confess, that having the occasion thus
forced upon me, I did the best I could, under its
pressure. The subject & the times have given it
a degree of circulation, which its own merits
could not have entitled it. Connected with
this subject, one good thing - excellent, & most
important - will ere long be made known.
At present, it is locked up in confidence. All
I can say is, & I w? not have that repeated,
                                                        except

FACSIMILE OF A LETTER WRITTEN BY DANIEL WEBSTER
Reproduced by permission of the Boston Public Library

perhaps, dear father, that the world will one
day - perhaps not a distant one - know Mr
Madison's sentiments on these constitutional
questions, fully & precisely; together with his
understanding of the Va. Resolutions of 1797 - 8
It will be an important paper.

It was thought, that pains are
taking to sound the Senate, with a view of ascertaining the expediency of a renomination of
Isaac Hill. No doubt, a great effort will
be made. I hope, not with success. - I never
shall believe he can either get thro' the Senate,
or get into it, till I see it.

It is difficult to get copies of the Executive
Journal. I have obtained one, this session, for
Ch. Kent. - If possible, I will hunt up another
for you; but if not this year, have little
doubt I

condo at next. If I can get it, will send it
sent, in a safe manner. —

It seems now to be understood that the actual
cumbent of the Presidency intends to stand for
a reelection. This disappoints more than one.

If that should not happen, I hesitate not
to say I think Mr Clay's chance much
the best. He is evidently gaining, in the West,
& among the political men here. What will
be advisable, if Genl. J. should be again can-
-date, cannot now be decided —

I shall be happy to hear from you, as
often as you will confer that favor. Have
the goodness to present my regards to your
father, & believe me, with much
sincere respect,
Yrs
Danl Webster

Hon Wm Plumer, jn
Epping N. H.

impression." To Mr. Ticknor he wrote: "I shall make no more speeches. What I have done, even, was not with malice prepense."

The big oratorical gun had been fired in the senate chamber at Washington, but its reverberations reached the ears of the aged Revolutionary War veteran, Captain Thomas, who lived in Webster's house in Marshfield. Webster's friend Peter Harvey vouched for the truth of this story which, in substance, follows:

Old Captain Thomas, at Webster's suggestion, had subscribed for the semi-weekly edition of the Columbian Sentinel, a Washington newspaper. In the Sentinel, Thomas read Hayne's first speech and confidently waited for a triumphant reply from Webster which, when it came, satisfied him. But the next number of the Sentinel contained a second speech by Hayne, which Thomas read with a degree of pain that, in a day or two, developed into consternation. Quoting Harvey:

> He was overwhelmed with grief. His hero, his great man, his beloved, almost worshiped friend, had been overthrown in debate by his southern antagonist. The kind old gentleman's pride was humbled; he was in despair. Casting away the paper, he rose and retired slowly to his room, directing someone to come and take his boots away, as he should never want them again. . . .
>
> For three days he kept his bed, mourning over the fall of his friend and refusing all consolation. His eldest son tried to persuade him that Webster was able to defend the cause of New England and would yet have his triumph. His only reply was: "It can't be answered, Henry, it can't be answered."
>
> The fatal semi-weekly came again in due course. It was evening. The captain still kept his bed and appeared to have determined to hold his vow never to rise from it. On opening the paper it was found to

contain Webster's second reply to Hayne. The family at once resolved that Henry should assume the task of carrying it to his father. Henry entered his father's room with a paper and a candle. The old man groaned and asked what was wanted. Henry replied:

"Father, I have brought you the *Sentinel;* I thought you might like to look at it."

"No, Henry, I don't want to see it."

"It contains a second speech of Mr. Webster in reply to Colonel Hayne."

"Oh, Henry," said the old man, "it is no use; it can't be answered; I don't want to see it."

But Captain Thomas consented to have the paper and candle left in his room and said that perhaps he would look at the paper. Henry went downstairs. . . .

Some time had thus elapsed when they were all suddenly startled by a shout from their father's room. They rushed upstairs. The captain was sitting on the side of the bed with the paper in one hand and the candle in the other. As Henry entered, the captain exclaimed:

"Bring me my boots, Henry; bring me my boots."

His recovery was complete.

The speech also profoundly affected another obscure man—a youth of twenty-one—of whom Webster had never heard. He lived out in Sangamon County, Illinois, and his name was Abraham Lincoln. William H. Herndon, Lincoln's law partner, testified to this in his biography of Lincoln. Webster, in his reply to Hayne, said that he hated slavery but would not lay a hand upon it in any state in which it existed, because he believed slavery, in such instances, was a state affair sanctioned by the Constitution. Years later, when Lincoln became prominent enough to be heard upon such matters, it was discovered that his views as to the fundamentals of the slavery question were the same as those expressed by Webster in 1830.

VII

DURING the following summer Webster made another speech that went straight into the school readers—the speech containing the words, "Murder will out." This address and another one in similar vein brought about the hanging of two brothers who were morally but not legally guilty of murder. To convict these brothers in the circumstances required the putting forth by Webster of every particle of his power in order to sway two juries. He had safely to lead them from one narrow, dangerous path of reasoning to another, failure to do which would have meant verdicts against him. Neither jury knew that the brothers were entitled to acquittal upon technicalities, nor is there proof that Webster knew it. What Webster must have known, however, was that, as to some vital matters, he lacked direct evidence which, had he possessed it, would have been very convenient. Not having such evidence, Webster used his great powers to make the jurors *believe* certain things, as to the truth of which no testimony had been given. If Webster knew that at moments he was skating on thin ice, he perhaps justified himself in doing so because of his belief that morally the brothers were guilty, as, indeed, they were. Yet such an explanation does not quite ring true. Webster, throughout his life, was a stickler for the observance of law *as law*. If, in this instance, he departed from this rule, he did so because his anxiety to convict men whom he believed to be guilty carried him across the line that should have given them protection.

The story of this celebrated case, which soon attracted

the attention of the entire country, may be briefly summarized as follows:

On the morning of April 7, 1830, Captain Joseph White, eighty-two years old and a wealthy resident of Salem, Massachusetts, was found dead in his bed. He had been struck on the head, perhaps with a hammer, and then stabbed thirteen times. Certain valuables, including money, lying about in his room were not touched.

A public meeting was called to consider the situation. A vigilance committee of twenty-seven prominent citizens was appointed at this meeting to solve the mystery and uncover the murderer.

The vigilance committee scoured the countryside but found nothing. This continued for weeks.

At length a rumor came that a man named Hatch, in jail at New Bedford, seventy miles away, knew something. He was visited and questioned. He said the murderers were Richard Crowninshield of Danvers and his brother George.

Hatch was brought before the grand jury, testified before it, and indictments for murder were brought against the Crowninshields.

Two weeks after Hatch's arrest, Captain Joseph J. Knapp, a shipmaster and merchant of good reputation, received a strange letter. It was from a man in Belfast, Maine, who signed himself Charles Grant, Jr. The writer intimated that he was familiar with the facts of the murder, intimated that Knapp had instigated it and threatened him with exposure if he did not pay Grant money.

Captain Knapp did not know what the letter meant. He showed it to his son, N. P. Knapp, a young lawyer of Salem, who no more understood the letter than did his father.

Captain Knapp then showed the letter to two other

sons, John Francis Knapp, and Joseph J. Knapp, Jr. The latter, whose wife was a daughter of the niece of the murdered man, read the letter, said it contained a "devlish lot of trash" and suggested that his father turn it over to the vigilance committee. The father did so.

The vigilance committee sent a man to Maine to see Grant. "Grant" proved to be a former convict named Palmer, who, during a term in prison, had become well acquainted with the Crowninshields. He said that on April 2 he had seen John Francis Knapp and the Crowninshields together and that he had heard George Crowninshield tell his brother Richard that John Francis Knapp wanted him to kill old Captain White. John Francis Knapp, according to Palmer, said that if White were killed J. J. Knapp, Jr., would pay one thousand dollars for the job.

The two Knapps were arrested. On the third day after their arrest, Joseph Knapp confessed. He said that Richard Crowninshield actually committed the murder, that John Francis Knapp engaged him to commit it, and that he, himself (Joseph J. Knapp, Jr.) had paid Crowninshield one thousand dollars for committing the crime. Joseph Knapp, in his confession, said that he desired to bring about White's murder so that his wife (the old man's grandniece) would inherit a large part of his estate, which was of considerable value. The idea had been to murder White, steal and destroy the unfavorable will, and thus cause the estate to be distributed according to an earlier will, which was more favorable to young Knapp's wife.

When Richard Crowninshield, locked in prison, heard that Knapp had confessed, he committed suicide.

When Knapp heard that Crowninshield had committed suicide, he repudiated his confession.

The confession had been obtained under a promise of immunity.

When the confession was repudiated, it became of prime importance, first to induce the trial judge to admit the confession as testimony and next to convince two juries that the confession was true.

There was another difficulty.

The Knapps had been indicted as accessories. The Massachusetts law at that time provided that no accessory could be convicted of murder unless the principal had already been convicted. In this case, the principal, Richard Crowninshield, was dead. It therefore became necessary to try to convict one of the brothers as a principal, thus opening the way to the trial of the other as an accessory. Frank Knapp was tried as a principal.

There was still another difficulty.

If Frank Knapp were convicted as a principal, the jury must be satisfied, the law said, that, since he did not actually commit the deed, he was nevertheless on guard in the vicinity to give assistance, if needed, to the actual murderer.

Webster convinced the jury at the trial of Frank Knapp that the accused was just outside the house when the murder was committed. The jury convicted Knapp and he was hanged.

The truth was that Frank Knapp was not in the vicinity when the murder was committed, therefore was not a principal within the meaning of the law; and, if he had not been convicted as such, his brother Joseph could not have been convicted of anything. Had Joseph, instead of refusing to testify, gone on the stand and told the truth, his story, if believed by the jury, would have freed both of them.

The statements herein made as to the technical innocence of the brothers are based upon declarations in George T. Curtis's biography of Webster. Curtis, himself a lawyer, was so close to Webster that he phrased the facts as gently as possible, yet there can be no mistaking their meaning. He said:

"The force of Mr. Webster's argument convinced the jury that Frank was, in this sense [near at hand, ready to give assistance] present at the murder. But the fact was otherwise. If Joseph Knapp had not refused to testify . . . it would have appeared that at the time Crownin-shield started to commit the murder he told Frank to go home and go to bed; that Frank did so."

Webster's task at the trial of Joseph Knapp was different but not less difficult. In the face of the fact that it is the law of the land that no accused man may be compelled to testify against himself, Webster succeeded in convincing the court that Joseph's confession, for which he was promised immunity provided he should testify against the others, should be admitted as evidence. This done, Webster convinced the jury that the confession was true, and Joseph Knapp was hanged on evidence given by himself and used against his will.

At the trial of Frank Knapp, Webster made a speech that was admirably suited to the task of creating among the jurors the hanging state of mind. It was so graphic a picture of a particular crime that little boys in school used almost to freeze in their seats when they heard older boys read excerpts from the speech aloud in class. Here are the paragraphs that made such urchins resolve to lead better lives:

An aged man, without an enemy in the world, in his own house and in his own bed is made the victim of a butcherly murder, for mere pay. . . . Deep sleep had fallen upon the destined victim and all be-

neath his roof. A healthful old man, to whom sleep
was sweet, the first sound slumbers of the night held
him in their soft but strong embrace.

The assassin enters, through the window already
prepared, into an unoccupied apartment. With noise-
less foot he paces the lonely hall, half lighted by the
moon; he winds up the ascent of the stairs and
reaches the door of the chamber. Of this he moves
the lock by soft and continued pressure, till he turns
it on its hinges without noise; and he enters and beholds his victim before him. The room is uncommonly open to the admission of light. The face of the
innocent sleeper is turned from the murderer and
the beams of the moon, resting upon the gray locks
of his aged temple, show him where to strike.

The fatal blow is given, and the victim passes
without a struggle or a motion from the repose of
sleep to the repose of death!

It is the assassin's purpose to make sure work, and
he plies the dagger though it is obvious that life has
been destroyed by the blow of the bludgeon. He even
raises the aged arm that he may not fail in his aim
at the heart, and replaces it again over the wounds
of the poniard. To finish the picture, he explores the
wrist for the pulse. He feels for it and ascertains
that it beats no longer. It is accomplished. The deed
is done. He retreats, retraces his steps to the window,
passes out through it as he came in, and escapes. He
has done the murder. No eye has seen him, no ear has
heard him. The secret is his own and it is safe.

Ah, gentlemen, that was a dreadful mistake. Such
a secret can be safe nowhere. The whole creation of
God has neither nook nor corner where the guilty
can bestow it and say it is safe. Not to speak of that
eye which pierces through all disguises, and beholds
everything as in the splendor of noon, such secrets of
guilt are never safe from detection, even by men.
True it is, generally speaking, that "Murder will
out." True it is that Providence hath so ordained,

and doth so govern things that those who break the great law of heaven by shedding man's blood seldom succeed in avoiding discovery.

Especially in a case exciting so much attention as this, discovery must come and will come, sooner or later. A thousand eyes turn at once to explore every man, every thing, every circumstance, connected with the crime and place; a thousand ears catch every whisper; a thousand excited minds intensely dwell on the scene, shedding all their light, and ready to kindle the slightest circumstance into a blaze of discovery.

Meantime, the guilty soul cannot keep its own secret. It is false to itself; or rather it feels an irresistible impulse of conscience to be true to itself. It labors under its guilty possession, and knows not what to do with it. The human heart was not made for the residence of such an inhabitant. It finds itself preyed on by a torment which it dares not acknowledge to God or man. A vulture is devouring it, and it can ask no sympathy or assistance, either from heaven or earth. The secret which the murderer possesses soon comes to possess him; and, like the evil spirits of which we read, it overcomes him and leads him whithersoever it will. He feels it beating at his heart, rising in his throat and demanding disclosure. He thinks the whole world sees it in his face, reads it in his eyes, and almost hears its workings in the very silence of his thoughts. It has become his master. It betrays his discretion, it breaks down his courage, it conquers his prudence. When suspicions from within begin to embarrass him, and the net of circumstances to entangle him, the fatal secret struggles with still greater violence to burst forth. It must be confessed, it will be confessed; there is no refuge from confession but suicide, and suicide is confession.

That speech hanged Frank Knapp, but what it had to do with his guilt or innocence no man can point out.

If there was ever a time when Webster appeared to play fast and loose with his conscience it was upon this occasion. He did and, we must presume, intended to do precisely what he told the trial judge he would not do. Knapp's attorneys objected to Webster's appearance in the case at all, on the ground that the prosecution had employed him to "hurry you [the jury] against the law and beyond the evidence." Webster replied that he hoped he had too much respect for his own character and too much regard for justice to do either, yet he straightway proceeded to do both. The men were legally innocent, yet he hanged them by bridging over with powerful oratory yawning gaps in his evidence. He said he was sure "that in this court nothing can be carried against the law," yet he hanged both brothers in spite of the fact that the law protecting accessories whose principals had not been convicted should have saved them. Moreover, Webster, though employed by the prosecution, was paid a fee in the first case, after the verdict was rendered, by a relative of the murdered man. At the second trial, objection was again made to the employment of Webster, and attention was called to a law prohibiting prosecutors from accepting money from private individuals interested in prosecutions. Webster thereupon assured the court that he had been employed by the attorney general, "without any pecuniary inducement." Granted that this was literally true in the Joseph Knapp case, it was not true as to the conviction of Frank Knapp, for which Stephen White paid Daniel Webster a fee. Webster's friend Curtis, in his biography, did his best to smudge over the situation, but with poor success. He said:

"It is quite evident that the court understood Mr. Webster as denying that he had received or expected any fee *in the case then on trial*. The application before the

COLONEL FLETCHER WEBSTER
Killed at the age of forty-nine at the Second Battle of Bull Run.
Reproduced by courtesy of Webster's great-grandson, Lewis A. Armistead

court involved no inquiry into the relations in which Mr. Webster had stood in the case of Francis Knapp."

The truth unquestionably was that Webster hanged two brothers who were morally but not legally guilty of murder, and that in violation of a state law he accepted a fee from a private person for assisting in the prosecution. Granted that at the second trial he accepted no fee, we are at a loss to understand why he did not accept one, since he had done so in the first case, unless it was to keep faith with the court, which permitted him to assist the prosecution upon the assurance that no outside person had employed him.

What does all of this prove? The most that it proves is that, in this instance, Webster, through an excess of zeal to serve a community much distressed by White's murder, and also to serve his friend Stephen White, did not give two blood-stained brothers their full legal rights. That money, promised or paid, determined Webster's action is not to be believed. He was not crooked, nor was he avaricious. But he believed the Knapps were guilty, the community believed they were guilty, the community wanted them hanged, and Webster hanged them. A hundred years later, in writing Webster's life, it becomes necessary to put upon white paper this stain that he placed on his record.

VIII

IT is now twenty years since Webster was first elected to congress. He is at the peak of his prestige, but does not know it. He believes the peak will have been reached when he moves into the White House; but fit, and more than fit, as he is for the place, he is never to get it. Instead, directly ahead of him, lie twenty terrible years, such as no man would care to know, ending at the grave. Nine years after his death, the drums are to begin to beat, and the great tragedy that he had tried to avoid is to take place.

Webster is at the peak of his prestige. His reply to Hayne has made him in the North and, indeed, in some localities in the South, the great man of the nation. From many places come demands that in this year of 1832 he challenge Andrew Jackson for the Presidency. Webster is more than willing, nor does he doubt that if nominated, he would be elected. His confidence is based upon the assumption that when one has earned the Presidency, it is given to him, which he believes has been the case, up to this time, except in the instance of Jackson. He does not know that the Presidency will often be decided henceforth by accident, and that as a rule the most prominent man in the country will be least likely to get it. Nor does he realize how poor a politician he is when his own presidential aspirations are concerned. With an adroit political manager he might easily win, but he has no manager and not the smallest prospect of success.

Webster, at four o'clock in the morning, begins to struggle with these questions—the White House for himself, the possible breaking up of the Union. It is his habit to arise at this hour, light a fire, write or read until six, have his breakfast, and then go down to the city market to buy the day's supplies. Followed by a colored boy carrying a basket, there he goes down Pennsylvania Avenue, thinking not of the fish, vegetable and meat stalls that he is about to visit, but of his country's plight and his own political fortunes. He no longer doubts that there is a serious prospect of civil war. Nullification and the outcry against northern opposition to slavery are, he believes, but screens back of which is hidden an intention to break the old Union and set up a new nation in the South. The southern people are not back of it, but some of their leaders are.

"In December, 1828," Webster wrote to a friend in South Carolina, "I became thoroughly convinced that the plan of a Southern Confederacy had been received with favor by a great many of the political men of the South, especially of your state."

It is a very different Pennsylvania Avenue, along which Webster swings as he muses, from what it will be in a century. It is not paved, which means that it is dusty in summer and muddy in winter. Cattle, which are per-mitted to go about, nibbling such grass as they can find, are called to the curb twice a day and milked. The side-walks, where there are any, are planks thrown down in the mud, flopping and splashing in wet weather as the pedestrian proceeds.

Webster picks his way, responding to the salutations of such early-morning milkers as he encounters (for they all know him, as do the tradesmen at the market), until he comes to the place where gardeners, butchers, fishermen, and others are gathered. He has a keen taste for the things he likes and, as he goes from stall to stall, makes careful selections of the best they have to offer. He pauses long-est at the fish stalls. He is wholly of the opinion that no fish ever swam in the Potomac, or adjacent waters, that could compare with those which swim along the Atlantic coast past Marshfield; but he must now eat Potomac fish or none at all, so he will take a shad. A four-pounder goes into the colored boy's basket, which, by this time, is filled. The homeward walk is begun. Fish fly out of his mind, and public questions fly back into it.

"It is just as I said in my Reply to Hayne. . . . The North is not opposing slavery and does not intend to. . . .

All assertion to the contrary is just a pretext for breaking up the Union. . . . What congress did, at its first session, shows how the North felt and still feels. . . . The Pennsylvania society for promoting the abolition of slavery petitioned congress to end it. . . . The petition was referred to a committee of seven members, all but one of them from the North. . . . The committee unanimously reported that congress had no power to interfere with slavery, and congress adopted the report. . . . There is no more to the nullification outcry. . . . It's all a sham to screen a plan to erect a Southern Confederacy."

So it is southern independence that is back of all this talk about nullification and northern interference with the legal right of slavery to exist? Webster's mind seizes the thought and carries it forward. When did this dream of a Southern Confederacy begin? His knowledge goes back only to December, 1828; but the attempt to stir up independence sentiment probably began somewhat earlier.

"It seems to be an inherent weakness of governments that, until they are thoroughly established, they shall be subject to sectional movements for independence . . . John Adams said it was so with regard to American independence. . . . Did he not make the statement in writing that, in his opinion, 'the American Revolution began as early as the first plantation of the country,' and that the real authors of independence 'were the first immigrants.' . . . Yes, Adams said that. . . . Perhaps, in the South, history is preparing only to repeat itself. . . . This must of course be prevented, if possible, but in doing so, there is no occasion for hating anybody. . . . The southern leaders are permitting ambition to carry them too far, but they are not bad men at heart and it is for us, here in the North, to convince them of their error. . . . The southern people? They are not back of this movement at all. . . . Like all peoples, they want peace. . . . It is true that they feel a degree of loyalty to their respective states that they should give only to the nation, but that is natural enough. . . . The same feeling nearly broke up the convention that framed the Federal Constitution. . . . In time it will pass away. . . . The thing to do, meanwhile, is to keep cool, be kind, try to smooth ruffled feelings instead of irritating them, and trust to quickened common sense, on both sides, to preserve both the Union and peace."

Webster sees clearly both what is happening and what may happen. He sees the possibility that, in the North, extreme opponents of slavery—abolitionists, they are to be called—will, by doing the right thing in the wrong way and by violating the very Constitution they urge others to obey, add to the difficulty of reaching a peaceful adjustment. The essence of his thoughts on this subject he is to put into a remarkable letter that he will write twenty years later, when upon the brink of the grave, to John Taylor, superintendent of his father's old farm at Franklin, New Hampshire.

John Taylor [that letter will say], . . . there are in New Hampshire many persons who call themselves Whigs who are no Whigs at all and no better than disunionists. Any man who hesitates in granting and securing to every part of the country its just and constitutional rights is an enemy to the whole country.

John Taylor, if one of your boys should say that he honors his father and mother and loves his brothers and sisters, but still insists that one of them shall be driven out of the family, what can you say of him but this, that there is really no family love in him? You and I are farmers; we never talk politics—our talk is of oxen; but remember this: That any man who attempts to excite one part of this country against another is just as wicked as he would be who should attempt to get up a quarrel between John Taylor and his neighbor, old Mr. John Sanborn, or his other neighbor, Captain Burleigh. There are some animals that live best in the fire, and there are some men who delight in heat, smoke, combustion and even general conflagration. They do not follow the things that make for peace. They enjoy only controversy, contention and strife. Have no communion with such persons, either as neighbors or as politicians. You have no more right to say that slavery ought not to exist in Virginia than a Virginian has to say that slavery ought to exist in New Hampshire. This is a question left to every state to decide for itself, and if we mean to keep the states together we must leave to every state this power of deciding for itself.

I think I never wrote you a word before upon politics. I shall not do it again. I only say, love your country and your whole country, and when men attempt to persuade you to get into a quarrel with the laws of other states, tell them that you mean to mind your own business and advise them to do the same.

John Taylor, you are a free man. You possess good principles. You have a large family to rear and to provide for with your labor. Be thankful to the government which does not oppress you, which does not bear you down by excessive taxation, but which holds out to you and yours the hope of all the blessings which liberty, industry and security may give.

John Taylor, thank God, morning and evening, that you were born in such a country.

John Taylor, never write me another word upon politics. Give my kindest remembrance to your wife and children, and when you look from your eastern windows upon the graves of my family, remember that he who is the author of this letter must soon follow them to another world.

Webster regards slavery as morally wrong, but nevertheless sanctioned by the Constitution, and he will countenance no violations of the Constitution to remove the wrong. Having an orderly mind, how can he believe otherwise? The Constitution provides orderly methods of doing whatever we wish to do—even to altering the Constitution itself.

Webster believes that honest but ambitious southern leaders, bent upon independence, are, one might say, almost the only ones in the South who desire to break up the Union. In this he is correct, but events will not prove it until nine years after his death. He will never know how reluctant were eight of the southern states to quit the Union, how their legislatures pigeonholed or otherwise delayed action for months upon ordinances of secession, how the people of Virginia, early in 1861, elected to pass upon secession a convention overwhelmingly in favor of remaining in the Union, and how this convention, as late as April 4, 1861, voted against the adoption of an ordinance of secession.

Nor does Webster, as he returns from market, realize how history is still further to justify his opinion that southern leaders, and not the southern people, are bent upon the destruction of the Union. To his mind comes no picture of the dramatic moment when some of these reluctant states will be driven into the secession camp and war made certain. He cannot hear the speech that former United States Senator Jeremiah Clemens, of Georgia, will· deliver at Huntsville, Alabama, March 13, 1864.* Clemens is to see a few men in a small room push the South into war, and in these words he will describe the scene:

"Before I declare this meeting adjourned, I wish to

* "The American Conflict," by Horace Greeley, Appendix, Volume I.

state a fact in relationship to the commencement of the war. Some time after the ordinance of secession was passed, I was in Montgomery and called upon President Davis, who was in the city. Davis, Memminger, the secretary of war, Gilchrist, the member from Lowndes County, and several others were present. Two or three of them withdrew to a corner of the room, and I heard Gilchrist say to the secretary of war: 'It must be done. Delay two months, and Alabama stays in the Union. *You must sprinkle blood in the faces of the people.*'"

The blood will be sprinkled at Fort Sumter.

IX

WEBSTER is at the peak of his prestige, but with such views about the slavery question and all that it involves, he might almost as well be at the bottom of the political sea. His views are correct and whatever of posterity is informed will justify him; but posterity is not present. Instead, he is living at a time when, to retain popularity, it is safest to assume that all the right is on one side and all the wrong on the other, which is not Webster's belief. In an age that is to be marked with increasing bitterness on both sides, he refuses to hate anybody; and who, at such a time, is likely to be more lonely than such a man?

Believing as Webster does, he hasn't a chance. The South will never have him because he abhors slavery, though he believes it has its legal sanctions, and because he is opposed both to nullification and to secession. The North will gradually turn away from him, not alone because he declares the South has some right on its side,

but because he regards the abolitionists as firebrands who
are willing to smash the Constitution to end an evil that
they are unwilling to eradicate in an orderly way. In a
hundred years, most of what Webster says will be cheerfully admitted by everybody, and a little later it will all
be admitted. The pity is that the change of heart will
come too late to prevent a civil war.

So, in 1832, we see the current gaining speed that is
to carry Webster forward to political destruction and
plunge the country into bloodshed. We shall also see how
poor a politician one man can be when his own presidential aspirations are concerned.

Webster is urged by many to seek to become the Whig
candidate for President, in opposition to Andrew Jackson; but Clay too wants it, and Webster is inclined to
defer to him. Some of Webster's friends tell him not to
let Clay stand in his way; that Clay cannot be elected
anyway because he is a Mason and there is now a great
tempest in a teapot about the Masons. It is charged that
six years ago, William Morgan, of Batavia, New York,
being upon the point of publishing a book revealing the
"secrets" of Masonry, was abducted by Masons and
drowned in Lake Ontario.

So great has become the opposition to Masons, by
some persons, that they are trying to make a national issue
of it. Webster is told that if he will take an Anti-Masonic
attitude, he can get their votes. This Webster declines to
do. In the first place, he does not believe the rumors
about Morgan's murder. Furthermore, he regards the
matter as too trivial to become a national issue. Still, being a poor politician, he flirts with the idea—just a little.
He permits it to become known that while he does not
believe the Masons murdered Morgan, and is opposed
anyway to making a national issue of the matter, he never-

theless considers the Masons and all other secret organizations as "objectionable." This statement naturally turns every Mason against him, without attracting a single vote from the Anti-Masons, who proceed to nominate for the Presidency, not one candidate but two, William Wirt and John Floyd, for whom they cast, at the election, 33,108 votes. The Whigs nominate Clay, who receives 530,189 votes, while Andrew Jackson is reelected with 687,502. The Anti-Masonic vote is so small that it would have done Clay no good if he had received it, but small as it was it was enough to make the needle of Webster's political judgment turn, for a moment, from its true direction. A good politician, in Webster's place, would have denounced both bigotry and murder and done it in such a way as to get the votes of both sides. Webster lost the votes of both sides.

Webster was disappointed but not sour. Immediately after Jackson's reelection an emergency arose that again disclosed the real Webster. A state convention in South Carolina declared the revenue laws of the United States to be null and void within the limits of South Carolina, and made it the duty of the legislature to pass such acts as might be necessary to resist the authority of the United States. The legislature thereupon made it a crime to attempt to enforce the tariff laws, and authorized the raising of military forces to maintain the state's attitude.

Jackson, in the White House, met the challenge by issuing a proclamation, under date of December 10, 1832, in which he told the South Carolinians that what they were fooling with was treason, and then repeating, in his own words, the precise arguments against nullification and disunion that Webster had used in his reply to Hayne. Indeed, Webster on his way back to the capital from Boston was told by a traveler who did not know him that

Jackson had "issued a proclamation against the nullifiers taken entirely from Webster's reply to Hayne."

Jackson's proclamation was good, but it contained a bad spot. After threatening the nullifiers with prosecution for treason, he bent his knee to truckle to them a little. Perhaps the tariff laws created excessive burdens. Perhaps they should be reduced. The subject should be investigated, and proper action taken.

What was Webster to do? He had no faith in Andrew Jackson as a thoroughgoing supporter of the Constitution. Jackson's attitude in the case of the Bank of the United States was such that Webster had been compelled to oppose him upon constitutional grounds. Both houses of congress had voted to renew the bank's charter, the United States Supreme Court had certified to the constitutionality of the bank's existence, yet Jackson had vetoed the bill to extend the charter on the ground that it was not constitutional. Jackson's contention was that each high official of the government was to judge for himself of the constitutionality of such measures as came before him. Furthermore, Jackson had not shown much concern when the state of Georgia refused to honor a decree of the Federal Supreme Court ordering the release of certain individuals held in prison by the state. As to these matters, Webster had opposed the President.

On the other hand, Webster thoroughly agreed with Jackson's proclamation to the nullifiers and, political opponent though Jackson was, lost no time in saying so. At a meeting held in Faneuil Hall in Boston, a week after Jackson's proclamation was issued, Webster said:

"I hope I may stand acquitted before my country of any negligence in failing to give the true character of this doctrine of nullification, when it was first advanced, in an imposing form, in the halls of congress. What it then appeared to be, in its very nature, it now proves itself, in this first attempt to put it in practice. It is resistance to law by force, it is secession by force; *it is civil war.* . . .

"I shall support the President in maintaining this Union and this Constitution; and the cause shall not fail for want of my aid, any effort, or any zealous cooperation of mine. . . . When the standard of the Union is raised and waves over my head—the standard which Washington planted on the ramparts of the Constitution—God forbid that I should inquire whom the people have commissioned to unfurl and bear it up; I only ask in what manner, as an humble individual, I can best discharge my duty in defending it."

That was to be Webster's course to the end. The right, as he saw it. Cooperating with those who were going his way, even if they were political opponents. Opposing those who differed from him, even if they were of his own party. Noble principles, but almost an impossible way to get to the White House.

In hewing to the line, regardless of friend or foe, Webster next encountered Mr. Clay, a fellow Whig. Clay, always a compromiser, yielded to the suggestion of Calhoun that congress back-track on the tariff. Clay therefore introduced a bill providing that the existing tariff laws should remain in effect until March 3, 1840, and then stand repealed; that in the meantime duties should not be increased, and that imposts thereafter should be laid solely for the purpose of raising needed revenue, and not for the purpose of encouraging domestic industry. In other words, the idea of protection, to which South Carolina objected, was to be yielded after 1840— eight years hence. How Clay expected to tie the hands of future congresses, each of which would have the power to legislate as it might see fit, is not clear.

Webster regarded it as highly dangerous to truckle to South Carolina as Clay's bill proposed to do. He believed that South Carolina, having defied the United States, should first be put back in her place, before making a move to consider whether the tariff laws of which she complained were, in fact, oppressive. Nor would he, to appease South Carolina, abandon the principle of a protective tariff and, by inference, brand it as an unconstitutional form of legislation. He did not regard a protective tariff as unconstitutional. He had not been, in the beginning, in favor of such a tariff, but since the nation had embarked upon a tariff and business had adjusted itself to it, he believed it should be continued. More important than all, he would not discuss the tariff with a state that was preparing to use force to nullify a law constitutionally enacted by the government of the United States.

Webster voted against Clay's bill, but the South swung in behind it and put it through both houses of congress.

South Carolina fired another legislative proclamation at Jackson, breathing defiance. Jackson, in a special message to congress, asked for special powers to deal with the situation. The powers that he asked were subsequently embodied in what came to be known as the "Force Bill." It sought only to modify the revenue laws in such a manner as to make possible the collection of tariff imposts in South Carolina notwithstanding the state's attempts at nullification.

Jackson sent a member of his cabinet to Webster to learn where he would stand with relation to this bill. Webster sent word that he would support it, and he did so. Clay privately said that he believed the bill should become a law, but he failed to vote either for or against it. Webster and Calhoun, who had retired from the Vice-

Presidency to resume his old place in the senate, came into head-on collision in debate. In favor of a state's right to nullify acts of congress and, if it desired, to secede, Calhoun made the strongest argument that was ever made— far stronger than the speech of Hayne. Webster replied in a speech devoid of rhetoric and wholly devoted to the task of proving both by fact and by reason that the doctrine of state rights had no legal sanction of any sort. Neither of the speakers fired at the other, as had Webster and Hayne. Each, in his attitude toward the other, was sincerely courteous. When Calhoun, in the course of his speech, said that he had a "deep conviction of the truth of my statements," Webster, from his seat replied, "I do not doubt it." Webster's thought and temper are admirably set forth in the following paragraph from his speech on the Force Bill:

Mr. President, I take this occasion to say that I support this measure, as an independent member of the senate, in the discharge of the dictates of my own conscience. I am no man's leader; and, on the other hand, I follow no lead but that of public duty and the star of the Constitution. I believe the country is in considerable danger; I believe an unlawful combination threatens the integrity of the Union. I believe the crisis calls for a mild, temperate forbearing, but inflexibly firm execution of the laws . . . I believe the people of the United States demand of us, who are intrusted with the government, to be just and fear not . . . For one, I obey this public voice; I comply with the demand of the people . . . I support the administration in measures which I believe to be necessary.

The bill to give the President power to enforce the tariff laws in South Carolina passed both houses of congress and became a law. Andrew Jackson personally thanked Webster for the support he gave it in the senate. Years later, Jackson expressed regret that he had not hanged Calhoun.

Jackson apparently did not know that ideas cannot be hanged. To have put Calhoun to death would have served only to make a bad situation worse. Jackson has been given far more credit than he deserved for the manner in which he handled the South Carolina nullification problem. He was entitled to praise for the firm manner in which he stood up for the right of the nation to enforce its laws within its own domain—but the next moment he weakened. So long as South Carolina challenged the right of the United States to collect any duties at all, there should have been no discussion of the justice of the particular schedules then in existence. Webster knew this. Jackson did not, nor did Clay. South Carolina was thereby emboldened to stand by her nullification ordinance. She abandoned her attempt to enforce it, but she never repealed it.

On the way to the Civil War there were many places to turn aside and escape the conflict. This was one of the places, but the turn was not taken. The South was encouraged to believe that the men of the North did not dare to fight. By forcing congress to modify the tariff laws against which she complained, South Carolina felt that she had won a victory; and she had.

Writing to a friend at this time, Webster said:

"A systematic and bold attack, now just begun, will be carried on, I apprehend, against the just and constitutional powers of the government, and against whatsoever strengthens the union of the states . . . I look forward to an animated controversy on these points for years to come."

X

ONE cannot be a great statesman all the time, however. One cannot remain incessantly upon his feet replying to Hayne or battling with Calhoun. One must have personal friends, relaxations, hours of ease.

About this time, Webster established a friendship with Philip Hone of New York, which lasted until Hone died, a year before Webster's death. This friendship will never, probably, be quite understood. Hone was not the kind of man whom one would expect to see Webster choose as a friend. He had left school at sixteen to become an auctioneer and grew rich at it—rich for those days; at one time he was probably worth half a million dollars. But he pursued business as an avocation rather than as a vocation. What really gave him joy was to dabble in politics (he was mayor of New York for a year), associate with great statesmen and thus get the feeling perhaps that he himself was a great man, which, as a matter of fact, he never was. But there was no man of his day, from the President down, whom he did not know, and Webster was his particular friend. It is more than suspected that Webster's chief interest in him was due to the fact that through Hone and his rich friends Webster and the political faction to which he belonged were able to finance their campaigns. In any event, it was for years the custom of Webster, when he was passing through New York and felt the need of a little recreation, to get in touch with Hone, who apparently could always be depended upon to arrange a small, interesting dinner party.

These parties, which began at six o'clock, usually lasted until long after midnight. Hone left a diary which tells a good deal about them. The best wines were served, and the best stories told; not off-color stories—Webster would never tolerate them—but reminiscences of all sorts, and particularly those that had a laugh in them. Webster's own preference was for stories of the old days back in New Hampshire, the odd characters he had known and the thrilling tales that some of them told of adventures with the Indians. Of such yarns Webster had a great supply, and they were always good. Webster's friend Peter Harvey seems to have been the only one who had the wit to put these things on paper, and when one reads them one does not wonder that Hone's dinners, when Webster was a guest, lasted almost until morning. Harvey speaks:

To illustrate the power of character and address upon a rabble, Mr. Webster related this anecdote. Shays's Rebellion, so-called, extended into New Hampshire, and the mob there, as in Massachusetts, resisted the law and would not permit the courts to sit. . . . The supreme court of the state hesitated to hold court in Sullivan County, the seat of the revolution. The judges were timid, and felt that they had no means of enforcing their authority. In this extremity, they sought the advice of old General Sullivan of Revolutionary fame, who, as the high sheriff, had charge of the court. He had a high reputation for personal courage, which he had won in the war, and was, withal, a high-toned, earnest Christian: When consulted by the court, General Sullivan said:

"We will go and open the court in Keene on the day when by law it is there to be held, and I will see that everything is right."

So they prepared to set out. In those days the stage accommodations were not good and most of the traveling by all classes was done on horseback. They put their clothes in the saddle-bags, and Sullivan, without the knowledge of the judges, put into his portmanteau his whole military suit—coat, epaulets and sword—that he had worn in the Revolutionary War. . . . They were a day or two making the journey, and were constantly getting reports from Keene as to the sentiments of the people. There seemed to be strong feeling of indignation and a determination to resist the holding of the court. The people were apparently resolved that the rebellion cases should not be tried, and this sentiment seemed to be unanimous. . . . When they got within four miles of Keene they got news that hundreds of exasperated people had gathered from the surrounding country to prevent any judicial proceedings. The judges turned pale and looked at Sullivan. One of them said:

"We don't wish to be mobbed, and nothing can be gained by going on. We have no civil posse or power to enforce respect."

The old hero replied:

"You follow me and it will end all right."

When within about four miles of Keene, he dismounted from his horse and took out his military suit. The judges looked at him in amazement while he attired himself in full uniform. He was a man fully six feet high, as straight as an Indian, as brave as a lion, and his military accouterments gave him a still more commanding appearance. When he was all ready, even to the spurs at his heels, he mounted his horse and told the judges to follow him and to keep close by him. He drew his sword and rode his horse to the front. On the outskirts of the village he met a crowd of men so dense as completely to block the road. General Sullivan shouted out:

"Make way for the court! Let there be no obstructing the court!"

The people recognized the old general, and one of the mob said: "I fought under him at such a place"; and they gazed at him. He bowed pleas-

antly to those he recognized. He halted to ask after
the health of some of them and that of their families;
and the old affection of his comrades in war was revived, apparently causing them to forget why they
had assembled. Before the party had reached the
hotel, the crowd was around old Sullivan, overwhelming him with attention. They found the hotel
full of people and crowds standing around, everywhere. The judges went into the hotel and sat down.
Sullivan said:

"I would open the court and immediately adjourn it, giving as a reason that there are no lawyers
present and no cases ready."

Acting upon this advice, they prepared to walk
over to the court-house. General Sullivan called for
the man who had the keys, who, when he came, said
it would not do to open the court. General Sullivan
replied:

"Take the keys of the court-house and go in front
of me."

So he drew his sword and they started, the janitor
leading the way, General Sullivan coming next, and
the judges following. When there appeared to be
the slightest attempt to crowd the path or obstruct a
free passage, the general would cry out:

"Make way for the court."

They finally reached the door. The frightened
janitor obeyed Sullivan's order to unlock the door,
the judges went in, the crowd pouring in after them
until every seat was filled. The judges took their seats
and the general sat down at the clerk's desk. He
then said, "The court is now open," and took off his
cap and sword and laid them on the desk; then he
called upon the chaplain to offer prayer. That over,
Judge Smith arose and said:

"There seem to be no suitors here and no clerk,
and I will therefore adjourn the court for three
months."

Sullivan got up deliberately, put on his cap and

sword and shouted, "Gentlemen, make way for the court," and they returned to the hotel, mounted their horses and rode off.

Webster said that the moral of this incident was the power of character over a mob. The mob felt that it was of no use to resist General Sullivan.

Sometimes it was the law business that pulled the trigger of Webster's memory and provided a yarn for Hone and his companions.

There was a lawyer who lived in his neighborhood in New Hampshire, he said, who was famous for his skill in collecting debts. There was a great deal of litigation in New Hampshire at that time, and almost everybody was sued before a debt was paid. If a note was given to this lawyer to collect, he was sure to get the money from the debtor. He snapped at that kind of business and everybody who had failed to get his money by other means went to him.

He was out fishing one day on a pond, when his little craft was wrecked and he was drowned. There was great consternation among his neighbors, and they went to raking and dragging the pond to find the body, working in this way for days without any success. At last a wag who had been sued a good many times by this lawyer was seen one morning standing on the bank of the pond with a fishing-line thrown into the water. Somebody came along and asked him what he was fishing for.

"Oh," said he, "for ———. There is a promissory note on the end of that line and, I think, dead or alive, if it gets to his nose, he will grab at it. If this won't fetch him, nothing will."

At one of Hone's parties, Webster's mind drifted back to his boyhood, and he told an Indian story that the faithful Harvey passed on to us.

In the neighborhood of Webster's father there lived a man named John Hanson, a laboring man who was often employed to work for the Websters. His boys were about Daniel's age. Hanson himself was somewhat addicted to strong drink and when in liquor was very quarrelsome and of great violence of temper. The Indian chiefs, particularly the young chiefs, often visited the white settlements, occasionally prolonging their stay for a week, at which times they were always treated with great hospitality. One of the old chiefs finally came and stayed eight or ten days, paying his visit chiefly to Hanson's house.

One morning Hanson and this old chief took their guns and started for Dover, a pretty long jaunt. The next day but one Hanson came back, but the Indian chief was not with him. Somebody asked him:

"Where is the Indian?"

"Oh," replied he, "he went home by another route."

But there was something about Hanson's appearance that led the people to fear that all was not right. Hanson had evidently been on a spree and was a little excited and did not give a very straight account of the Indian. In the course of a week or ten days, some men, as they were crossing a stream on a little log bridge about four miles distant, looked down and saw the remains of the old Indian. They took the body out and found a bullet hole in it. As it proved afterward, Hanson and the Indian had got into an altercation, both being full of liquor, and Hanson had shot him.

The whole settlement was filled with excitement. It was a bloody, murderous and wicked deed in itself, and its consequences were alarming. The vindictiveness of the Indians was proverbial. They were bound by their code to take vengeance upon anybody who had slain an Indian, and this was an old chief; so that everybody in the settlement looked for an immediate attack from the tribe.

Hanson was at once arrested and sent to the Dover jail. A committee was then chosen to visit the tribe and apprise them of the facts. They proceeded to the Indian encampment, carrying with them the remains of the chief. They told them of the murder; that John Hanson had committed it, and that it was probably done in liquor. They added that Hanson would be tried for his life and, if found guilty, would be hung; and they wished the tribe to know that this man's life would just as soon be taken for killing an Indian as for killing a white man. This was said to propitiate them and seemed to have its effect.

But by and by the sentiment that a white man's life should never be taken for that of an Indian gained ground among the settlers, and a reaction took place in favor of Hanson. The result was that in the course of a few weeks a dozen stout fellows painted their faces black, signed a round robin, and started for Dover jail. They tore out the side of the jail and set Hanson free.

The whole region was greatly excited, but Hanson got away. The pursuit was not very vigorous, for the feeling was strong that perhaps Hanson, after all, might have had real provocation from the Indian. The excitement gradually died out, but Hanson had a son, named for his father, who began to express the fear that the Indians would visit the iniquity of the father upon the son, which was a part of their code. He said:

"My father has escaped jail. The Indian says he will have revenge upon the next of kin."

He could not work or even sleep. He imagined that every noise he heard was a band of Indians coming to take revenge. He was a strong, stalwart fellow, but he began to lose flesh, so that his mother and friends became alarmed at his condition.

At last he came to the conclusion that he would go and deliver himself up to the Indians. He said nothing of his purpose until he had resolved upon it.

Then he told his mother and started for the Indian camp, forty or fifty miles distant. He arrived there and presenting himself to the chief, said:

"I am the son of John Hanson, who slew your chief. My father has escaped, and I have come to offer myself in his stead. You may take me and do what you please with me."

This touched the magnanimity of the Indians, and they asked him how he would like to be adopted into their tribe. He replied that, if such was their wish, nothing would please him more. So they made an Indian of him. He put on the Indian costume, married a squaw, was made a chief, and spent the remainder of his life among the Indians.

Usually the Hone dinners to Webster were private, select, confidential and protracted. Occasionally a hall was hired and two or three hundred of the best people were invited. It was at such a dinner that Webster made his celebrated reference to Alexander Hamilton:

"He smote the rock of the national resources, and abundant streams of revenue gushed forth. He touched the dead corpse of the public credit, and it sprang upon its feet. The fabled birth of Minerva from the brain of Jove was hardly more sudden or more perfect than the financial system of the United States as it burst forth from the conceptions of Alexander Hamilton."

Though Hone was perhaps a bit of a bounder, something about him must have appealed to Webster, who often had him as a house guest at Marshfield. We shall later often see them fishing on Cape Cod Bay. Usually, however, their meetings were in New York. Their small dinners we can still understand, but some of the larger ones would now be impossible. Think of 220 men paying from $30 to $40 each to dine with Webster at the Astor House, and remaining all night to listen to speeches. Hone tells of an occasion when Webster did not begin to speak until two o'clock in the morning. Because of the lateness of the hour he said he would be brief, but the audience would not have it that way. The guests kept urging him to go on, with the result that he spoke two hours. Even then they had not had enough. More speakers were called out, and more speeches were made. Hone was so worn out that, at the conclusion of Webster's speech, he went home, but the others remained until daybreak.

Of course the explanation must be found in the alcoholic customs of those far-gone days. The habit of drinking—and drinking too much—was general. Champagne, Hone tells us, was two dollars a quart. A tolerable grade of whisky or rum could be obtained for fifty cents a gallon. Guests sat up all night, not because they were so deeply interested in affairs of state, but because they were having a good time and hated to quit. Perhaps nobody was less inclined to quit than was Webster himself. He never outlived that liking for spirits which was developed in him when a young man by a gift of wine from old Christopher Gore.

At the Hone dinners Webster was introduced to a cocktail that he liked so much that it was named after him. Every bar in Washington and New York thereafter served "Daniel Webster cocktails." What they were made of, nobody now knows. Whatever their ingredients, they did no good to Daniel Webster. An occasional man appears to have a porcelain stomach and asbestos kidneys, but Webster was not thus equipped. He lacked the physique, but even more than that, he lacked the temperament. He was unfitted, as was Poe, to stand alcohol. Sober, he was an imposing, magnificent human being. When too much stimulated he became, by turns, ridiculous and pathetic. Hone nowhere says so, but between his lines one can see that he felt it. While Hone's attitude toward Webster was always that of respect, he occasionally referred to him as "the immortal Dan." There would seem to be a little slur in that word "immortal." Up in New England when Webster was making his great orations and had better habits, people spoke of him as the "godlike Webster." Between the two phrases is the awful chasm that lies between respect and ridicule.

Into this pit it was Webster's misfortune to plunge. If he had been a cheap politician, his fall would not have seemed so deplorable. Instead, he had such a combination of gifts as no other American has ever had. We have never produced another just like him. If he had had one more gift he could have saved himself and probably achieved the Presidency. What he lacked was will-power. He did not follow through. He liked his ease too well. He cared too much for the companionship of good fellows. Hammer Hayne and then go out for a night with Hone. No continuity. A giant at his best, but only a broken-winged bird at his worst.

Yet America will always honor the memory of Daniel Webster, and those who feel the warmth of his personality will always love him—faults and all.

XI

DANIEL WEBSTER was himself and looked his best in the senate. Always carefully dressed, he made an impressive figure. Early in his public life he had adopted what was known as the Whig uniform, consisting of dark blue broadcloth coat and trousers, gilded buttons on the coat, a fancy waistcoat, perhaps of yellow, black silk socks, highly polished black shoes, a high white collar and a fancy cravat. When he arose to speak he seemed to do so with some embarrassment. His voice was moderate and his manner subdued, his right hand resting upon his desk and his left hanging by his side. Ordinarily he spoke infrequently but in the fight that he had come back to make against Andrew Jackson he, within a year, spoke sixty-two times. The thing that spurred Webster to such activity was Jackson's determination to destroy the Bank of the United States. The bank's charter would not expire for two years, but Jackson was unwilling to wait for it to die a natural death. He wanted to kill it now, and he determined to do so by withdrawing from it the deposits of the government of the United States. The law said that the secretary of the treasury *might* withdraw such deposits, but it did not give this permission to the President.

That was what the trouble was about. Jackson took the position that if the secretary of the treasury would not do what he wanted him to do, he would remove him and appoint another. This took place. Mr. Duane, having refused to do the President's bidding, was removed and Mr. Taney (later Chief Justice of the Supreme Court) was placed at the head of the treasury department. Secretary Taney ordered the government's deposits transferred from the Bank of the United States to a selected list of state banks. This was done on October 1, 1833. Jackson's opponents attributed his enmity toward the bank to the fact that he held it responsible for certain political activity that had been centered upon him by the bank when he was a candidate for reelection to the Presidency.

Jackson moved rapidly but no more rapidly than Webster. Jackson was to win the fight and retain power long enough to install Martin Van Buren as his successor, but he was to bring upon his party troubles that, at the close of Van Buren's term, would bring defeat.

WEBSTER AT SIXTY-THREE
During his second period of service in the United States Senate
From a painting by Chester Harding

Webster predicted that the shifting of the government's funds from the Bank of the United States to a group of state banks would shake the country's credit and have an adverse effect upon business. Jackson said it would not, but Jackson was wrong. The effect was worse, if anything, than Webster had feared. The crippled bank called its loans, and a panic swept over the country. When congress assembled in December, it was confronted by a mass of memorials from business organizations, all over the country, urging the return of the government's funds to the Bank of the United States. Webster, who had been chosen chairman of the committee on finance of the senate, led the fight to do this. Clay (always an ardent poker player) saw a mêlée in prospect and introduced two resolutions, as he would have sat down at a card table and bought two stacks of chips. The first resolution scored Jackson for violating the Constitution by insisting upon exercising discretion that congress had lodged with the secretary of the treasury. The second resolution declared that Taney's reasons for withdrawing the deposits were unsatisfactory and insufficient. Both resolutions passed the senate and died on the house's doorstep. The house, controlled by Jackson, would not touch them.

The first resolution brought promptly from Jackson a sharp message of protest addressed to the senate. In this protest, Jackson set forth a view of presidential powers that went far and away beyond anything contained in the Constitution. The Constitution made congress—not the President—the great driving force behind the government. Jackson sought to make the President the great power.

Jackson's assertions brought sparks from the senate. Speech after speech was made in contradiction of his claims. None of the speeches entirely satisfied Webster.

None of them seemed quite to cover the ground. Writing to his friend Jeremiah Mason, he said: "I fear I shall be obliged to make a speech on the Protest. I have heard nothing yet which puts the case on such grounds as you and I should approve."

Webster made the speech. It was a logical, lucid statement, carefully set forth and following closely the spirit of the Constitution. That he was right is indicated by the fact that his views are now generally accepted. Once in a while, a really powerful man gets into the White House and, in the face of a great emergency, temporarily enlarges the power of the Presidency; but on the whole, Jackson's view has not been able to make a place for itself. The power of congress is, if anything, increasing.

As a phrase-maker—as a master of succinct expression—Webster, on this occasion, fairly outdid himself. As he warmed to his subject, that excellent mind of his began to throw off sentences that seemed white-hot.

"They went to war against a preamble," said he, speaking of the colonists who defied England because she had burdened them with taxes, not burdensome in themselves, but dangerous because they carried with them the assertion of the power to tax.

"They fought seven years against a declaration," he continued, praising the colonists for standing upon principle just as Jackson's opponents should now stand upon principle.

"They saw in the claim of the British Parliament a seminal principle of mischief, the germ of unjust power; they detected it, dragged it forth from underneath its plausible disguises, struck at it . . . till they had extirpated and destroyed it to the smallest fiber."

Then he added what is without doubt the greatest single gem of all his oratory:

"On this question of principle, while actual suffering was yet afar off, they raised their flag against a power, to which, for purposes of foreign conquest and subjugation, Rome in the height of her glory is not to be compared; *a power which has dotted over the surface of the whole globe with her possessions and military posts, whose morning drum-beat, following the sun and keeping company with the hours, circles the earth with one continuous and unbroken strain of the martial airs of England."*

What a magnificent picture of the dawn sweeping around the world to the accompaniment of music! No Englishman ever painted British power in such colors. When Webster was an old man, Peter Harvey read the foregoing paragraph to him and asked him how he happened to utter it. Webster turned toward Harvey and with a half-smile said:

"That is pretty fine. Did I say all that?"

Harvey solemnly assured Webster that he had once uttered those very words.

"Yes," said Webster, "and I got the impression as I stood on the walls of Quebec for the first time; and casting an imaginary glance over the broad extent of that dominion, thought of the magnitude of the power that governed half a civilized globe by her superior intellect. And I was proud that the blood of the Englishman flowed in my veins."

Webster won the thanks of Englishmen for his oratory, but got a brickbat from some of Jackson's supporters in York County, Pennsylvania, who in a communication to the senate declared that Webster's opposition to Jackson in the bank matter was due to discreditable motives; that he was the attorney for the bank, which was described as a "good fat client," having paid to Webster more than fifty thousand dollars in fees. Martin Van Buren, Vice-President and presiding officer of the senate, considered the charges libelous and refused to permit them to be read. Webster dragged the slander into the open by insisting upon the reading of it in the senate. It was true, he said, that he had acted as the attorney of one of the officers of the bank, but his employment was due, not to the favor of the bank, but to that of a number of Boston merchants who, in placing in the bank's hands a number of claims arising under the French treaty, specified in the contract that Webster should be engaged to prosecute them.

But the serpent had many heads, and the cutting off of one did not kill it. At various times and places it was declared that the Bank of the United States held mortgages upon Webster's property and that it carried his notes for various amounts, one story setting the figure at fifty-six thousand dollars. Webster, over his own signature, denied all of these fabrications. His transactions with the bank had been only those of an ordinary customer; it held no mortgage upon anything that he owned and had extended to him no special favors.

The house being unwilling to join the senate in upsetting Jackson's bank policy, congress adjourned with nothing done, which was a victory for the administration. During the next few months, Webster became convinced that the bank's charter, when it expired, would not be renewed. State banks, issuing currency of fluctuating and uncertain value, must be tolerated but, if possible, regulated. Webster believed, however, that such a system would never be successful and it was not. It was a failure that, until remedied, caused untold misery.

XII

THE Whig party, in 1836, had a chance to win. Daniel Webster, in 1836, had a chance to get the Whig nomination. All the Whig party needed was cohesion and energy intelligently exerted; all Webster needed was political sagacity. Neither the Whig party nor Webster measured up to these requirements. The Whig party, instead of uniting its forces behind one candidate, nominated four, of whom Webster was one. These four candidates received, in the aggregate, 736,656 votes as against 761,549 cast for Martin Van Buren. A shift of fewer than 13,000 votes would have elected a Whig candidate. If four Whigs, none of whom had a ghost of a chance of winning, could come within 25,000 votes of equaling the Democratic vote, a single Whig candidate, with energy and political intelligence behind him, might reasonably have expected to switch the few votes required to spell victory. But the Whigs were bankrupt of political sense, and so was Daniel Webster.

Nothing about Webster was more remarkable than the rapidity with which he shriveled when transferred from the arena of statesmanship to that of politics. Most members of congress have no difficulty at all in playing the parts of politicians; it is only when they desire to be considered statesmen that they fall flat. With Webster, the reverse was true. As a statesman, he was superb. He had a penetrating mind and a level head. Altogether, he would have made such a President as we have seldom had. But the Presidency is a political office, and he who achieves it must have either instinctive or acquired knowledge of how to go about it to play the political game successfully. Of such knowledge, Webster was innocent. All he knew was how to stand stedfastly for what he believed to be right. He could have done this and still been elected President if he had known how to handle himself. He did not know. Where Lincoln would have succeeded, Webster failed. But in his failures there was something beautiful. It is always an inspiring sight to see a man set his course by his conscience, and sail on—even to the rocks.

This Webster did. The Presidency was just ahead of him. He wanted it. It was a noble aspiration for which no man who has it need apologize. It was also an aspiration that a majority of the voters of his day, if they could have been properly assembled, probably would have been proud to indulge. An adroit political manager could have assembled them properly. Lacking such sagacious advice, Webster's hopes crashed. If he had gone down because he was wrong there would have been nothing to regret, but the pity of it was that Webster was never so right as he was when he was wrecked. He was right with regard to the manner in which slavery and the menace of disunion should be dealt with. To this day, the credit that belonged to him has not been given. The fortunes of war obscured a great service that he tried to render and gave credit to a group of men who should have been censured.

Reference is here made to the abolitionists—John Brown, Garrison, Wendell Phillips, and others. We now honor the memory of these men. Our homage is misplaced. If one believes in hanging at all (which the present writer does not) John Brown deserved to be hanged. He had blood on his hands. Determined to right a great wrong in his own way, he brought death to others. Garrison and Phillips openly advocated violation of the Constitution. They called it a "covenant with hell." What they particularly disliked about it was its sanction of the Fugitive Slave Law. They swore that "Constitution or no Constitution," no negro who ever walked the streets of Boston a free man should be sent back into slavery. That was no way to talk. When any man declares that, law or no law, he will do as he pleases, it is time to lock him up. Nor does it matter that his purpose is commendable. It is never right to do the right thing in the wrong way. The Fugitive Slave Law was just as bad as the abolitionists said it was —but it was the law. Granted that the public sentiment for its repeal existed, there was a lawful, orderly way to get rid of it. If such sentiment was sufficient there was even a lawful, orderly way so to amend the Constitution that such a law could never again be enacted. If there was not enough such sentiment (which there was not) delay would have been necessary until more could be generated.

That was exactly what Brown, Garrison, Phillips, and the rest were unwilling to do. They were unwilling to wait. They were unwilling to abide by the orderly methods provided by the Constitution. Instead, they chose to be a constitution unto themselves. They sought to substitute their will for the public law.

Some persons honor their memories by reason of the fact that the fortunes of war worked to their advantage. The Emancipation Proclamation gave the abolitionists a place in history to which they are not entitled. Lincoln issued it, not because the abolitionists desired it, but because he believed he could thereby cripple the striking power of the South. Lincoln hated slavery as much as did any abolitionist, but he recognized its constitutional sanction and was willing to wait to get rid of it by constitutional means. Until he issued the proclamation, he would have consented to end the war, at any time, with slavery left intact, provided only that the South would recognize the federal authority. He said so, many times. Once he said that he would ask to write but one word in the peace treaty—the word "Union"—and the South might write all the rest. Only the obstinacy of the southern leaders prevented the war from being ended with slavery intact. If it had so ended, the abolitionists would not have stood so well in history. If the South had won the war, the abolitionists would have stood forth in their true colors—as reckless law-breakers and agitators who had brought disaster to the country. If the Civil War had begun in 1850 instead of in 1861, it is very likely that the South would have won it, as the South at that time was economically stronger than the North. That the war did not begin in 1850 was due more to the mollifying measures of Webster than to the acts of any other man.

The point that every generation of Americans should keep clearly in mind is that under our Constitution there is never any justification for violating the Constitution to redress grievances. The Constitution itself provides an orderly way to do this. If we do not believe in orderly processes, we need no Constitution; let everybody do as he pleases and use such force as he can command to compel others to obey him. If we do believe in orderly processes, we should always obey the law whether we like it or not, knowing full well that when enough of us want to do so we can always change the law in the manner that is provided by law. This method may not suit impatient minorities, but it is the only safe way to proceed; and impatient minorities have no right to rule the United States.

It was necessary to make this digression to enable the reader to understand and to appraise at its true value Webster's attitude toward the various matters that led up to the Civil War. Presently we shall see the southern slaveholding oligarchy begin to maneuver to get Texas into the Union, and we shall now be able to understand why Webster opposed the admission of the Lone Star state.

Webster's statesmanship, while correct in principle, failed because he lacked the power to induce the North and the South to follow his lead. His straight, middle-of-the-road course ultimately left him with few followers anywhere. The kindliness of his nature and his recognition of the South's legal rights brought him friendly cheers from southern crowds, but no votes; while the abolitionists would have none of him. Perhaps the task of reconciling the extremes of opinion in the North and in the South was too great for any man to accomplish. Certainly it was too great for Webster.

It is pathetic, now, to see how Webster in 1835-36 tried to move upon the White House. There were great difficulties in his way, but he so met them as to make them greater. The machinery of national conventions not having been invented, it was necessary to adopt what we should now call cumbersome methods to bring about a nomination. The practice was to light a fire somewhere in the political grass and see if it would not spread. So we see Webster, in January, 1835—twenty-two months before the election—writing to his friend Mason urging that the Massachusetts legislature place him in nomination. Curiously enough, he asked that his letter be burned, though there was nothing in it that required burning. Politicians seem never to learn that the surest way of preserving a letter for remote posterity is to ask that it be burned. Webster apparently wished his letter to be destroyed because he was unwilling that anybody should ever know that he had made a move to get the Presidency. Webster was so impatient for action by the Massachusetts legislature that a month later he wrote again to inquire why nothing had been done. A few days after the receipt of the second letter, the legislature placed him in nomination. Present-day politicians would probably consider it unwise to launch a candidacy twenty-one months before election. There is too much danger of such a candidacy growing cold. But the idea then was to give the other states a lead and see if they would not follow Massachusetts.

Pennsylvania perhaps would have followed if Webster, himself, had not made a hash of the situation. Asked by the Anti-Masonic faction, which was strong in the state, whether, in the event of his election, he would appoint Masons to office he replied, in a letter marked "confidential," in an unsatisfactory manner. After saying between the lines, as plainly as he could, that he would appoint no Masons, he refused to make the flat statement that he would not do so, on the ground that he had no right to make such a pledge. The result was that the Anti-Masons nominated William Henry Harrison, and a day or two later, the Pennsylvania Whig convention did the same. This amazed Webster as he had looked upon Harrison as an outsider who had no chance at all.

Webster had not the slightest ability as a political organizer. The commonest tricks of party leaders and politicians generally were never practiced by him. As an illustration: it was the custom in Washington then as it is now, and has been ever since his time, for country visitors to seek introductions to great men, usually through the intercession of their congressmen. When Clay was thus approached he was at once all amiability and attention. He shook hands in his most gracious manner, smiled his broad smile, made numerous inquiries as to the visitor's family and sent the caller away happy. Webster was quite different. Sometimes, when he was writing at his desk, and visitors were introduced, he would merely extend his left hand, permit it to be shaken, and never look up, with the result that the caller went away humiliated and, perhaps, angry. It was not that Webster meant to be discourteous or unkind, but he seemed to think that handshaking was a cheap political trick to which he did not care to descend. Webster was the soul of courtesy, but he would not capitalize it for the sake of votes.

As the months wore on it became apparent that the Webster fire that had been set in the grass of Massachusetts was not going to spread. The Whig party, lacking leadership, spawned forth two more candidates, making four in all. The other two were Hugh L. White and W. P. Mangum.

Webster's uncompromising attitude toward the problems growing out of slavery had, by this time, begun to produce a fine crop of enemies—gentlemen who seized upon every trifle they could pick up to embarrass him. One of these trifles had to do with a remark that Webster, in the heat of debate, made upon the Fortifications Bill. Believing that it contained an unconstitutional provision, Webster said he would not vote for it even "if the guns of the enemy were pointed against the walls of the capitol." Out of this molehill, some of Webster's enemies tried to make a mountain. The best evidence that the remark was, from a political point of view, a mistake, was that Webster wrote a speech explaining it, which his friends induced him not to deliver. Whatever has to be explained would always better have been left unsaid.

Petitions poured into the senate from northern abolitionists. Some of these petitions asked that slavery be done away with entirely, while others called for its elimination in the District of Columbia. If the District of Columbia could not be made free, it was even demanded that the national capital be removed to the North. Such petitions gave Webster further opportunities for hewing to the line, but decreased his chances for the Presidency.

He offended the abolitionists by taking the ground that the senate was quite right in refusing to refer to committees and consider, in the regular manner, petitions to end slavery, giving as his reason that, under the Constitution, congress had no right to interfere with slavery where it already existed. The next moment, he offended the South by declaring that congress had the power to prohibit slavery in the District of Columbia, and that petitions to do so should therefore he referred to a committee and take the regular course. What he sought was an opportunity to bring the subject up in the senate for such extended discussion as might lead to a better understanding on both sides. The senate would not have it so. The petitions were received and laid on the table, where they remained until the blasts of the Civil War blew them away.

The long-cherished southern plan for the acquisition of Texas as a slave-holding state had come from beneath the surface into the open. First, Southerners had gone to Texas as settlers and, as soon as they felt strong enough, had gone to war with Mexico and achieved their independence. The next step was to obtain the recognition of the United States. Webster was in favor of this. But he was not in favor of the step that followed, which was to bring Texas into the Union. He opposed it. Petitions from the North backed him up. President Van Buren, always with his ear to the ground, waved Texas away. The United States did not want her. Keep out.

Almost a century later, it may seem to some as if Webster, in opposing the admission of Texas, was wrong. Is not Texas now a great state? Is not its civilization superior to that of Mexico? Did not the admission of Texas set in motion a train of events that brought into the Union California, Utah, Arizona, New Mexico and other territory? Are not these, too, great states? Is not their civilization superior to that of Mexico?

We believe the civilization of these states is superior to that of Mexico. But if the seizure of the lands of other nations is to be justified on the ground that the civilization of the aggressor is declared by him to be superior to that of the victim what nation would be safe? The opinion of the aggressor then becomes the rule of action, and fundamental right and wrong are forgotten. Probably every nation believes its civilization to be superior to that of any other. Would the United States care to be attacked on no better moral ground than that its assailants believed that by conquering us and annexing our territory they could establish a superior civilization? Within limits, there is such a thing as having the right to be what we are, and the original settlers of Texas, under Mexican rule, had this right.

Webster could not undo what the southern revolutionists in Texas had done, but he was in favor of stopping them in their tracks before they could bring their loot into the United States. He and those who agreed with him kept Texas out for ten years, and when at last they failed the prospect of peace between the North and South failed almost to the same extent. The admission of Texas, in 1845, brought on war with Mexico, and war with Mexico was a long step toward the Civil War.

In the summer of 1837, Webster made a trip to the West that was remarkable for the widespread manifestations of affection and respect upon the part of the people. He was received as no public man, up to that time, had ever been received. On his way out he stopped overnight at North Bend, Ohio, to visit William Henry Harrison. Proceeding to the banks of the Mississippi, where he turned back, he rolled along in his carriage to the accompaniment of ringing bells and booming cannon. Bryan, who was to come along sixty years later, could have told him the difference between cheers and votes. Ten miles out of Chicago he was met by a long string of carriages that escorted him into the city. Along the way, he spoke in all the great cities and, at that, had to reject nine-tenths of the invitations he received.

Of course, Webster, on such a trip, would naturally have to fall into a pit of some kind that would cost him money. The worst business man in the world, he always had great undertakings swimming in the back of his head. His particular weakness was for agriculture on a great scale, and while he was in Illinois somebody sold him a thousand acres of land in Sangamon County. His two farms in the East were drawing more and more heavily upon his purse, but such a small fact constituted for him no reason why he should not commit himself still further. On such a stretch of Illinois prairie what cattle and what oxen could be raised! Webster was overwhelmed at the prospect. And what a site for a town! There was nobody within gunshot who wanted to live in a new town, but that did not prevent the platting of a town-site, which, in honor of his birthplace, was named Salisbury.

Webster's will, which often wobbled, began to wobble again. Perhaps it was his investment in Illinois lands that made him feel the need of more money, but at any rate, he determined to resign from the senate, service in which had so interfered with his law business that his income was comparatively small. He resigned, but his friends in Massachusetts protested, and so did his friends in New York. It was a great tribute for citizens of a neighboring state to pay him. Webster withdrew his resignation, and in January, 1839, the legislature of Massachusetts reelected him for a term of six years.

Webster had long wanted to visit England. There was a boundary question to be settled between Maine and the British territory to the north; and some of Webster's friends believed that it would be well to kill two birds with one stone by appointing him a special commissioner to go to England and make the settlement. Such an appointment would give him an official status that might be pleasant, and he could furthermore do good work for his country. Webster was willing, but the President would not appoint him. So Webster, in the spring of 1839, sailed away, not exactly like a common tourist, but as a United States Senator for whom a Democratic administration had little use.

PART FOUR

NOR to business a drudge, nor to faction a slave,
He strove to make int'rest and freedom agree;
In public employments industrious and grave,
And alone with his friends, Lord! how merry was he!
— MATTHEW PRIOR (1664-1721).

I

WEBSTER'S visit to England was one of the happiest events of his life. He was fifty-seven years old, his health was still good, he had a reputation that had leaped the Atlantic, which meant that he would be well received; and thwarted ambition had not yet dulled the edge of his capacity for enjoyment. Mrs. Webster accompanied him, and so did his daughter Julia, who had grown into a fine young woman of whom her father was very fond. Julia was about to be married to Samuel A. Appleton of Boston, but her father, feeling that he must have her company on the journey, induced her to sail with him and be married in London. Mrs. Page, the wife of Webster's brother-in-law, was also of the party. Edward Webster, the youngest son, then a student at Dartmouth, was to sail a little later and join his father in London.

Webster was in gay humor, and it was good that he could be, for this trip to Europe was to be the last great moment of happiness he was ever to have. Everything that could crush a man was about to close down upon him, but he did not suspect it.

England gave Webster all it had to give; gave it gladly, almost proudly, as if recalling what blood was in his veins. Every door that he could have wished to enter was opened to him. More than that: when he occasionally desired to be by himself he was let alone. Politeness and consideration can go no further.

Webster's letters to friends in America accurately describe the picture as it was unfolded to him and also throw an interesting light on the writer. What sight might one suppose he would mention first? A glimpse of the queen? Not Webster. The great varieties of fine cattle that he saw around Liverpool and in Cheshire! Some of them were the best he had ever seen, but, on the other hand, some were not so good. He viewed every bovine with a critical eye, as if to give it accurate classification.

The general aspect of the countryside mightily pleased him. Such fields of wheat and potatoes! They looked as if they had been stamped as people stamp butter. The green grass, the hedges—everything about the country took Webster by storm.

And London. What a city!

"For the two days we have been here," he writes, "I have been poking about *incog.,* going into all the courts and everywhere else I chose with the certainty that no one knew me. That is a queer feeling to be in the midst of so many thousands and to be sure that no one knows you and that you know no one . . . A stranger in London is in the most perfect solitude in the world. He can touch everybody, but can speak to nobody. I like much these strolls by myself."

When Webster tired of solitude he had plenty of companionship—Dickens, Wordsworth, Carlyle, Sydney Smith, Tom Moore, the poet, and everybody else who was worth meeting. Almost every morning, he was invited out to breakfast.

"An English breakfast is the plainest and most informal thing in the world. Indeed, in England, the rule of politeness is to be quiet, act naturally, take no airs and make no bustle. This perfect politeness has, of course, cost a good deal of drill. Fuss and fidgets can be subdued only by strict discipline."

As the news began to spread about that a distinguished

visitor had come from abroad it at length reached a news-paper office. The London *Gazette* said:

"We cordially welcome to our shores this great and good man and accept him as a fit representative of all the great and good qualities of our trans-Atlantic brethren."

The day after the publication of this paragraph, the press of carriages at the door of his hotel blocked traffic. "Our heads are rather turned at present, but we hope to get right soon," Webster remarked.

It seemed as if almost all of his visitors bore titles, but Webster found society "more free and easy" than he had expected.

"Not that there is not, as I presume there is, a good deal of exclusiveness, but the general manners, when people meet, are void of stiffness and are plain and simple, in a remarkable degree.

"It is the height of what they call 'the season'; London is full and the hospitalities of friends, the gaieties of the metropolis, and the political interests of the moment keep everybody alive . . . I have been to the courts, made the acquaintance of most of the judges, and attended the debates in both houses of parliament . . . I have liked some of the speeches very well. They generally show excellent temper, politeness and mutual respect among the speakers. Lord Stanley made the best speech which I have ever heard. I was rather disappointed in Macaulay; but so were his admirers and I have no doubt that the speech I heard was below his ordinary efforts."

What ill luck for Macaulay, with a distinguished member of his own trade-union sitting in the gallery, to make a poor speech! Well, no clock can strike thirteen all the time, but it is too bad to strike three when company is present.

"Among the great men here," said Webster, "Lord

Wellington [Napoleon's conqueror] stands, by universal consent, far the highest . . . If he were to die now he would depart life in the possession of as much of the confidence and veneration of the British people as any many ever possessed."

Late in June, Carlyle wrote to a friend in America:

"Not many days ago I saw at breakfast the notablest of all your notables, Daniel Webster. He is a magnificent specimen. You might say to all the world, 'This is our Yankee Englishman; such limbs we make in Yankee-land.' As a logic-fencer, advocate, or parliamentary Hercules, one would incline to back him at first sight against all the extant world. The tanned complexion; that amorphous crag-like face; the dull black eyes under the precipice of brows, like dull anthracite furnaces needing only to be *blown;* the mastiff mouth accurately closed; I have not traced so much of *silent Berserker rage* that I remember of, in any other man. 'I guess I should not like to be your nigger.' Webster is not loquacious, but he is pertinent, conclusive; a dignified, perfectly bred man, though not English in breeding; a man worthy of the best reception among us and meeting such, I understand."

Which was a good deal to say, considering that Carlyle usually carried a heavy hammer and knocked everybody. Once he said to an American: "There is another country-man of yours that needs taking down a peg—George Washington."

About this time, John Kenyon, a wealthy, cultivated Englishman, met Webster, soon became very friendly with him, and afterward related many interesting anecdotes of their association. Kenyon, though rich, sometimes criti-cized English economic arrangements in what might now be roughly described as communist fashion. Once, when he had done so, Webster placed a hand upon each of Kenyon's shoulders and said: "Don't talk so. Depend on it, if you put the property into one set of hands and the political power into another, the power won't rest until it has got hold of the property."

Kenyon asked Webster if it was true that he received the largest professional income in the States. Webster replied that it was not true, though it might have been if he had not sacrificed a considerable part of his legal income to serve in congress.

"Coleridge used to say," said Kenyon, "that he had seldom known or heard of any great man who had not 'much of the woman in him.' Even so, that large intellect of Daniel Webster seemed to be coupled with all the softer feelings; and his countenance and bearing, at the very first, impressed me with this. I find this memorandum in my note-book: '7th June—Called on the American Webster; much struck with him, had fancied that he was a powerful but harsh-looking man, but found him kindly and frank. A commanding brow, thoughtful eyes, and a mouth that seemed to respond to all humanities.' "

Almost a hundred years later, many Americans still believe that Webster was austere and cold. He could be both, but it was his nature to be neither. He was a kindly, cordial, and sometimes a playful man. The following entry from Kenyon's diary shows how light-hearted this man of fifty-seven could sometimes be:

Went to Oxford to join the Websters at the Angel. We had been invited to a huge agricultural meeting and dinner, which were to take place at Oxford the day after. They dined together—gentry and yeomanry—to the number of twenty-five hundred or more. I was to have dined with them, but as the

dinner hour came on, my courage oozed out (I prefer parties of six or eight at most). So I surrendered
my ticket to some applicant not so intolerant of dinners of twenty-five hundred, and dined with Webster's agreeable family party—his wife and daughter
and relative, Mrs. Page—at the hotel. He returned to
us early in the evening, sliding into the room joy-
ously, half as if he were dancing, and as if to tell,
good-naturedly, that he was glad to come back to us.
After a little while, I said, "But I am sorry to have
missed your speech, which they say was a capital
one." "Order in some wine and water and I will
speak it over again"; which he did most festively.
. . . Fancy how delightful and attaching I found all
this genial bearing from so famous a man; so affectionate, so little of a humbug.

This was the day of autograph albums and Kenyon
asked Webster for his autograph. Webster wrote:

> When you and I are dead and gone,
> This busy world will still jog on,
> And laugh and sing, and be as hearty,
> As if we still were of the party.

It is significant that the only public address Webster
made in England was to this assemblage of farmers.
Wherever there were fat cattle, Webster would be if he
could get there. Of necessity, his head was kept most of
the time in law books—"in the everlasting company of
plaintiff and defendant," he often said—but his heart was
in the soil. Dining in the open, with twenty-five hundred
farmers, was just to his liking. Webster's sense of modesty
prevented him from making much of a speech, but what
he said was good. Perhaps the thing that most endeared
him to the crowd was what he said about himself and his
reasons for going to England:

The noble chairman was pleased to speak of the people of the United States as kindred in blood with the people of England. I am an American. I was born on that great continent, and am wedded to the fortunes of my country, for weal or for woe. There is no other region of the earth which I can call my country. But I know, and am proud to know, what blood flows in these veins.

I am happy to stand here today and to remember, that, although my ancestors, for several generations, lie buried beneath the soil of the western continent, yet there has been a time when my ancestors and your ancestors toiled in the same cities and villages, cultivated adjacent fields, and worked together to build up that great structure of civil polity which has made England what England is.

When I was about to embark for this country, some friends asked me what I was going to England for. To be sure, gentlemen, I came for no object of business, public or private; but I told them I was coming to see the elder branch of the family. I told them I was coming to see my distant relations, my kith and kin of the old Saxon race.

The English apparently liked Webster as much as he liked them. "I must say," he wrote to a friend in Boston, "that the good people have treated me with great kindness. Their hospitality is unbounded."

About the first of August the Websters went to Scotland. They were greeted by such continuous downpours of rain that Webster must have recalled the reply of Samuel Johnson, when he first visited the country, to the inquiry of a clergyman as to what he thought of the place. Johnson tactfully replied that, without doubt, it was the most horrible country in the world. The clergyman reeled for a moment, but when he recovered his balance, said:

"Yes, but God made it." "Indeed He did, sir," replied Johnson, "but remember that He made it for Scotchmen. And God made hell."

The tourists, too, bothered Webster. Wherever there was enough water to float a ship, steamboats came, loaded down with passengers who when they were ashore crowded the hotels.

"This takes off much of the romance and much of the interest," Webster wrote home to a friend. "All travel together, and everybody is in a prodigious hurry. The decks of the steamboats are covered with a mass of men and women, each with a guidebook in his hand, learning what to admire! . . . The great majority of travelers only wish to 'get on.' The first inquiry is, how soon they can get to a place; the next, how soon they can get away from it. They incur the expense of the journey, I believe, more for the sake of having the power of saying afterward that they have seen sights than from any other motive."

The Websters returned to London in the middle of September, where Julia was married on the twenty-fourth. Edward had come on, and except for Fletcher the family was complete. But the family had no more than been assembled when it was time to begin thinking of returning to America. Webster's last days in England were spent at the country home of Mr. Denison, a member of the house of commons. "While he was with me," said Mr. Denison, "he talked continually of his intention to quit public life, both professional and political, and to withdraw to a property he had purchased in the western country."

Fat cattle! Big oxen! Crops! Green fields!
Dreams!

II

AFTER a trip of thirty-five days, Webster landed in New York on December 29, 1839. The first news he heard was that, on the fourth of the month, the Whig national convention had nominated William Henry Harrison for the Presidency. Webster instinctively knew well enough what this would mean to him. He had no doubt that Harrison would be elected and felt sure that the new President would offer him a seat in his cabinet. What Webster expected was what happened. Van Buren had made a mess of his administration. His attitude toward the currency problem had kept the country in a continuous panic; the people were tired of it all and wanted a change. After rather a dull winter in congress, in which minor aspects of the eternal slavery problem were the chief subjects considered, Webster plunged into the Harrison campaign with a will. He was everywhere in demand and flittered from New England to the east shore of Maryland as rapidly as trains could carry him. Fifteen cities asked him to deliver Fourth of July addresses.

What a tantalizing spectacle! On all sides were proofs of the existence of a degree of popularity that would have put him into the White House if it had been properly organized and directed. Lacking such organization, it had become his fate to campaign for a man whom he obviously considered his inferior. The subject must have been discussed more or less in Webster's family, because we find his daughter Julia bursting out with it in a letter in which she called the country "ungrateful." For the purpose of becoming better acquainted with Julia, as well as to show how she felt about the country's failure to elect her father President, her letter is given:

I thank you, dear father, for your kind letter from Philadelphia, which I received today, and still more for the verses enclosed in it. I think them beautiful, dear father, and thank you for associating me in remembrance with my dear mother. I have never thought of her so often as I have since I have had a child of my own, and could I be but half as good a mother as she was, I might hope to fulfil my duty to my little girl, but hers, I fear, was a goodness which I cannot attain.

We are all quite well here. My strength increases gradually and I hope, before long, to be quite myself again. I wish you could see my baby. She has improved very much since you left and begins to show some signs of intelligence. Everybody says she is a very bright child, but of course everybody would tell its mother so and she, of course, believes it. . . .

You are now, I suppose, immersed once more in the cares and excitements of public life. Do not let it interfere with your health, dear father. Pray let that be your greatest consideration. Surely you have done enough for your country, did you never utter another word in its behalf, to be considered the best and the noblest among the noble sons of America. Has not the fame of your greatness extended to the uttermost parts of the earth? It cannot be increased, and do not, dearest father, wear yourself out for the good of a country ungrateful at best. What is the whole country to your family when weighed in the balance with one hour of sickness or anxiety which it causes to you? I am no great patriot, I do not love Rome better than Cæsar; the advancement of party better than my own dear father. . . .

Don't you think you would be happy to live once more at home with your old friends? Do come back to us, dear father, and do not be persuaded to stay in Washington by persons who may not be altogether disinterested in their motives, who may look to you to advance them further than their own unassisted efforts could ever do. . . . I am not naturally suspicious, but I do mistrust some of your friends.

Webster often momentarily deceived himself into believing that what he really wanted to do was to get out of office and the law business and be a farmer, but the fact was that the holding of high public office had for him an irresistible lure. When the President-elect, in a letter written December 1, 1840, offered him a place in his cabinet, the vision of a great stock farm in Illinois was permitted quickly to fade out. Not only did Webster accept a place in the new cabinet, but he did so in a way that he would have scarcely employed if his respect for the character and abilities of the President-elect had been greater.

What happened was this: Harrison wrote to Webster offering him either the secretaryship of state or of the treasury, but plainly indicating that he would prefer him to take the latter, which Clay had refused and which seemed likely to be difficult acceptably to fill. Webster, by letter, promptly accepted the secretaryship of state. It is true that he did so in such a manner that Harrison, if he chose, might still urge that he accept the treasury portfolio. But it is also true that when a definite office has been definitely accepted, it becomes a little harder for the appointive power to ignore the acceptance and continue conversations. In an adroit way, not any too gentle, Webster forced Harrison's hand. In such circumstances, Harrison did what Webster apparently believed he would do, and without further words Webster became secretary of state. Obviously, Webster's idea was that the country was to have at its head an old man, inexperienced in statesmanship, and that he (Webster) would be the big man of the administration. It was true that Harrison was but little more fitted for the Presidency than he was to sing in grand opera, but he had a will of his own as Webster soon discovered.

How little respect Webster had for Harrison's abilities is indicated by the fact that he had the amazing nerve, without having been asked to do so, to write Harrison's inaugural address. Harrison, when he met Webster in Washington a week or so before the inauguration, was told this by Webster himself, who took care to attach to the bomb many little blue ribbons of apology to the effect that he knew the President, at such a time, would be overwhelmed with callers and would hardly have leisure to write an address.

The little blue ribbons meant nothing, however, to Harrison. He bluntly told Webster that it was unnecessary for him to write an address; that he had written one for himself.

In the face of this rebuff, Webster had the audacity to ask Harrison to let him see his proposed address.

That Harrison did not here turn his back upon Webster and leave him out of his cabinet proves something, but it is difficult to tell just what. Disrespect could hardly have gone much farther. Webster should have been instantly put in his place, but Harrison was apparently too old, or appreciated too little the dignity of his office, even to refuse Webster's request. On the contrary, he granted it without hesitation, asking only that he be permitted to read the speech that Webster had prepared. That night, each read the other's address.

Webster told his friend Peter Harvey that General Harrison, when they met the next morning, said to him:

"If I should read your inaugural instead of mine, everybody would know that you wrote it and I did not. Now this is the only official paper which I propose to write, for I do not intend to interfere with my secretaries; but this is a sort of acknowledgment on my part to the American people of the great honor they have conferred upon me in elevating me to this high office; and, although it is not as suitable as yours, still, it is mine, and I propose to let the people have it just as I have written it. I must deliver my own instead of yours."

Webster was in a pickle. He knew now that he was dealing with an obstinate old man who, perhaps, would be as good as his word and insist upon reading the address as it stood. After reading the document, Webster knew that it was very bad, having, as he said, "no more to do with the affairs of the American government and people than a chapter in the Koran." Harrison had gone deeply into the histories of ancient Greece, Athens and Rome without saying anything about the United States. The subject of Rome seemed especially to fascinate him. The word "proconsul" was music to his ears, which he indicated by using it again and again. In short, he had made of his address a terrible hash, which Webster would have been ashamed to have made public. Still, the old gentleman seemed determined to read it, so there was nothing to do but to ascertain whether he would not tolerate a few additions and subtractions. Webster wanted to cut out some of the references to ancients and substitute a few paragraphs about America. Harrison was at first reluctant to consent to any alterations, but finally permitted Webster to indicate what he would strike out and what he would add.

The day that Webster edited Harrison's "copy" was a hard day in Webster's life. Coming home, late for dinner, he threw himself on a couch and was so obviously worn, worried, and tired that a member of his household expressed the fear that something had happened.

"You would think something had happened," he replied, "if you knew what I have done. I have killed seventeen Roman proconsuls as dead as smelts, every one of them."

Harrison may have flinched when he saw the slaughter, but at his inauguration he read the manuscript that Webster handed back to him.

Webster resigned from the senate on March 3, 1841, and the next day took the oath of office as secretary of state. On his desk, awaiting him, was a problem of the first magnitude. The United States and Great Britain were on the brink of war. Three serious disputes contributed to the creation of a bad situation, but the thing that threatened peace had to do with the killing of an American by a party of Canadians, and the arrest, on a charge of murder, in the state of New York, of one of the attacking party. The seriousness of the arrest lay in the fact that the British Government promptly assumed responsibility for the act that brought death to an American, and let it be understood that serious results would follow if the man accused of the murder were put to death. Great Britain's acknowledgment of responsibility for the casualty made of the incident a matter for settlement by America and Great Britain; and upon ascertainment of this fact the authorities of the state of New York should have washed their hands of it and turned it over to the Federal Government, which alone was competent to deal with it. But when this suggestion was made by Webster to Governor Seward, the governor refused to act upon it.

The trouble grew out of the rebellion that took place in Canada in 1837. Some of the rebels, after their defeat, removed to the United States, enlisted the aid of sympathizers, and organized raids across the Niagara River upon the Canadian shore. They used, for this purpose, an American steamship called the "Caroline." The Canadians, justly indignant at such raids, crossed the river and burned the "Caroline," and, in the fighting that accompanied the fire, killed a man named Durfee. Alexander McLeod, a Canadian, in a few days entered the state of New York, boasted that he had killed Durfee, and was arrested.

In this problem, as here stated, is nothing so intricate that two men of good will, representing the governments in interest, might not hope to reach an amicable agreement. The American citizens who attacked Canada did wrong. The British Government did wrong in using force against the "Caroline." The matter should have been left to diplomacy. Nor was Governor Seward justified in offering no objection to the prosecution of the murder charge by the state of New York. British acceptance of responsibility for the killing made it an international matter with which no state was competent to deal.

But what might have been settled so easily by men of good will was not settled at all during the Van Buren administration. There was bad feeling between the two nations. The British regarded the American spirit as too ruthless and too aggressive. Lord Palmerston, British Foreign Secretary, made little if any effort to conceal his dislike of America. On the other hand, Americans were irritated by the disagreement as to the proper boundary line between Maine and the British possessions to the north. There was also a difficulty, felt keenly in the South, about a slave ship, the slaves on which had overcome the master and crew of the ship and put into the British port of Nassau. There the authorities, instead of freeing the sailors and restoring to them their ship, freed the slaves and helped them to escape.

It now seems incredible, but it is nevertheless a fact that the British Government intended, in the event of the conviction of McLeod on a charge of murder, to declare war upon the United States. Mr. E. Vernon Harcourt said as much in a private letter to Webster; and Lewis Cass, American Minister to France, wrote again and again to Webster, informing him of Britain's warlike preparations, including plans to send a fleet of fourteen steam frigates to Halifax. After telling Webster that war with America would be popular in England, Cass said:

"Bend all your efforts to steam. Equip all the steam vessels you can. Establish the most powerful steam batteries in the exposed ports, and especially in New York. If you depend upon stone walls and fixed fortifications to keep steam vessels out of your harbors, you will, in the hour of trial, be disappointed."

During the last days of the Van Buren administration congress came near to declaring war. The house committee on foreign affairs, which had been making a survey of the situation, submitted to the house a warlike report. The Van Buren administration went out in peace only because the question of whether it would be wise to prepare for war was referred to the committee on military affairs.

Webster, the new secretary of state, therefore had on his hands a difficult problem of first importance. During his first week in office, the British Government demanded that the murder charge against McLeod be dropped because of the governmental capacity in which he had acted.

Webster believed that the attack upon the "Caroline" was without justification, but he also believed that a man, acting under the orders of his government, should not be prosecuted for murder. He could not halt the prosecution; but he did cause the Attorney-General of the United States to be sent to Lockport, New York, where McLeod was imprisoned, with instructions to arrange for the employment of proper counsel for the prisoner, to provide materials for his defense, and if necessary to appeal the case to the United States Supreme Court.

While matters were at this stage, President Harrison died; but John Tyler, who succeeded him, asked the Harrison cabinet to remain in office, and Webster continued his efforts to avert war with Great Britain. Webster, in pursuit of his invariable policy of fair dealing and honest statement, replied to the British demand for McLeod's release on the murder charge by admitting that the charge was without justification. The charge having been made, however, it could be dealt with only by action of court where the plea could be entered upon behalf of the prisoner, that he was not guilty of murder by reason of the fact that he had acted upon the orders of his government.

That an American statesman should concede anything to Great Britain, however, was not to be tolerated by some of the Democratic members of the house of representatives. All of the right must be on America's side, and all of the wrong on Britain's. In harmony with this idea, some of these gentlemen attacked Webster's policy in speeches in the house, thus imperiling delicate diplomatic negotiations that were proceeding. To make a bad matter worse, the President and some of the Whig leaders who elected him fell out over the question of whether a charter should be issued to another Bank of the United States. Tyler was opposed to this and vetoed the bill. Another bill of the same general nature was quickly put before him, and again there was a veto. All of the members of his cabinet resigned, and many Whigs believed

Webster, too, should have relinquished his office. But, as to this Whig opinion was divided, and Webster agreed with those who believed he should remain. Webster, of course, did not agree with the President about the bank; but he took the ground that Tyler's opposition to a bank was well known before his election, that if he were treated with consideration some sort of acceptable compromise might be obtained, and that, in any event, it was wrong to seek to drive the President against his conscience.

As to the McLeod matter, the New York courts insisted upon a trial and then acquitted him, thus ending the threat of war.

In this forgotten story of a war that never happened is seen what excitable men of bad will can do to break the peace. It was never true that the people of either country wanted war. Lord Palmerston, who seemed to want it, was put out of office by his own people before the New York jury acquitted McLeod. Before McLeod was acquitted, Webster's friend Denison, a member of the British House of Commons, wrote Webster a long letter about farming, stock-raising, and kindred subjects in which they were mutually interested, that included this political paragraph:

"If we had not seen each other so lately, and if you had not had the opportunity of seeing with your own eyes, and hearing with your own ears, how the United States and everything that belongs to them are regarded in this country, I might perhaps have thought it worth while to enter at some length on that topic and tell you, not only how completely all bad and jealous feelings are cured, but how sincere and universal the desire is to cultivate the most friendly and intimate relations with you, our brethren, on the other side of the water. I make no doubt that among the great body of the American people, the same feeling of good will toward us prevails, and I cannot therefore entertain a doubt that our differences may be honorably and peaceably adjusted."

Webster's will was good; British statesmen knew and respected him; and one after another the matters as to which the two nations differed were amicably adjusted. The same difficulties, if handled by men like Palmerston and the Democratic members of the house who flayed Webster for admitting that there was any right at all on Britain's side, would likely have resulted in war.

The acute tension between Great Britain and America having passed, machinery was set up to adjust all outstanding differences between the two nations. Lord Ashburton, an amiable, fair-minded man sixty-seven years old who, years before, had married a Philadelphia heiress, was authorized by Great Britain to go to America and enter upon negotiations. After many months of hard labor, Ashburton and Webster agreed upon what is known as the Treaty of Washington. When this treaty came before the British Parliament for ratification, some members denounced Ashburton for his part in it, declaring that he had surrendered everything to America. When it came before the United States Senate, some senators denounced Webster for surrendering everything to Great Britain. The truth is that, so far as boundary lines were concerned, the treaty was a compromise.

In this connection, there is an interesting story. While negotiations were proceeding, Webster had in his possession an old map which indicated that the line claimed by Great Britain was correct. About this map, he kept very mum. When Edward Everett, our minister to Great Britain, wrote that he was in search of old maps, Webster wrote back to him: "I must tell you, in particular confidence, that I hope you will *forbear to press the search*

for maps, in England or elsewhere. Our strength is in
the letter of the treaty." At the same time, Lord Ashburton had in his possession an old map that indicated
that the boundary claimed by the Americans was correct,
but he said nothing about it, and the facts on each side
did not come out until years afterward. The situation had
its humorous aspects—the picture of two crooked poker
players comes readily to mind—but there was really nothing about it that reflected upon the negotiators. Neither
could know whether the old map that gave the case away
to the other side was correct. Each had great responsibilities to his nation. It was not the duty of either to give
away his case because of a map that nobody could be sure
was correct. But Webster believed in taking no chances.
He warned Everett to "lay off" in his search for old maps.

As to other matters, Great Britain expressed her regret
at the burning of the steamship "Caroline" and the landing upon American territory. Webster did not ask that
the slaves who had murdered captain and crew and seized
a ship be captured and returned to the United States. He
asked only that Great Britain agree, in future, to consider such persons criminals and hand them over to the
United States for trial. This was done.

The treaty was fought in the United States Senate by
James Buchanan and others, the debate lasting for days,
but when the vote came it was thirty-nine for ratification to nine against it.

During this period, Webster also disposed of the
British claim of "right of search," which, though it
caused the War of 1812, was not settled by it. Webster
did this, not by including in the Treaty of Washington
a clause of renunciation, but by making a statement of
American views and intentions, which the British Government never found it expedient to answer. Webster in-

sisted that a ship flying the American flag would be protected by the United States Government, and that whoever should molest it, would do so at his peril. Peter Harvey, years later, told the whole story as Webster told it to him:

Webster wished, after settling the boundary question, to discuss the question of the right of search. He said to me that he had long wished for an opportunity to express his views in a way that would have weight on that long-disputed subject. Nothing had surprised him more than the failure upon the part of eminent American statesmen to get at the real point of the controversy.

"Even John Quincy Adams," said he, "with all his knowledge of diplomacy and international law, failed, I think, to meet the case. Mr. Adams talked about latitudes and longitudes; that conceded away the whole case. In my judgment there was but one course—flatly to deny the right. Nothing short of that would meet the trouble. Every ship that sails the ocean must find its protection in its flag.

"Well, when I proposed, after the boundary question was done with, to settle this disputed question, Lord Ashburton said he did not wish me to write him any letters upon that subject. Consequently, the dispatch which I wrote on the right of search was sent to our minister to present to the British minister. Mr. Everett was then our envoy at the Court of Saint James. He told me that he read the dispatch to the Earl of Aberdeen, who was the foreign secretary, and who was a tough-headed, bluff old Scotchman. As usual, he did not pay much attention at first to the reading; but finally he became interested and, interrupting, said: 'Won't you read that again, Mr. Everett?' He did so and as soon as he had finished reading, Lord Aberdeen asked for a copy of the dispatch. 'Mr. Everett,' said he, 'that American Secretary of State writes very extraordinary papers. That is a remarkable document. The argument in that paper cannot be answered. Mr. Webster has got the right of it.'

"The next time they met the earl said: 'I have not altered my opinion about that dispatch. It has been before Her Majesty's ministers and they say it must be answered; but I do not know who is going to answer it.'

"And Lord Aberdeen was right; the argument is unanswerable. There was no very extraordinary ability in my paper, but the common sense of the thing was apparent. The English Government turned around and attempted to say: 'Then you will allow your flag to be desecrated to the practices of piracy. A suspicious-looking craft may be sailing under the flag, and a cruiser may have every reason to suppose that she is a pirate and she cannot be brought to.' Now, I claim no such thing as that. If there is a robber in a man's house, and you break down the doors and go in and find you have got a robber, you are all right, but if you find he is not a trespasser, you must pay the damage, and that is precisely what I say in this matter. You can stop and search this supposed pirate, and if she is a pirate and has assumed a flag that does not belong to her, then let her be dealt with as such. But suppose it turns out that you were mistaken; that she is no pirate but a lawful ship, pursuing her voyage for her owners with regular papers, and that the cruiser was mistaken? What then? Pay the damage, just as you would in any other case of trespass. That is the distinction. If you had the right to stop everything, it would kill commerce."

The dispatch of Mr. Webster was never answered. He said: "There is one thing you may rely upon. The British Government have never answered that dispatch of mine denying the right of search because they cannot. The common sense of the thing settles that. But they will, perhaps, never

admit it, either. The English minister probably will
not sit down and write a dispatch saying that he is
convinced that the English view is wrong. But they
will never again attempt to exercise the right of
search. When the issue arises again, they will
abandon it."

The result has so proved. During Mr. Buchanan's
administration, the question did come up, and when
our government called England to account for attempting to exercise the right of search, they hastened to disclaim it, and at once gave orders to their
cruisers not to touch any ship sailing under the
American flag.

III

WHILE Webster was settling his country's differences with Great Britain and winning for himself world-wide renown as secretary of state, three great
storms were bearing down upon him. The first had to
do with the action of certain Whig leaders in his own
state of Massachusetts, who, two years ahead of time, had
called a state convention and put through it a resolution declaring it to be the sense of the party that in
1844 Henry Clay should be the Whig candidate for President. This act probably had more to do with keeping
Webster out of the Presidency than anything else that
ever occurred to him. As secretary of state he had added
to his already great fame, and, more than ever, was the
man of the hour. But the stab in the back from his own
state made his nomination unthinkable. He was stabbed
because a majority of the Whig leaders in Massachusetts
were displeased that he had chosen to remain in President Tyler's cabinet after all the other Whig members
had resigned.

The second storm was the Massachusetts flurry on a larger scale. A great many Whig leaders throughout the country were incensed that Webster should remain with an administration that they believed had been false to the party. It was never the custom of Webster to pay attention to political attacks made upon him, but in this case he eventually unbent to the extent of going into Faneuil Hall to meet his critics and reply to their criticism. The audience was unquestionably hostile. The speaker was conciliatory and polite, but firm. He had remained in the cabinet after the other Whigs had left, because he believed he could adjust the differences with England. He had adjusted them, and he would leave to the audience the question of whether his work in this respect had been of any value. As to whether he would remain in Mr. Tyler's cabinet, he gave not the slightest intimation. He would do as he believed proper and best. "I am, gentlemen, a little hard to coax, but as to being driven, that is out of the question." The speech produced a very good effect.

Webster resigned from the Tyler cabinet a year later in May, 1843. The following winter, the legislature of Massachusetts elected him to the United States Senate to take the place of Rufus Choate, who had resigned.

The third storm that blew up against Webster in 1842 was the worst of all. It consisted, not of a whispering campaign against him, but a shouting campaign. From a thousand directions, it seemed, stories came that, if true, were discreditable. He was said to be a drunkard, and a conscienceless, unscrupulous man in money matters; one might almost say a fraud. Some of Webster's friends, who wrote biographies of him within a few years of his death, referred bitterly to these scandals, but tried to do Webster a service by refusing to put upon paper the nature of the charges that had been made against him. That was a mistake. Such things cannot be covered up. The best way is to meet them. After more than seventy years, one may still hear in that great whispering gallery which we call Washington, stories about the drunkenness and the slack financial practices of Daniel Webster. The echoes reverberate. The explanatory facts to which the memory of Webster is entitled are not heard. It is one of the great glories of the United States that it was capable of producing Daniel Webster. History should give him a square deal. It cannot be done by leaving the floor to his detractors.

As to the exact charges that were made against Webster we shall perhaps find the most accurate statement in a book written by James Parton fifteen years after Webster's death. Parton did not like Webster, but he was a biographer of note, an intelligent man, and, though plainly biased, he tried to tell the truth as he saw it.

From a book published by Parton in 1867, the following paragraphs indicate the nature of the scandalous charges that swept over the country in 1842:

> He never appeared to know how much money he had nor how much he owed; and what was worse, he never appeared to care. He was a profuse giver and a careless payer. It was far easier for him to send a $100 note in reply to a begging letter than it was to discharge a long-standing account; and when he had wasted his resources in extravagant and demoralizing gifts, he deemed it a sufficient answer to a presented bill to ask his creditor how a man could pay money who had none? . . .
>
> From 1832 to the end of his life it appears to us that Daniel Webster was undergoing a process of deterioration, moral and mental. . . . Naturally inclined to indolence, and having an enormous capacity

for physical enjoyment, a great hunter, fisherman and farmer, a lover of good wine and good dinners, a most jovial companion, his physical desires and tastes were constantly strengthened by being keenly gratified, while his mind was chiefly fed upon past acquisitions.

His pecuniary habits demoralized him. It was wrong and mean in him to accept gifts of money from the people of Boston; it was wrong in them to submit to his merciless exactions. What need was there that their senator should sometimes be a mendicant and sometimes a pauper? If he chose to maintain baronial estates without a baron's income; if he chose to maintain two fancy farms of more than a thousand acres each; if he chose to keep two hundred prize cattle and seven hundred choice sheep for his pleasure; if he must have about his house llamas, deer, and all rare fowls; if his flower garden must be one acre in extent and his books worth thirty thousand dollars; if he found it pleasant to keep two or three yachts and a little fleet of smaller craft; if he could not refrain from sending money in answer to begging letters, and pleased himself by giving away to his black man money enough to buy a very good house; and if he could not avoid adding wings and rooms to his spacious mansion at Marshfield and must needs keep open house and have a dozen guests at a time—why should the solvent and careful business men of Boston have been taxed, or have taxed themselves, to pay any part of the expense? . . .

During the land fever of 1835 and 1836, he lost so seriously by speculations in Western land that he was saved from bankruptcy only by the aid of that mystical but efficient body whom he styled his "friends"; and from that time to the end of his life he was seldom at his ease. He earned immense occasional fees—two of $25,000 each; he received frequent gifts of money, as well as a regular stipend from an invested capital; but he expended so profusely that he was sometimes at a loss for a hundred dollars to pay his hay-makers, and he died forty thousand dollars in debt. . . .

We heard one of his last outdoor speeches. It was near Philadelphia in 1844 when he was stumping the state for Henry Clay. How poor and pompous and pointless it seemed. Nor could we resist the impression that he was playing a part, nor help saying to ourselves as we turned from the scene: "This man is not sincere in this. He is a humbug." And when, some years later, we saw him present himself before a large audience in a state not far removed from intoxication, and mumble incoherence for ten minutes, and when in the course of the evening, we saw him make a great show of approval whenever the clergy were complimented, the impression was renewed that the man had expended his sincerity and that nothing was real to him any more except wine and office. And even then, such were the might and majesty of his presence that he seemed to fill and satisfy the people by merely sitting there in an armchair, like Jupiter, in a spacious yellow waistcoat with two bottles of Madeira under it. . . .

He was not one of those who find in the happiness and prosperity of the country and in the esteem of their fellow citizens, their own sufficient and abundant reward for serving her. He pined for something lower, smaller—something personal and vulgar.

He had no religion—not the least tincture of it, and he seemed at last, in his dealings with individuals, to have no conscience. What he called his religion had no effect whatever upon the conduct of his life; it made him go to church, talk piously, puff the clergy and "patronize Providence"—no more.

He would accept retaining fees and never look into the bundles of papers which accompanied them, in which were enclosed the hopes and fortunes of anxious households.

He would receive gifts of money and toss into his waste-paper basket the list of the givers, without having glanced at its contents, thus defrauding them of the only recompense in his power to grant, and the only one they wished.

It shocked him if his secretary came to the dinner table in a frock coat, and he would himself appear drunk before three thousand people.

And yet, such was the power of his genius, such was the charm of his manner, such the affectionateness of his nature, such the robust heartiness of his enjoyment of life, that honorable men who knew his faults best, loved him to the last—not in spite of them but partly in consequence of them. What in another man they would have pronounced atrocious appeared in him a kind of graceful helplessness to resist.

Such, as it seems to our very imperfect judgment, was Daniel Webster, one of the largest and one of the weakest of men, of admirable genius and deplorable character, who began life and served his country well and often, but held not out faithful to the end. . . .

A rhymed fling also was taken at Webster by the Quaker poet, John Greenleaf Whittier, who had in him some of the Batchelder blood that was in the veins of Webster's black-haired grandmother. Whittier's poem, under the devastating title of "Ichabod!" ("The glory has departed") was understood to be aimed at Webster.

> So fallen! so lost! the light withdrawn
>   Which once he wore.
> The glory from his gray hairs gone
>   Forevermore!
>
> Revile him not,—the Tempter hath
>   A snare for all;
> And pitying tears, not scorn and wrath,
>   Befit his fall!

Oh, dumb be passion's stormy rage,
  When he who might
Have lighted up and led his age
  Falls back in night.

Scorn! would the angels laugh to mark
  A bright soul driven,
Fiend-goaded, down the endless dark,
  From hope and heaven!

Let not the land once proud of him
  Insult him now,
Nor brand with deeper shame his dim,
  Dishonored brow.

But let its humbled sons, instead,
  From sea to lake,
A long lament, as for the dead,
  In sadness make.

Of all we loved and honored, naught
  Save power remains,—
A fallen angel's pride of thought,
  Still strong in chains.

All else is gone; from those great eyes
  The soul has fled:
When faith is lost, when honor dies,
  The man is dead!

Then, pay the reverence of old days
  To his dead fame;
Walk backward, with averted gaze,
  And hide the shame!

Enough charges to sink a ship! What were the facts, and how should they be appraised? Before proceeding with this inquiry, let it be asked how many men of the present day would care to be judged by an old Quaker like Whittier, and, if so judged, how many might reasonably expect to go unpunished.

A man's contemporaries always have the right to appraise him according to the standards of their day; but so has posterity. Each man is a part of the world of his day, and what he was should be considered in relation to what his associates were. We all take on more or less of our color from those who are about us.

What, then, was Webster—a teetotaler? Not unless water be the thing from which he be said to have abstained. When Webster was a pale, serious youth, old Christopher Gore set him to drinking, and he never stopped until he died. There can be no question whatever that he both drank and ate too much. When he was old he became paunchy and elephantine, with such a tendency to fall asleep that, after his midday luncheon, he sometimes dozed on a bench in Lafayette Square, midway between his own home and the White House.

Did Webster, even once, appear drunk before an audience, and utter incoherent sentences? Parton says he once saw him and heard him do so. Parton, at the time, was twenty-two years old. Perhaps he was an accurate observer and correctly reported what he saw; perhaps not. If Webster, even once, did such a thing, those who still honor his memory can only profoundly regret that he should have done so. It is by no means unlikely that Parton was substantially correct in saying that he saw Webster appear drunk before an audience. If so, it was the only time he ever did so; at least no other such occasion is recorded.

But what was the world in which Daniel Webster lived and, particularly, what was Washington? Perhaps we may find the best answers to these questions by glancing at a series of moving pictures. We walk into the White House in Andrew Jackson's day when Daniel Webster, a member of the house of representatives, is in his late forties. What is that huge thing placed upon saw-horses and planks in the East Room? It is a cheese weighing twelve hundred pounds that admirers of the President have sent to him. What are the people who crowd the room doing? They are struggling to get near the cheese, so they may cut off huge hunks and eat them with the crackers they hold in their hands. Why are they so noisy? Because several sideboards are heavily stocked with liquor of which everybody may have all that he wants, and nobody seems to want less than all he can hold. What makes the walking on the rugs so hard? The fact that the rugs are slippery with the cheese and crackers that have been ground into them—and more cheese is falling every minute.

Three days of this sort of thing before the cheese was gone! Three days of drunkenness, clownishiness and uncouthness, not only before the President's own eyes, but in his very house! Imagine such a thing now.

Let us call again during the administration of President Polk. A reception is in progress. Everybody who is anybody and a good many who are not are lined up before the President awaiting an opportunity to shake his hand. President Polk is in great good humor. With a word and a smile and a quick clutch of the hand, he moves the line along, and it proceeds like clockwork.

But the line has ceased moving. Something has gone wrong. What is it? Nothing except that a gentleman who is about to introduce two ladies to the President is in difficulties. What are his difficulties? They are many. In the first place, he appears to be drunk. In the second, he is clad in a blue swallow-tailed coat, light cassimere pantaloons, a scarlet waistcoat, and is thus so conspicuous that he is attracting the attention of everybody. Furthermore, having escorted two ladies over to the President and in stentorian tones begun to introduce them, he is suddenly halted by the fact that he does not know their names. Who are these ladies? Call them ladies if you like. They are two French milliners whom this gentleman, a member of congress, has picked up to take to the reception. They are milliners employed in the building in which he rooms, whom he, being a bachelor, suddenly conceives the brillant idea of taking to meet the President. We hear him bellow in tones that drown every other sound:

"Mr. Polk, allow me the honor of introducing to you my beautiful young friend, Ma'm'selle,—Ma'm'-selle,—Ma'm'selle—*parley-vous Français?*—whose name I have forgotten."

Turning to the other young milliner, he says: "Will you introduce your friend?"

The President, of course, realizes what is the matter, but acknowledges the introductions and laughs it off.

Imagine such a thing taking place now.

We pass into an aristocratic Washington club. As we enter a large room, gales of laughter come from a group seated around a man, somewhat slumped down into his chair. He seems to be amusing the others. The man is Webster. What is he saying? He does not exactly know, but he thinks he is making a speech. As he proceeds, one of the guffawers—one of the aristocratic members of the club and one of the respectable men of the day—is prompting him by suggesting points upon which it is desired that he express himself. A stenographer might perhaps take down something like this:

Prompter: "Tariff."

Webster: The tariff, gentlemen, is a subject requiring the profound attention of the statesman. American industry, gentlemen, must be— (Nods a little.)

Prompter: "National debt."

Webster: And, gentlemen, there's the national debt—it should be paid. [Loud cheers which arouse the speaker.] Yes, gentlemen, it should be paid [cheers] and I'll be hanged if it sha'n't be [taking out his pocketbook] —I'll pay it myself. How much is it?

Who will not do decent men of the present day the honor to believe that none of them who could get into a respectable club would, in such circumstances, fall so low as to place upon exhibition and make a mockery of an honored citizen? Today, if such a man were encountered in such a condition, he would be quietly put to bed at his club, or got into a taxicab and accompanied home by a friend. The last thing that anyone would think of doing would be to place him upon exhibition in a club-room and make sport of him. It is not that the men of the present day are any better than were the men of a hundred years ago, but they have different opinions about drunkenness. In Webster's day, to be drunk was nothing to conceal—excessive drinking was common. Now drunkenness is not the rule, members of congress do not "tank up" and take strange women to presidential receptions. The world has changed, and we who wish to know what Webster was, and why he was, must, if we would do him justice, also look back to the world in which he lived.

Webster was one of the last men who should have drunk at all. He had neither the physique, the temperament nor the will to make the use of alcoholic liquors even moderately safe. There is no evidence that he drank more than did most other men of his day, but liquor went to his head, and his high station made him a marked man. If Philip Hone got drunk nobody cared and few heard about it, but if Daniel Webster drank too much everybody heard about it.

The reply, then, to the charge that Webster drank too

much is that it is true. It is also true that alogether too
much was made of his drinking. Bad though such indul-
gence was, it was not bad enough to justify the withering
blast that Whittier gave him, nor the merciless scoring
of Parton. Parton said that Webster began to decline in
1832. What did he mean by decline? Did he mean that
he had done his best work by 1832, when he was fifty
years of age? Did he mean that after reaching the age of
fifty he did little or nothing that was important? He made
the Webster-Ashburton Treaty when he was sixty. Anyway, what if it were true that Webster did his best work
before he was fifty? Is not the same true of most men?
Were not all of Edison's greatest inventions made before
he was fifty?

The fact is that no accurate appraisal of Webster's
work can be made without first ascertaining and considering what his work was. It was of two kinds. There was
the work that consisted purely of intellectual effort and
the work that consisted of intellectual effort combined
with emotionalism. His oratory, which played so large
a part in his first fifty years, was made possible by the
play of intellect upon his emotional nature. Time dulled
his emotions, as it does everybody's, and the quality of
his oratory deteriorated. By the time he was fifty, the best
of it was gone. But time did not dull his intellect, nor did
what alcohol he drank. Moreover, experience and reflection added to his wisdom. As an intellectual machine,
he functioned at high speed to the last. To the last he saw,
as did no other man of his time, the rights and wrongs of
the quarrel between the North and the South and the
way through this quarrel to safety. To the last he was
such a lawyer as no lawyer who did not wish to lose his
case cared to meet. Within six months of his death, he
wearily left his desk at the state department, in the midst

of a busy Washington season, to go to Trenton and try a case for the Goodyear rubber interests—ten thousand for going; five thousand more if he should win—and he won! To the day of Webster's death, he was "all there" mentally. Only his physical strength declined. Parton was wrong.

Parton and others said that Webster had no religion; that so far as his religious pretensions were concerned, he was a fraud. Perhaps Parton and others knew. Perhaps they could read his innermost thoughts. If so, they had the right to speak. But who can be so sure that he knows whether a man who says he is religious is lying or telling the truth? Is it quite safe to be so sure? It is true that public men, even to this day—and perhaps even more now than in Webster's time—profess an adherence to religious beliefs that they do not feel. It is considered politically wise to seem to be a devout, orthodox Christian. It is more likely that Webster was an orthodox Christian than it is that any politician or statesman of our day is such, though most of them pretend to be.

Parton said that Webster accepted retainers from clients, put their money into his pockets, and then never looked at the papers they gave him upon which their cases rested. How did Parton know this? Was Webster in the habit of calling witnesses when he was about thus to betray clients? Did he ever call Parton into his office and say, "Parton, I am about to steal some money that has been paid to me; watch me steal it"? Or did Webster, when he robbed clients, commit the theft alone in his office? If he committed it alone, did he afterward tell others, including Parton?

Parton neither had nor could have had any justification for asserting that Webster accepted retainers from clients and never read such documents as they left with him. Parton's spleen carried him too far; but such stories spread and added to the great clamor of 1842.

Parton said that in money matters Webster seemed to have no conscience. Every cent of the fifteen-thousand-dollar fee that Webster received from the Goodyear rubber interests went to his creditors. Webster was trying hard to pay his debts when he died.

The charge is true that Webster, for perhaps the most of the last twenty years of his life, received a "subsidy" from rich men in Boston and New York. Webster's misfortune would seem to have been that, in this matter, as in some others, he was weak and self-indulgent. He once resigned from congress to make more money practicing law, but his business friends would not permit him to remain out. They caused the legislature of Massachusetts to elect him to the senate, and, by private contributions to him, they made up part of the difference between his senatorial salary and what he could have earned at the law. It is definitely known that Webster believed he had rendered to this nation and to his state great services of incomparable value, and when contributions were offered to him to induce him to continue such services it seems likely that he accepted them as belated payment for services already performed. Certainly, he was not a crook.

Parton criticized Webster for handing out money right and left to beggars, when he himself owed money that he could not pay—or had not yet paid. That Webster was what we should now call an "easy mark" for beggars was true. To a strange woman who once wrote to him requesting money he sent a reply severely reprimanding her for making such a request of him merely because he was a public official of whom she had heard; and, having reprimanded her, he enclosed a $50 bill!

Webster lacked the callousness of Henry Ward Beecher who, importuned to send a strange lady $50 on the plea that, if she did not receive it, she would be compelled to "sell her honor," replied that if her honor was worth only $50 to her he did not care whether she sold it or not. Webster was always more or less a fool with regard to women —particularly those who were or pretended to be in "hard luck." Women always were to him only a little lower than the angels, nor did it seem ever to dawn upon him that occasionally there was a woman who was quite a bit lower. So when a woman came to Webster with a pitiful story and wanted money, or sought his patronage to advance her in her work, she usually got it.

If he had not been a man about whom no one could gossip, this tendency would, again and again, have caused scandal. One such incident occurred during the administration of Van Buren when a very lovely Italian lady came to Washington who said she was a descendant of Amerigo Vespucci, the gentleman who first set his feet upon the mainland of the western world and gave his name to it. Just to prove that her ancestry was what she said it was, she declared her name was America Vespucci. All she wanted was to be naturalized as an American citizen and to be given a "corner of land" in the country that bore her ancestor's name and her name.

Webster and John Quincy Adams both implicitly believed her story, as did many others; and Miss Vespucci was soon flitting about in fashionable society, a new, strange star of the first order. Her petition to congress for a "corner of land" was rejected, because of lack of power to give away any part of the public domain, but refusal was accompanied with eulogy and regret. Perhaps no congressional committee, before or since, ever took time to describe a petitioner as "a young, dignified and graceful lady, with a mind of the highest intellectual culture, and a heart beating with all our own enthusiasm in the cause of America and American liberty." The committee suggested that perhaps the American people, by direct contributions, would provide her with means to make a real-estate investment in the land of her distinguished ancestor. The committee babbled on: "The name of America—our country's name—should be honored, respected and cherished in the person of the interesting exile from whose ancestor we derive the great and glorious title."

The sergeant-at-arms of the senate at once started a subscription to provide land for Miss Vespucci. Congressmen, judges, Webster, John Quincy Adams and many others put their names on the dotted line for such sums as they were willing to give. Subscription ink was flowing freely until a chill wind from across the water froze the fluid on the pens. Word came that the lady had borne a bad reputation in Florence and in Paris; that she had been paid by the Duke of Orleans, whose mistress she had been, to break off relations with him and go to America. A little later, the duke's younger brother came to America and refused to speak to Miss America. Of course, these disclosures put an end to her social career in Washington. She went to New York, became the mistress of a wealthy citizen, lived with him until he died, and then returned to Paris.

So far as women were concerned, Washington, in those days, was apparently full of fools. Women still can make their way in Washington, but they have had to change their technique. Such a yarn as Miss Vespucci told would not now deceive an office boy.

Keeping always in mind the fact that in order to judge Webster fairly we must take into consideration the time in which he lived, we find interesting another situation that could not take place now.

A gentleman named Pendleton, who belonged to one of the first families of Virginia, and whose wife was the daughter of Robert Mills, the architect of the Treasury Building, had a desire to live magnificently. Perceiving no other way to gratify his desire, he opened, upon Pennsylvania Avenue, a magnificent gambling house composed of several large rooms and such a staff of chefs and other servants as only a rich man could employ. The furnishings of the room were luxurious enough to satisfy the desire of the guests for ease and also to gratify any artistic tastes they might have. All this was, of course, not for the regular run of humanity, which, if it had darkened the doors, would have been sent on its way. Pendleton's place—known as the "Hall of the Bleeding Heart" and the "Palace of Fortune"—was designed for the socially elect, and by such persons was it patronized. Barring only the President himself, there was nobody in Washington who might not at any moment be seen either among the chattering, drinking throngs in the parlors or with the silent ones seated around the tables where games of chance were proceeding. Present were gentlemen who in the near future hoped to be President; at their heels were high federal officials from the various departments of the government; while threading their way through the crowds were notorious lobbyists, bent upon combining business with pleasure. But the social aspect of the place was quite incidental to the gambling aspect. What had drawn this fine flower of Washington society was the hope of exchanging dimes for double-eagles. Of course, Mr. Pendleton had so arranged matters that in individual cases this could only seldom be done and, as to patrons generally, never.

This well-known fact did not, however, prevent them from trying. Occasionally, they tried too hard and at inopportune moments, as did Mr. Humphrey Marshall, in 1852, when he had just been appointed minister to China. He had drawn from the government six months' pay in advance, and was ready to sail, when it occurred to him that it might be well somewhat to increase his cash balance by trying a little adventure at Mr. Pendleton's. Mr. Marshall's luck was, from the beginning, such as did not justify high hopes of his ultimate success, but he nevertheless kept on, as men, in such circumstances, usually do. He kept on with the result that, in a few hours, he had lost his six months' advance salary and everything else with it. Mr. Pendleton, however, was a good sort and lent him enough money to go to China.

There came a day when Mr. Pendleton could run the place no more. He was dead. Of course everybody who is dead must have a funeral, but what a funeral Mr. Pendleton had! Official Washington turned out to do him honor. Among those present was James Buchanan, later President of the United States.

In similar manner, bad fortune once came to a certain Baron Bodisco, representative in America of the Czar of Russia, who had married the beautiful Miss Williams, a lady of great charm. It was their custom to entertain their friends royally, which meant not a little but a good deal of gambling on the side. The czar in fact provided the baron with a certain allowance to offset such losses as he might sustain at the gaming table. The usual game was whist; this perhaps explains why Daniel Webster was often a guest. At any rate, the game went bad for the baron. Either he was not good enough for it or his guests were too good. The last stroke of ill luck took from him a thousand dollars. Arising from the table, he said:

"Ladies and gentlemen: It is my disagreeable duty to make the announce that these receptions must have an end, and to declare them at an end for the present, because why? The fund for their expend, ladies and gentlemen, is exhaust, and they must discontinue."

When Millard Fillmore became President, his father, eighty years old, came to visit him. A week in Washington was quite enough for the old gentleman, and he packed his bag to depart. A visitor to the White House suggested that he remain a few days longer.

"No, no," he replied, "I will go. I don't like it here; it isn't a good place to live. It isn't a good place for Millard. I wish he was at home in Buffalo."

Such was Washington in the days when it was the home, the greater part of each year, of Daniel Webster. What has been set down here is not in justification for anything he did that was wrong, but in explanation of why he did wrong at all.

The worst of the rumors about Webster circulated irresponsibly, though political enemies were usually back of them. Webster was an easy man to beat down with blackguardism, because he considered it beneath his dignity to fight back. Perhaps it hurt him most that when a particularly foul blow was aimed at him it usually came from a political enemy in his own state. Representative Charles Allen, of the Worcester district, made in the house a vicious attack upon Webster, in whose honesty he expressed an utter lack of faith. He accompanied his attack with no evidence, and as to one matter he was later revealed as the teller of a premeditated falsehood. So malignant and unjustified were his utterances that several other members came to Webster's defense. Hilliard of Alabama declared that if Massachusetts repudiated Webster, the rest of the country would take him up.

Such attacks deeply wounded Webster, but he gave no outward sign of his pain. He gave no outward sign except such as his body gave. He was sixty years old, and in the most favorable circumstances must have begun to show his age. Stung to the quick as he was, he lost weight, the color faded from his cheeks, the lids of his eyes became tinged with black and blue. But he kept on.

IV

WEBSTER resigned from Tyler's cabinet because Tyler—bent upon making the preliminary moves for the admission of Texas, which Webster opposed—froze him out. After Webster's resignation, there was the usual exchange, between the President and himself, of complimentary letters, but the fact remains that the President and the other members of his cabinet studiously went about it to make Webster's place in the cabinet untenable. A. P. Upshur, a Virginian and an extreme advocate of slavery and state's rights, was appointed to succeed Webster, but he was soon killed by the bursting of a gun on the warship "Princeton," and John C. Calhoun was placed at the head of the state department.

Webster retired from Tyler's cabinet in the spring of 1843 and had the following summer to himself. Some of the time was spent at Marshfield, where, in the company of his much-loved daughter Julia, he built a spacious library which she had designed. He tried a lawsuit or two, but do what he might, he could not get his mind off Texas. While a cabinet officer he had learned things about plans under way that frightened him, because he knew—or believed he knew—what the annexation of Texas would mean. It would mean war. One day a friend met him on State Street in Boston and asked him what, if any, truth there was in the report that Tyler's administration was secretly moving to bring Texas into the Union.

I felt [said this friend] his arm press mine spasmodically as he said in a low tone, but with great emphasis, "That is not a matter to be talked about on the street; come to me this evening and I will tell you about it."

I went at the appointed time. He was in his chamber alone. He looked concerned and troubled. He began abruptly by saying that he and Mr. Upshur, notwithstanding the differences of their political opinions, had always been good friends, and that one day when he was sitting with that gentleman, who was then secretary of state in Mr. Webster's place, he told him that he thought Mr. Tyler was going on unwisely. Mr. Upshur replied that he was of the same mind, and that he was so little satisfied with the condition of affairs that "he would not continue in office a fortnight if he had not a particular object to accomplish."

Mr. Webster said that he conjectured in a moment what this object must be. His phrase was, "I felt Texas going through me." He said, however, nothing further to Mr. Upshur upon the matter, but he said that in two days he knew all about it. He went on earnestly, telling me that he was astounded at the boldness of the government. They had absolutely been negotiating with Mr. Van Zandt about Texas, which then anxiously desired the protection of the United States against a threatened invasion from Mexico, and had persuaded our government to agree to give such protection, so far as was possible, by the United States vessels then in the Gulf of Mexico, if that invasion should take place.

We might therefore, Mr. Webster said, be in a war with Mexico at any time, with or without the authority of congress, and he did not doubt that the administration would be willing to have such a war. Indeed, he said he felt sure that war would be the inevitable consequence of the annexation of Texas without the consent of Mexico. He then went on and described the troubles that would follow any great enlargement of our territory in the southern direction. He thought it would endanger the Union. He became very much excited. He walked up and down the room fast and uneasily. He said he had not been able to sleep at night, and that he could think of little else in the day. . . .

His object, he said, was to rouse the whole North upon the subject. An election was about to take place in Connecticut and he alluded to it. "If I had the means," he said, "I would send men to Connecticut who should run through the state from side to side, with their arms stretched out, crying "Texas, Texas"; and he suited the action to the word in the most fervent and impressive manner.

Webster was excited, but his friends were not. Among the politicians and business men of Boston it was the general opinion that he was taking Texas altogether too seriously. Once, when he addressed a small group, a little laugh followed his statement that "I do not say Texas will be annexed within a year, but I do say that I think I can see how it can be done, and I have no reason to suppose that the administration sees less clearly into the matter than I do." The laugh was not quite respectful, and Webster soon left. After he had gone, one man said, "He ought to come out for Clay." It was not that New Englanders and New Yorkers differed from Webster as to the undesirability of the admission of Texas, but they did not consider such an event within the realm of probability. The legislatures of most of these states—and particularly of Massachusetts—had adopted resolutions declaring that the annexation of Texas would be both unconstitutional and unjustifiable. What the New Englanders did not know was that there was an underground movement in administration circles to get past all such resolutions.

While the Texas situation was simmering, the Massachusetts political situation began to boil. Rufus Choate, who had kept Webster's senatorial seat warm, was about to resign. The business interests of Boston quickly moved to put Webster back in his old place. Moreover, a widespread feeling had grown up throughout the state that Webster had not been treated quite fairly by the group of political enemies who, by taking snap action in convention, had sought to commit the party, two years in advance, to Clay. It was felt that this wrong could perhaps be undone by restoring Webster to his place in the senate and giving him, at least so far as Massachusetts was concerned, a fair chance at the Whig nomination. In a speech at Andover, Webster flatly said that he was a candidate for no office whatsoever. Later, in reply to a letter from some political friends who asked him to become a candidate, he made the same reply and requested them to look elsewhere for a candidate. Toward the close of his Andover speech, he showed how sorely he had been wounded by criticism of his course in remaining in the Tyler administration so long. For some of his critics he had respect, because he knew they were honest, but for those who had indulged in "coarse vituperation" he had nothing but contempt.

"Gentlemen," he said, "I thought I saw an opportunity of doing the state some service, and I ran the risk of the undertaking. I certainly do not regret it and I never shall regret it. And it is in no spirit of boasting or vainglory, it is from no undue feeling of self-respect, that I say now that I am ready to leave it to the public to decide whether my remaining in the cabinet was best for the country; or whether, on the other hand, my leaving it would have been better for the country. On this question, I am in the judgment of this generation and the next generation, and I am willing that my name and fame and character shall abide the result."

Concerning the determination of some persons to return him to the senate, he would not, for the moment, hear a word. He was in debt and wanted to get out. He was earning, at his law business, fifteen thousand dollars a year. He must continue to earn money at his law business, at least for a while. If Mr. Choate would consent to remain in the senate until March 4, 1845, the thing might be arranged. Mr. Choate consented to remain. The legislature of Massachusetts elected Webster to succeed him.

While these events were taking place upon the national stage, a private sorrow came upon the man whom sorrow had so often stricken. Fletcher Webster's little daughter Grace died. Three had borne the name, not one of whom survived.

V

PARTON said that when he heard Webster speak in Philadelphia in 1844 in behalf of the presidential candidacy of Henry Clay, Webster seemed to have no heart in what he said and therefore appeared to Parton to be a humbug. What this youth of twenty-two did not then know may be put down here. As between Clay and James K. Polk, his Democratic opponent, Webster was emphatically for Clay. That did not mean, however, that upon what Webster conceived to be the great subject of the threatened annexation of Texas, Clay's position satisfied him. Indeed, it fell far short of that. Clay opposed the annexation of Texas solely upon the ground that such action would be offensive to Mexico. Webster went much further. He saw in the contemplated move part of a great southern policy to retain political control of the nation upon behalf of slavery by bringing into the Union more slave states. As to this Webster was, of course, absolutely right. He was not a particle too much excited about Texas. But Clay apparently did not see the danger, nor did the Whig party. Clay was actually sent into the national campaign of 1844 without a word about Texas in the Whig platform upon which he ran. His blindness was equalled only by that of his party.

When the campaign opened there were but three courses that Webster might take: he might keep out of it altogether; he might support Polk; he might support Clay. Feeling as deeply as he did about Texas, he found it impossible either to keep out of the campaign or to support Polk. There was nothing left for him to do but to support Clay as best he could, and try to be thankful that matters were no worse. If Parton, when he heard Webster speak in Clay's behalf, had been familiar with the facts and been old enough to understand them, he might not have been so quick to brand Webster a humbug. It is a very difficult thing for an honest man to stand before an audience and support a candidate whom he only partly approves. His conscience prevents him from going too far, and if he go not far enough to please the striplings he lays himself open to the charge of insincerity. The difficulties of the position in which he found himself, were illustrated in a speech that he made at Valley Forge. Though Clay's platform was silent upon the subject of Texas, Webster felt that he must say something; so he said:

It has always appeared to me that the slavery of the blacks and the unavoidable increase both of the numbers of these slaves, and of the duration of their slavery, found an insuperable objection to the annexation of Texas. For I will do nothing now nor at any time that shall tend to extend the slavery of the African race on this continent. Now our opponents are in favor of immediate annexation at all hazards. The secretary of state says . . . that the annexation of Texas is necessary to preserve the domestic institutions of the two countries; that is, to preserve slavery in the United States and to preserve slavery in Texas.

Now, slavery, in this country, stands where the Constitution left it. I have taken an oath to support the Constitution and I mean to abide by it. I shall do nothing to carry the power of the general government within the just bounds of the states. I shall do nothing to interfere with the domestic institutions of the South; and the government of the United States has no right to interfere therewith. But that is a different thing, very, from not interfering to prevent the extension of slavery by adding a large slave country to this.

The Webster policy! Straight through the middle of the road along the line marked out by the Constitution. But it did not please anybody, either in the North or in the South, who cared less for the Constitution than he did for the quick victory of his political purposes.

Polk was elected President, but his vote was 24,000 less than the combined votes of Clay and the abolition candidate, Mr. Birney. The opposition vote was an anti-annexation vote. If it had been combined upon one man, the Civil War might have been averted. But Clay, with his limited opposition to annexation, was not the man upon whom to combine it. Webster was the man. But when Webster talked about Texas, even in his own state, solid business men felt that he was becoming "excited" and some of them laughed.

In this connection, it is interesting to note how the abolitionists, in this campaign, cut off their own noses. The 63,000 votes that they gave to Mr. Birney would have elected Clay and put into the White House a man opposed to the admission of Texas. But the abolitionists knew their business best. Whenever is sought the reason why the United States, alone of the great nations of the world, was unable to get rid of chattel slavery without bloodshed, look into the history of the abolitionists. They were both poor citizens and poor politicians. When they had the majority of the country with them, as they did have in the matter of the annexation of Texas, they did not know enough to take advantage of it. Nor had they time to remove slavery by legal political process. "To hell with the Constitution." They had their way, but their way brought unnecessary war.

Very ancient history—why not forget it? First, because in a community in which orderly, lawful methods are provided for the working of the public will, the advisability of adhering to these processes is always both a live question and a duty incumbent upon good citizenship. Second, because repetition of the mistakes that produce war may sometimes so penetrate the intelligence of peoples that they will realize how upon the stages of all wars stride the same characters. Their names change but all else remains the same.

At one time these characters appear upon the programs as "Jefferson Davis," "Robert E. Lee," and "John C. Calhoun"; at another time as "Emperor William," "Ludendorff" and "von Hindenburg," but whatever the names upon the programs, the real names are, Greed,

Power, Selfishness, Fear, Revenge, and Mistaken Patriotism. All wars are caused by various proportions and combinations of certain primary impulses. Therefore, the history of no war, however far removed in time, is ancient history. The same thing, in another form and with different names upon the program, may recur tomorrow. Nothing is more important than to study the blunders and the wrongful acts that, at one time or another, have produced war. Understanding is our best defense.

VI

LOVE and politics occupied the mind of John Tyler during his last days in the White House. At the age of fifty-five, he was married to a woman of twenty who, during her husband's last fortnight in office, was the belle of two balls held in the East Room. She and Mr. Tyler were subjected to a great humiliation the day he relinquished the Presidency. Following the precedent set by John Adams when Jefferson was inaugurated, Tyler, who heartily disliked Polk, refused to take part in the ceremonies with which he was inducted into office. Instead of going to the Capitol in the morning, Mr. and Mrs. Tyler and a large retinue of colored servants hastened to the dock to board a Potomac River steamship. As they arrived, the ship was just backing away from the wharf. A man in the crowd called out to the captain on the bridge to wait a moment; that former President Tyler was coming. "Damn former President Tyler; let him stay," exclaimed the captain as the ship proceeded on its way. The captain was a Whig who resented Tyler's failure, after he became President, to live up to Whig principles. People then took their politics seriously.

Mr. Tyler had not quitted office without doing what

from the first he had most wished to do. He had brought Texas into the Union. This was done in a manner that occasioned surprise. It had been supposed that custom would be followed and a treaty negotiated; this would have required a two-thirds vote in the senate. Instead, a simple resolution of admission was introduced in congress on March 1, rushed through both houses, and signed by the President before he went out of office.

Less than a year before, Webster had been laughed at in Boston for expressing the fear that such a thing might be done, but what he feared had become a reality. The North had the power to prevent it, but the North was asleep. The vote in the senate was twenty-seven votes for admission and twenty-five opposed. Thirteen of the votes for admission were from free states and four of them were from New England. A change of two votes from the affirmative to the negative would have kept Texas out. But the North was asleep. Opposed as it was to admission, it had not deemed such a thing possible and said little about it; even the Whig platform the year before had contained no reference to it. Added to this was the desire that perhaps the young are most likely to feel to add territory; to increase the grandeur of the country by enlarging it.

Anyway, the resolution admitting Texas got past; and it was a very bad resolution. Not only did it admit Texas as a slave state, but it pledged the United States not to object to the division of Texas into four states, either slave or free, which meant that they would be slave. Mexico filed a diplomatic protest to which Mr. Polk's secretary of state replied in a mild and conciliatory manner, the substance of the reply being that the thing had been done and it was too late to protest. Webster, on March 4, had resumed his seat in the senate, but there was nothing that he could do; and the special session of the senate that had been called to confirm the new President's nominations for places in the cabinet soon adjourned. Webster returned to Marshfield for the summer.

VII

IF ever a man loved a place, Webster loved Marshfield, and the older he grew, the more he liked it. When he was away it called to him, and when he returned the resounding waves of the ocean seemed to welcome him home. *"The sea, the sea!"* he had exclaimed in his youth in a moment of ecstasy, and now, at the age of sixty-three, he felt the same thrill. Everything about the place had some interest for him—even the burying of a dead horse. If the horse was just a horse—a horse, one might say, without a history—it was put away almost any place. But if it was a horse that had long served its owner well, it was buried with what Webster called the "honors of war," which meant that it was buried standing up with its harness on its back. We may well believe that, for such occasions, old harnesses were found, because Webster, in small matters, disliked waste. Big wastes usually got past him.

When Webster was at Marshfield his first thoughts were about farming. He always had a thousand and one ideas as to what should be done next, and these ideas kept his workers busy. Arrayed in old clothes, he worked among them—long enough, at least, to get them started on the tasks. Such matters attended to, he devoted the remainder of each day to his guests, of whom he always had a houseful. Much fishing, some hunting, and, in the evening, a great deal of talk.

Webster did most of the talking; not because he wanted to, but because his guests seemed to desire that he should. During his long life, many things had come under his observation that were either instructive or amusing. About this time, he often repeated a witty remark that Rufus Choate had made a few years before with regard to the boundary line between Massachusetts and Rhode Island. It was an old boundary, made in colonial days, and so poorly described that no one could say exactly where it was. Choate had said that it "began at a hive of bees in swarming time, and ran thence to a hundred foxes with firebrands tied to their tails."

One evening, Webster's mind drifted to the age in which they lived, comparing it with the past and speculating as to how it might compare with the future.

"I think," said he, "our lines have fallen in pleasant places, and in a pleasant period of the world's history. I have reflected much upon the past and upon the future, in connection with events that are passing before our eyes, and I am rather inclined to the belief—though all generations of men think they are wiser than those who have preceded them—that for discovery, this age has certainly surpassed every other of which history renders us an account. And I doubt whether any century in the future will be so prolific in discoveries beneficial to the race as ours has been. . . . The miracle of miracles is the telegraph. Whatever improvements may be made in the instrument of telegraphic transmission, the agent itself cannot be improved. It is impossible, because it is as quick as thought. Steam, electricity, ether, and the ten thousand things that have grown up from them—think of it. . . . I thank God that it has pleased Him to assign my life to just this age of the world."

The "pleasant period" of America's history of which

Webster spoke was marked by wars and by rumors of war.

The only railroads that Webster ever knew would to-day be regarded as intolerable; poor coaches, low speed, change of cars every little while to get anywhere. Webster always spoke of "the cars," not trains. This custom still prevailed in the early eighties.

The telegraph that Webster considered remarkable is today regarded as no more remarkable than a door-bell, which in fact it somewhat resembles. Nor was it much of a telegraph at that—one message at a time, slowly pounded out on a "key." Four messages are now sent each way at the same time on the same wire, with perhaps a telephone conversation thrown in, while telegraphic messages are recorded at the receiving end upon automatic typewriters.

Webster believed that no similar period in the future would equal the period in which he lived, yet the first seventy-five years after his death produced marvels beside which nothing that was evolved in his day was worth mentioning.

Guessing at what the future holds is and always has been a favorite though a dangerous pastime. What if one were now to guess that the greatest inventions of the next hundred years will have nothing whatever to do with material things—that they will have to do with the readjustment of human relationships and the revision of human ideals? There will be plenty of material inventions too, but sometime or other we shall have to learn how to get happiness from what we already have. Invention is now outrunning assimilation.

As Webster grew older he became more and more inclined to revisit the scenes and friends of his boyhood. One day when he was at his father's old home in Salisbury, New Hampshire, he determined to make a journey to visit John Colby, his brother-in-law, whom he had not seen for more than fifty years. Colby had married one of Webster's half-sisters. She was considerably older than Webster, and Colby was perhaps twenty years older. She died within five or six years of their marriage, and the Webster family thereafter paid no attention to Colby.

Webster took with him on the trip his old friend Peter Harvey and, as their horse jogged along, told him why he was making this belated call upon his brother-in-law. He had heard that Colby had "got religion" and he wanted to see with his own eyes what had happened. In the old days, Colby was regarded in the Webster neighborhood as a very wicked man; bad temper, swearing by note, and all that. Webster wanted to see to what extent the power of religion had transformed the bogy of his childhood.

Arrived at the village in which Colby lived, Webster inquired of a boy the way to the house and was directed to it. Colby himself, more than eighty years of age but still sprightly, came to the door.

"This is Mr. John Colby, is it not?" asked Webster.

Colby replied in the affirmative.

"I suppose you don't know me?" continued Webster.

"No, sir, I don't know you," said the old man, "and I should like to know how you know me?"

"You married my eldest sister, Susannah," said Webster.

"I married your oldest sister! Who are you?"

"I am 'little Dan,'" replied Webster.

Amazement and incredulity struggled for mastery of the old man's face.

"*You* Daniel Webster?" said he. "Is it possible that this is the little black lad that used to ride the horse to water? I cannot believe my senses. Now sit down. I am so glad to see you, Daniel. I never expected to see you again. Why, Daniel, I read about you and hear about you in all ways; your name seems to be constantly in the newspapers. They say you are a great man, a famous man, and you cannot tell how delighted I am to hear such things. But, Daniel, the time is short—you won't stay here long— I want to ask you one important question. You may be a great man, but are you a good man? Are you a Christian man? That is the only question that is worth asking or answering. You know, Daniel, what I have been. I have been one of the wickedest of men. Your poor sister, who is now in heaven, knows that. But the spirit of Christ and of Almighty God has come down and plucked me as a brand from the burning. I would not give what is in the Bible for all the honors that have been conferred upon men from the creation of the world until now. Are you Christian? Do you love Christ? You have not answered me."

"John Colby," replied Webster, "you have asked me a very important question, and one which should not be answered lightly. I intend to give you an answer and one that is truthful, or I won't give you any. I hope that I am a Christian. I profess to be a Christian. But while I say that, I wish to add—and I say it with shame and confusion of face—that I am not such a Christian as I wish I were. I have lived in the world, surrounded by its honors and its temptations; and I am afraid, John Colby, that I am not as good a Christian as I ought to be. I am afraid I have not your faith and your hopes; but still I hope and trust that I am a Christian, and that the same grace which has converted you, and made you an heir of salvation, will do the same for me."

As they drew near to Salisbury on their return, Webster halted the horse to point out to Harvey a tree on

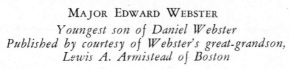

MAJOR EDWARD WEBSTER
Youngest son of Daniel Webster
Published by courtesy of Webster's great-grandson,
Lewis A. Armistead of Boston

a small island in a river. There was a story in connection with the tree that had come down from old Ebenezer Webster, Daniel's father. Before Bunker Hill Ebenezer and the soldiers under him used to use this tree as a target, shooting from a distance. If they hit the tree nothing happened. If they did not, there was a splash in the water where the bullet fell. When old Ebenezer shot, there were never any splashes, as the result of which he gained the reputation among his men of being a dead-shot.

"How did you do it?" Daniel, as a little boy, had once asked his father.

"I never used to put any bullets into my gun," replied Ebenezer with a smile.

When they returned to the old farmhouse, Webster said to John Taylor, his boss farmer:

"Well, John Taylor, miracles happen in these later days, as well as in the days of old."

"What now, squire?" asked Taylor.

"Why, John Colby has become a Christian! If that is not a miracle, what is?"

During the evening, the conversation shifted to potato-bugs. Taylor said he had never seen so many bugs in his life as there were on that year's crop—at least a million bugs to each vine.

"Not a million, John Taylor," said Webster, "not a million."

"Well, half a million, anyway."

"John Taylor, you remind me of a man whom I knew when I was a boy. Never did he go hunting or fishing that he did not return with some marvelous story of what he had seen. Once his story had to do with snakes that he had encountered along the road. There were at least a hundred of them, lined up beside the highway, each twenty feet long. My father, to whom this man told the story, expressed doubt that he had seen so many. 'Maybe there weren't a hundred,' said the man, 'but there were seventy-five.' My father said he did not believe there were seventy-five. 'You may be right,' said the man, 'but there were fifty.' Again, my father expressed disbelief, while the teller of the story, in the face of my father's incredulity, gradually reduced the number of snakes he had seen to two, and then blurted out: 'That's as far as I will go. I'll give up the story first.' "

Over at Marshfield, a few evenings later, Webster permitted a group of guests to draw him out as to what he thought of many noted men with whom he was, or had been, in contact. He did not think much of James Buchanan.

"Buchanan is a good politician," he said, "but he is no statesman. He merely looks at things as they affect the party."

Webster, in private, spoke freely of Henry Clay and frankly admitted that he did not like him. One might suspect that the personal dislike arose chiefly if not solely from the fact that for many years they had been rival contenders for the leadership of the Whig party and for the Presidency of the United States; but such was not the case. Clay could never quite forget that he was a politician and therefore occasionally treated friendships in a manner both fast and loose. Webster, on the other hand, always supported Clay, when he was a candidate, even though he did not like him. In the campaign of 1844, when Harvey advised Webster to "let Clay get elected in his own way" without Webster's help, the latter, who was about to begin a campaign tour, replied:

"It is not Mr. Clay, it is the cause, the great cause,

the success of which I believe to be for the best interest of the country. Men are nothing, principles everything. Besides, Mr. Clay is fit to be President. His principles are such as I can approve, and his ability no one can question. Therefore, I am bound, as an honest man, to do everything I can. And when I say that, I am perfectly aware that Mr. Clay would not do the same thing for me."

As to this, Webster was right. In 1852 Clay advised his friends to vote for Fillmore rather than for Webster. This hurt Webster terribly.

Webster and Clay, as lawyers, had many times appeared as counsel for the same client. Webster said that, in such cases, when the time came for him to speak, he had often been compelled to work hard to undo what Clay had said.

"The fact is," Webster said, "that Mr. Clay is no lawyer. He is a statesman, a politician, an orator, but no reasoner."

Calhoun, Webster said, had the best mind of any man he had met in the senate. Webster, who always judged men by their virtues rather than by their defects, ranked Calhoun somewhat higher than history now regards him. Webster considered Calhoun to be a patriot. Calhoun's admiration of Webster also went to great lengths. "Mr. Webster," he said, "has as high a standard of truth as any statesman whom I have met in debate. Convince him, and he cannot reply; he is silent. He cannot look truth in the face and oppose it by argument."

Webster said that Thomas Jefferson had more deeply impressed his ideas upon the government and the people than any other man who ever lived. In his early days, Webster had heartily disliked Jefferson and, in a sense, feared him. The old Federalist slanders that Webster had repeated, in his Dartmouth College argument, to inflame Chief Justice Marshall, Webster at that time accepted as truths. But after Webster had spent a week with Jefferson, at Monticello, he departed with an entirely different conception of the man. He had seen that the founder of the Democratic party was no firebrand, no anarchist, no demagogue, but a sincere promoter of what he conceived to be the public welfare. Webster regarded it as fortunate that Jefferson had stripped the government of all the pomp and ceremony that grew up under Washington and Adams.

The name of Silas Wright, Senator from New York, was mentioned. Wright's chief distinction, up to that time, was that when nominated for Vice-President, on the ticket with Polk, he had declined on the ground that he "did not propose to ride behind on the black pony [slavery] at the funeral of my slaughtered friend, Van Buren." Webster had no high opinion of Wright.

"He is the most overrated man," he said, "that I ever met. He is oracular, wise-looking, taciturn, and cunning as a fox, but the most inferior man in debate in the senate. You have seen boys in school who would contrive in some way to skip the hard spelling. Wright always skipped the hard places. His arguments, beside being weak and evasive, were always fallacious. He would try to make the crowd think he had answered when he had not touched the point."

Somebody brought up the subject of memory. Webster said that Senator Thomas H. Benton of Missouri had the most marvelous memory and the greatest accumulation of facts that he had ever encountered. Even John Quincy Adams, who was regarded as a walking encyclopedia, could not hold a candle to him. Webster said that, upon a certain occasion, he was at a loss to recall a certain geographical fact having to do with a discussion that was proceeding from day to day in the senate. Somewhere he had read this fact, but he knew neither the name of the book nor the name of the man who wrote it. Upon this small basis of recollection, Webster had made inquiries among his friends and at the Congressional Library without learning anything to his advantage. Finally, he went to Benton.

"You know everything, colonel," he said, "and where everything is. I have told you the general nature of the book I want. Do you know what book I mean and where I can get it?"

The colonel stopped a moment to think and then replied:

"I know what you want. I'll see if I can find it."

An hour later, Webster returned to his seat in the senate.

"There, lying on my desk," he said, "was an immense book, with a leaf turned down to the place that I wanted to find, although I had not said a word as to the particular *part* of the book that I wanted to consult. I looked up from my desk to his and there he was, bowing to me, as if to say, 'That's it.' I do not suppose there was another man who could have found that book for me."

The question arose as to what was the greatest speech Webster had ever made. Peter Harvey thought the Reply to Hayne had been read by more intelligent persons than any other address ever delivered in the English language.

"Oh no," replied Webster, "I think you must be mistaken about that. You must remember that the speeches of English orators and statesmen are not reported as ours are; neither are the English people, to a great extent, a reading people. Everything that is worth reading and is eloquent, our people read."

Harvey stuck to his point. No speech had been read by so many persons as the Reply to Hayne. Moreover, it had the greatest fame.

"I suppose it has," replied Webster. "As a popular effort, it was undoubtedly more read than any other speech. Nevertheless it was not, in my opinion, the best speech I ever made."

Harvey asked him what speech he placed first.

"My forensic efforts," he replied, "have been those which have pleased me most. The two arguments that have given me the most satisfaction were the argument in the steamboat case and the Dartmouth College argument. The steamboat case, you remember, was a question of the constitutionality of the act of the State of New York in giving a monopoly to Fulton and his heirs, forever, of the privilege of plying the waters of the State of New York with his steamboats. The value of the right was not then and could not have been, from the nature of the case, fully understood. But it seemed to me to be against the very essence of state rights, and a virtual dissolution of the Union in a commercial sense. If New York had a right to lay tolls upon her rivers for everybody that should pass, then all the other states that had great waterways would have the same right, and we could not be one as a commercial people. The people of New York felt that their rights were at stake in the contest, and their great lawyers, of whom there were many, were engaged on that side—the Livingstons and Clintons and others of like caliber. Mr. Wirt and myself were employed against the monopoly."

It will be recalled that this was the case in which Wirt, having asked Webster upon what grounds he purposed to argue it, replied that he saw in the argument no leg upon which they might stand, and Webster, having heard what Wirt purposed to say, made the same comment to him. Each argued in his own way, and Chief Justice Marshall, in writing the opinion of the court, followed Webster's reasoning without indicating that the court had paid any attention to Wirt.

Thus did the summer pass—and the autumn. December came and with it the necessity of bidding adieu, for a time, to Marshfield, and returning to Washington.

VIII

WHILE Webster was away on vacation the administration of President Polk had got under way. One incident in connection with the making of the cabinet is worth recalling, because such an incident could not now take place. John Y. Mason of Virginia, who had been secretary of the navy in Tyler's cabinet, appealed to the President not to remove him because he needed the salary that was attached to the office. Mason appealed to influential friends to help hold his job for him, to one of whom he wrote:

"Imprudence amounting to infatuation, while in Congress, embarrassed me, and I am barely recovering from it. The place is congenial to my feelings, and the salary will assist Virginia land and negroes in educating six daughters. Although I still own a large estate, and am perfectly temperate in my habits, I have felt that the folly of my conduct in another respect may have led to the report that I was a sot—an unfounded rumor that originated with a Richmond paper."

Mason's pleading and wire-pulling were not without

favorable result. The President retained him in the cabinet, but transferred him from the navy department to the department of justice.

Polk came to the Presidency with two great purposes in his program, one of which was secret.

The purpose that was known was to bring about the settlement with Great Britain of the northwestern boundary question upon the basis of the fifty-fourth parallel of latitude. James Monroe, during his Presidency, had offered to accept the forty-ninth parallel; but Great Britain held out for the Columbia River, which would have given her the present states of Washington and Oregon. The country became much worked up about the matter. "Fifty-four forty, or fight," was the cry. War was threatened. For the second time within ten years, hostilities with Great Britain became a prospect.

Webster regarded this as all nonsense. He believed Monroe's offer of the forty-ninth parallel was a reasonable and just compromise. Very fortunately for both nations, Webster was held in such high respect in England that his opinion carried great weight there. By private correspondence with British statesmen, Webster contrived to get an offer from Britain to accept the forty-ninth parallel which, though it was at first rejected by the Polk administration, was later accepted and, to this day, constitutes the boundary line.

The secret part of Polk's program had to do with the raiding of Mexico for the purpose of despoiling her of some of her territory—lands that might later be converted into slave states. The annexation of Texas, which had been boldly proclaimed by Polk and already brought about, was not enough. Webster, with his invariable tendency to give every man a little more than a square deal, gave Polk altogether too much credit for peaceful intentions. Writing to his son Fletcher, a week after Polk's inauguration, Webster had said: "That Mr. Polk and his cabinet will desire to keep the peace, there is no doubt." What Webster had in mind at the moment was whether Mexico would attack the United States for annexing Texas. Mexico made no attack.

This forced Mr. Polk's hand. If Mexico would begin no war and thus give him an opportunity to seize and hold parts of her territory, he would begin it himself. This he did. As to what he did, Ulysses S. Grant, who as a young soldier was on the spot, gave interesting testimony. Writing in his "Memoirs," he said:

> We were sent to provoke a fight, but it was essential that Mexico should commence it. . . .
> The army did not stop at the Nueces and offer to negotiate for a settlement of the boundary question, but went beyond, apparently to force Mexico to initiate war. . . .
> The occupation, separation and annexation were, from the inception of the movement to its final consummation, a conspiracy to acquire territory out of which slave states might be formed for the American Union. . . .
> The Southern Rebellion was largely the outgrowth of the Mexican War. Nations, like individuals, are punished for their transgressions. We got our punishment in the most sanguinary and expensive war of modern times.

Polk's party did not declare war but utilized the familiar device of putting through congress a resolution declaring that war "existed"—of course as a result of the acts of Mexico, which was not true. Grant knew better, and so did everybody else who was informed.

In the late winter of 1846 another furious onslaught upon the character of Webster was made by a small but

malignant group in the house of representatives. He was
accused of stealing an indefinite part of a seventeen-
thousand-dollar fund that had been put into his hands
for secret service purposes, when he was secretary of
state under Tyler; he was criticized for the manner in
which he had settled the trouble with Great Britain arising from the burning of the "Caroline"; and he was
taken to task for the part he had played in the negotiation of the Treaty of Washington. Moreover, it was
said that he was secretly in the pay of a group of New
England manufacturers who sought higher tariffs upon
the commodities they produced.

For weeks, the house was full of sound and fury, the
malignant group scorching Webster as best they could,
while many others, particularly those from the South,
took his part. Webster, in the senate, took notice of what
was going on in the other house and lashed back at
Ingersoll and Dickinson, his chief accusers, in language
so pointed that he later eliminated from his "Works" the
most severe things he had said about them. The house
called upon the President to throw such light as he could
upon the situation, with the result that it was discovered
that the great sum that Webster had "stolen" dwindled to
forty dollars that he had, as a matter of fact, actually paid
out, but for which he could not get a voucher because
of the disappearance of the man to whom it had been
paid. The charges concerning the "Caroline" affair and
the Ashburton treaty also blew up. A few years later,
Dickinson of New York, who had reviled Webster foully,
did something that Webster so approved that he wrote
him an appreciative letter. Dickinson very humbly replied that he had often grieved at his former mistake,
asserting that it was "divine" in Webster to forgive him
and declaring that Webster's letter would be handed

down in the Dickinson family as its most cherished possession.

As to the charge that the manufacturing interests of Massachusetts had bribed Webster, there was no truth in it at all. What was true was that Webster had again been so foolish as to accept from a group of well-meaning friends an annuity that was meant to help him out in his chronic financial troubles. This annuity never exceeded $1,135 a year and was usually $900 or $950. It was produced by the deposit of $37,000 with the Massachusetts Hospital Life Insurance Company, notice of which was given to Webster by David Sears in a letter containing the purposes of the donors. "This fund has been created," wrote Sears, "freely and cheerfully by your friends, in evidence of their grateful sense of the valuable services you have rendered to your country."

It seems to have been the habit of Webster's New England friends at that time to rush to him with money whenever they thought he was in trouble. When he was on his death-bed, there was a knock at his door, and a large roll of bills was thrust in by an old gentleman who said that "at such a time as this, there should be no shortage of money in the house."

It was their way to give, and it was Webster's way to accept. That he should have done so was undoubtedly a mistake, but it is even a greater mistake to assume that in such transactions there was anything crooked. If Daniel Webster had been crooked, nobody could have hired him for $1,100 a year! As we look back almost a century at the towering figure of Webster it seems astounding that he should so often have been the object of malignant slander. We are a better people than were our ancestors—not so credulous, at any rate.

Webster was not in Washington on May 11, 1846,

when the Democrats hastily introduced and passed through both houses of congress a resolution declaring that war with Mexico existed. In a speech in Philadelphia, a few months later, he severely criticized Polk for precipitating war by advancing troops into contested territory. The point he raised then will always be of interest and importance. He denied the constitutional power of the President to take a position that made war inevitable, or even probable. Such steps should not be taken without the prior approval of congress. Otherwise, there would be no safety in the constitutional provision that only congress may declare war.

But nobody paid any attention to him. Few persons ever pay attention to such a warning until it is too late. In the meantime, precedents are formed that are cited, in the future, as justification of the assumption by the President of what is, in fact though not in form, the power to declare war. The President's control over foreign relations, as it now stands, gives him power to bring on war, leaving to congress only the rubber-stamp function of recognizing and approving something that has already happened.

Webster believed that the power to declare war should actually rest where the Constitution placed it; but this point never received a hearing in his day, nor has it had one since. When there is no war, nor any prospect of any, the people are not interested in what appears to them to be useless discussion of fine points of law. And when wars come, with their draft laws, it is too late to talk! Wars could not persist if those who are opposed to them were always and forever alert.

As the war proceeded and the prospect of land-loot became more apparent, the fears of Webster and those who shared his views became greater. Mr. Wilmot of

Pennsylvania introduced a resolution in the house (the Wilmot Proviso) providing that slavery should be prohibited in all territory that might at any time be annexed. This resolution was defeated.

Webster went further and introduced a resolution in which it was proposed to declare that the war was not being waged to gain territory, that no territory would be accepted, and that the Mexican Government be so informed. This resolution, too, was defeated. Northern Democrats, as well as those from the South, voted against it. Northern Democrats wanted no extension of Slavery, but they hungered for land and were not above seizing it from a neighbor. The stain is upon them and must always remain. Desiring to honor their country by increasing its dimensions, they dishonored it by subtracting from its reputation for fair dealing. Webster said, in a speech in the senate, that the country, with eyes wide open, seemed to be rushing headlong into perils. It was rushing headlong, without doubt, but its eyes were not open. Both North and South were preparing a war that neither of them wanted. Nor were the hands of either of them clean. The blood of Mexico was smeared upon both.

What the situation summed up to was, in brief, this:

The idea of looting Mexico originated in the South among the leaders of the slave interest.

The looting having begun, certain northern political interests were in favor of going through with it, though they hoped so to arrange matters that the South would not get the only advantage.

The common peoples of both the North and the South had no part in beginning the war, nor much understanding of what it was all about, though they furnished the blood that bought the loot.

IX

THE son named Edward, born to Daniel Webster in 1820, lived to become the apple of his father's eye. Nature gave him intelligence, good looks, a gentle, kindly spirit, and to these assets the elder Webster added everything within his power. First, he gave him the advantage of his own fine companionship. During the long summer months, they were playfellows together upon the great estate at Marshfield, one vying with the other in flying leaps over cocks of hay piled in the meadows. A little later, the boy was started by the father down the old road that the father knew so well—to Exeter Academy and then to Dartmouth. Then the boy was given a year or two in Europe, spending most of the time in the family and under the sheltering wing of Edward Everett, whom Daniel Webster had induced a President of the United States to make Minister to England.

To such favorable influences the young man responded adequately. He became just such a young man as every father would wish his boy to be—a splendid, affectionate, well-bred human being. Only as to one matter did he fall short, and that was in determining what he should make his occupation. Here the father jumped into the breach. He would get Edward a job; this, in view of the fact that Daniel Webster at that time was secretary of state, was not difficult to do. Edward was appointed to a civil engineering position in connection with the commission that was to determine the boundary line between the United States and Canada.

Edward Webster was engaged at this work when word came to him in Canada that war between the United

States and Mexico had broken out and that General Scott's army was in danger! What strange "news" sometimes hurtles across frontiers in war-time when the press is not free and military gentlemen are engaged in the task of creating the sentiment necessary to the conduct of warfare. Edward Webster, from his post in Canada, heard that General Scott's army was in danger, and no sooner did he get this word than he resigned his position, hastened to Boston, and raised the first company of volunteers that was accepted by the State of Massachusetts.

Edward had raised his company, but when he had done so, the "extreme danger" in which General Scott's army found itself did not seem to be quite so great. For reasons that were not, of course, communicated to Edward, he and his company did not, at the moment, appear to be wanted. There was delay that ran into weeks and months, during which time many of Edward's enlisted companions scattered to the four winds and he himself engaged in private employment.

Eventually word came to get the company together, and Edward with difficulty did so. During the long months of waiting, Edward's war-ardor had somewhat cooled (perhaps his father had told him the "inside" of the whole story), but Edward felt that he must stick to his word. Holding, as he did, a commission as a major, he might have resigned, but such an idea never entered his head. He went to the war, landed in Mexico, immediately had the misfortune to develop malarial fever, and was returned to the United States, where for many months he lay in a hospital.

Again, the day came for him to sail for Mexico, but this time he had with him, as protector and personal servant, a negro named Henry Pleasants whom Daniel

Webster many years before, while living in Washington, had for $500 bought out of slavery and given his freedom. This negro felt a degree of affection for the Webster family, and particularly for young Edward, to which it is difficult if not impossible to pay adequate tribute. Asked if he could leave his wife and go to the front with Edward he replied that he would go to the ends of the earth with him.

This fine young man and this admirable negro reached Mexico in the fall of 1848. During the weeks that followed, it sometimes seemed to Daniel Webster, engaged in his work in the senate, as if his son had gone to the moon. A great silence had settled down between them, broken only at long intervals by a letter. War-time in Mexico, almost a hundred years ago, was neither a good time nor a good place for the quick transmission of intelligence. Each letter from the boy said he was all right, but there were many weeks between letters.

Christmas came and went; New Year's; the month of January; twenty-three days of February, and then to the desk of Daniel Webster came a notice from the war department that seemed at first so to stun him that his full measure of suffering did not come until later. Edward was dead; he had died in camp of typhoid fever, on January 23, just a month before.

As soon as Webster had rallied enough from the shock to hold a pen he wrote as follows to his son Fletcher:

February 23, 2 o'clock, 1848.

My Dear and Only Son: I have just received this; when shown to Julia and the rest of the family, send it back safely to me.

My own health is pretty good, but I hardly know how I shall bear up under this blow. I have always regarded it as a great misfortune to outlive my children; but I feel now, more intensely, as when Grace and Charles died.

But the will of Heaven be done in all things!

Yours Affectionately,

DANIEL WEBSTER.

This man who could write so well, could, at the moment, write almost nothing.

Julia, as soon as she heard the news, hastened to strive to comfort her afflicted father.

"It is," she wrote, "indeed a sad affliction, but, thank God, I feel such trust in His mercy and love, and know so well that 'He doth not willingly afflict or grieve the children of men' that I feel assured that it was for Edward's good and happiness, as well as for ours, that he was taken away. . . . God bless and keep you, dearest father, may you long, long live; and may your remaining children be spared to be a comfort and a solace to you."

Daniel Webster, sixty-six years old, shattered in spirit and somewhat impaired in health, buckled down to the problem of how to exist during the maddening months that must elapse before his son's body could be returned from Mexico. Under much depression, he tried to keep up his work in the senate, but, try as he would, he could not disengage his mind from his grief. Wherever he was, he was always thinking of his dead boy. Healy, who made the great painting of Webster replying to Hayne that is in Faneuil Hall in Boston, was commissioned to paint a portrait of Edward from a daguerreotype.

"I have not seen it," Webster wrote to Fletcher on March 12, "but it is thought to be very good. I have been meditating upon something which I wish should be thought of. Edward was ten years old when I made the Hayne speech in the senate. Why should not Mr. Healy make a picture of him, as of that age, from the daguerreotype, and from Miss Goodrich's little miniature, and place him at my feet?"

Three days later, Webster wrote to Fletcher that he had seen Healy's portrait of Edward and that it was "most beautiful." "I shall take it home," he continued, "and keep it before my eyes as long as I live."

It seemed as if the winter would never end and the body of Edward never come. Moreover, something else had arisen to worry the stricken old man. Julia was not well. Early in the winter she had caught a heavy cold which, instead of subsiding, steadily grew worse. Every day she had a little fever, and high color settled upon the upper part of her face. Tuberculosis had seized upon her, but nobody suspected it. She had her ups and downs, as such patients always do, and every time she seemed to improve a little, her father, who watched carefully over her, thought she was about to recover. But such vitality as had been born into her had been given to the five children to whom she had given birth, and she lacked the stamina to make the fight. On April 28, 1848, she died. "Let me go, for the day breaketh" were her last words.

Edward was still unburied. Webster was reeling from the first great shock when the second one came. "Never was a daughter more loved than I loved Julia," he wrote to one friend. What recollections, too, rushed in upon him. Only a few weeks before her death when she, out for an airing with her father, was driving past the burial ground near the Common in Boston, she had pointed to a modest monument and expressed the wish that at Marshfield one like it be erected for Edward and another one for herself. Her father told her it should be done and later it was done. Webster, whose love for his family was one of his most marked characteristics, was overwhelmed by his new sorrow, but nerved himself to bear it.

"I did not look for these calamities," he wrote to his old friend Mrs. Lee, "but I pray for a submissive and reconciled spirit. I know that I must follow my lost children soon, and that we must all be diligently preparing for a change of worlds."

The day after Julia's death, Mr. Ticknor found him walking nervously about the room with a copy of the Bible in his hand.

Julia was buried on Monday, May 1. A few hours before her burial, the body of Edward arrived. He was buried on Thursday. Two of Webster's children buried in one week. His first wife and four of her five children in the tomb. Only one left—Fletcher—and he, to be killed in 1862 at the second battle of Bull Run.

The weary old man followed his dead to their resting-place, at every sight of him the people along the streets respectfully and sympathetically removed their hats, and when these sad duties had been performed he went to Marshfield. What he immediately did there was told by his secretary, Charles Lanman:

Directly in front of the Marshfield mansion, in a sunny and pleasant locality, are two small elm trees, which were planted by Mr. Webster in memory of his children, Julia and Edward. The ceremony of their planting was as follows: Mr. Webster had been missing from his study for an hour or more when he suddenly made his appearance before his son Fletcher with two small trees and a shovel in his hand and summoned his attendance. He then walked to the spot already designated, and having dug the holes and planted the trees without any assistance, he handed the shovel to Fletcher and remarked in a subdued voice, as he turned away: "My son, protect these trees after I am gone. Let them ever remind you of Julia and Edward."

These trees came to be known as "The Brother and Sister." In 1929, the trees were still standing.

Webster was never the same after the death of Julia and Edward. He could work, but he could not play. Joy seemed to have been crushed out of him. Julia was thirty when she died; Edward twenty-eight. He had come to know them, whereas Grace, at seven, and Charles, at two, had passed away after so brief a residence upon earth that their loss was not felt so keenly.

X

THE slip of a girl who died at thirty was the only one of Daniel Webster's children who, in 1929, had a living descendant. Two of Webster's children died in infancy, a third died unmarried, Fletcher had a number of children, most of whom died in infancy and none of whom had children. Julia Webster Appleton became the mother of five children, one of whom died in infancy, one in 1872, another in 1911, another in 1921 and another in 1925. In 1929 there were living nine great-grandchildren and fifteen great-great-grandchildren of Daniel Webster, all descended from his daughter Julia. One of Webster's great-grandsons is Jerome Napoleon Bonaparte of New York, the son of Julia Webster Appleton's daughter Caroline, who married one of Napoleon's Baltimore grand-nephews. The other eight great-grandchildren of Webster are: Constance Edgar, Convent of the Sacred Heart, Baltimore; Webster Appleton Edgar, Cazenovia, New York; Samuel A. Appleton, Warrenton, Virginia; Esther Heaton, Fairfield, Iowa; Robert E. Appleton, Ann Seabury, St. Paul, Minnesota; Lewis Addison Armistead, Boston; Daniel Webster Appleton Armistead, Bethlehem, Pennsylvania.

PART FIVE

FOR what wears out the life of mortal men?
  'Tis that from change to change their being rolls;
'Tis that repeated shocks, again, again,
  Exhaust the energy of strongest souls,
    And numb the elastic powers.
Till having used our nerves with bliss and teen,
  And tired upon a thousand schemes our wit,
To the just-pausing Genius we remit
  Our worn-out life and are—what we have been.
                              —MATTHEW ARNOLD.

I

SOME men, who were not born until after Webster died, say that to the year of his death he pursued the Presidency; and saying thus, they do but repeat what was said by some men who lived in Webster's time—men who did not like him. It is true that in 1848 and, again in 1852, in the autumn of which Webster died, he hoped to be nominated by the Whig party, but men who knew Webster well, and liked him, say that even in 1848 personal ambition no longer moved him. What he saw plainly, they say, and feared much, was the likelihood of civil war; and he desired the Presidency only because he believed that, as the head of the state, he could bring the country through its difficulties without bloodshed. A man who loved his country as much as Webster undoubtedly did would naturally wish to be President if he believed that he could thereby keep the peace.

As to whether personal ambition continued to the last to spur him on, each of us can now do no more than consider the facts and draw such inferences as may seem justifiable. Webster, in 1848, was sixty-six years old; in 1852 he was seventy. How much interested in the Presidency is a tired old man likely to be who, for forty years, has known each President well; and who knows how much of worry and care attend the office and how little of satisfaction it yields in comparison with the sacrifices that it involves? The White House had long since ceased to be to Webster a place of mystery and enchantment. Does it tax imagination too much to assume that Webster during his later years sought the Presidency solely as a means of doing good? Webster had been stricken both by age and by private sorrows. Enough had happened to him to kill ambition. It is not difficult to accept the statement of Webster's friends as true.

The weakness of this theory is that Henry Clay, who knew the White House as well as Webster did, tried, at the age of seventy-one, to get the Whig nomination. In the case of Webster, perhaps the shrewdest guess would be that while ambition, during the latter part of his life, bulked small and sometimes seemed to have disappeared, it never quite died, and occasionally flared up. When great matters, involving principle, were concerned, Webster, having taken a position, always stood fast, but in relatively small matters that had to do only with his personal inclinations he was oftentimes as changeable as the wind. Whatever he was doing, it eventually seemed desirable to him to do something entirely different. If he was in the senate, the wisest move would be to drop everything and go out to Illinois to operate a thousand-acre farm. When he was in the house of representatives, he refused reelection that he might practice law, after six years of which he permitted himself to be placed in the senate. Sometimes agriculture and the law were forgotten in his desire to be President.

There was never anything mean or low about Webster's presidential aspirations. He was not like some Presidents during his time, and others to come after him, who, though utterly unfitted for the office, nevertheless desired it as a means of achieving what they perhaps believed to be their own immortality. Webster believed that he was "fit to be President," that as chief of the state he could serve his country well. The Presidency is an awful measuring stick to place behind the back of a short man, but Webster had the height. We who have come after him know that he had it. As President, he would have taken rank with Washington, Jefferson and Lincoln —a very select company.

Webster got into the swing of life in Washington again just as plans were developing to make General Taylor the Whig candidate for the Presidency. Taylor was a slave-owner from Louisiana about whose politics no one knew anything, least of all the Whigs. Webster was appalled by the prospect. He objected to a candidate who had no other qualification than a great military record; Taylor had no other qualification. Webster also felt that it was insane for the Whigs to nominate a man of whose political beliefs they knew nothing. But the Whigs, believing that Taylor could win, and apparently caring for little else, refused in convention to declare what Whig principles were, and nominated Taylor without seeking to commit him to anything. The convention succumbed to what Webster bitterly described as the "sagacious, far-seeing doctrine of availability." Webster said Taylor's nomination was one "not fit to be made."

At once Webster was confronted by a number of very practical questions. What was he to do? Should he drop out of public life? His fear for the Union forbade this. Should he support the Democratic candidate, Lewis Cass, who was committed to the extension of slavery to the limit, throughout the conquered and purchased territories? Support of Cass was out of the question. The only other course was to support Taylor, the candidate of a party that, in the North at least, was opposed to the extension of slavery, and hope for the best. Webster therefore, during the campaign, gave qualified and limited support to Taylor. Ben Perley Poore, a Washington newspaper correspondent for sixty years, said in his "Reminiscences" that Webster received a large sum of money for

supporting Taylor, but he neglected to refer to the slightest corroborative evidence. There was no such evidence.
Webster supported Taylor because it was the only course
left open to him.

Taylor was a rough old fellow who scattered boxes
of sawdust throughout the parlors of the White House to
catch tobacco juice (Mrs. Fillmore, when she became the
"First Lady," had much carpet-cleaning to do) but he
was nevertheless an agreeable surprise to Webster and
other northern Whigs. He readily subscribed to Whig
doctrine, as it was made known to him, and pledged himself to resist to the uttermost any attempts that might
be made to break up the Union. Perhaps such sentiments
explained why he and his son-in-law, Jefferson Davis,
were not on speaking terms.

During the first session of congress after Taylor's inauguration, the battle began in the senate to determine
whether the territories obtained from Mexico should be
kept free or held in readiness to convert into slave states.
One day, Horace Greeley was in the senate when Stephen
A. Douglas sought to edge into the picture by making a
motion. Webster, who was in his seat, glared at him and,
without rising, said:

"We have no such practice in the senate, sir."

Douglas changed the substance of his motion a little.

"That is not the way we do business in the senate, sir,"
said Webster, still without rising.

"The 'Little Giant,' " said Greeley, "was a bold, ready
man, not easily overawed or disconcerted; but if he did
not quiver under the eye and voice of Webster, then my
eyesight deceived me—and I was very near him."

Webster and Calhoun, too, had a sharp passage at
arms, but nothing immediately came of all the talk except abundant proof that the spoliation of Mexico was

destined to bring great trouble to the United States. Congress adjourned without taking action.

II

ONE by one, Webster's old-time friends were passing away. John Marshall had died in 1835, Justice Story in 1845, and in 1848 came Jeremiah Mason's time to go. Death took him at eighty, and when he went a flood of memories poured in upon Webster. When Webster was a young man Mason had been the first to teach him, by demonstration in open court, exactly how law should be practiced, and Webster had proved so ready a pupil that Mason, who usually faced him as opposing counsel, soon said of him: "He is the very devil in any case whatsoever." Together they had practiced law, together they had spent their vacations, riding over the hills of New England, together they had sat at table with John Marshall and old Christopher Gore when they all boarded together in Washington at the Congress Hotel; together they had served in congress and lived their lives; and when Death intervened, Webster felt that something very real and important had been taken from him. Before the Massachusetts Supreme Court, Webster delivered a eulogy of Mason in which he told how Mason had seen and talked with George Washington. Webster also gave advice to old persons as to how to be happy. "Depend upon it," he said, "whatever may be the mind of an old man, old age is only really happy when, on feeling the enjoyments of this world pass away, it begins to lay a stronger hold upon another." Fame was nothing, riches were nothing, "but a conscience void of offense before God and man is an inheritance for eternity."

Webster's activity in public affairs, however great, never prevented him from carrying on an enormous correspondence. It was his custom, when the proceedings in the senate did not interest him, to sit at his desk and write letters, sometimes for hours at a time. Considering that typewriters had not yet been invented and that he had to write each letter by hand, it is difficult to understand where he found the time or how he discovered the strength to do what he did. Letters literally fluttered from his desk to the superintendents of his farms, to whom he gave the minutest directions about their work. Also, he wrote upon a great variety of subjects to other persons. A cross-section of the letters that Webster wrote in 1849 shows how many things besides statecraft occupied his thoughts:

To Fletcher Webster:

I send a quarter of lamb to roast; and if not too rainy, will come and dine with you.

Potatoes. Let these be peeled early and thrown into a basin of cold water, till time to cook them. Let them be boiled in a good deal of water. When done, pour off all the water, shake up the potatoes a little, hang on the pot again, and let the potatoes dry two or three minutes, and then bring them to the table. I remember that when we heard Hannah Curtis shaking the pot, we knew that dinner was coming.

To Mrs. Page:

A century hence, when negro labor shall have been done away with, and white men become willing to work, this [Virginia] will be a most agreeable region.

To John Taylor, at Elms Farm, New Hampshire:

I suppose the ox is dead. You did all you could. If you have another creature sick in the same way, treat him as you did this except (1) Repeat the bleeding; bleed him very freely. (2) Cut off the end of his tail. (3) Put red pepper into vinegar and dash it up his nostril frequently, with a syringe or some such thing.

To Porter Wright at Marshfield:

I wish you would tell me the weights of the hogs and the cow. I am sorry the ox does not thrive better. Mr. Thomas thinks he is not yet fit to kill. It will be best therefore to keep him a little longer than we talked of.

I wish to inquire of Mr. Willis about ashes. I want to know how many bushels he can let us have and at what price. I have written to Boston to inquire about crushed bones.

Please look well after all the cattle. Henry says the Phillips cow looks thin. James must give her more meal.

To Mr. Blatchford:

. . . I am willing to confess to the vanity of thinking that my efforts in these two cases have done something towards explaining and upholding the just powers of the government of the United States, on the great subject of commerce. . . . Whatever I may think of the ability of my argument, and I do not think highly of it, I yet feel pleasure in reflecting that I have held on and held out to the end.

To Mr. Charles March:

At that poor place called Marshfield, which you have never thought it worth your while to visit and I am afraid never will, there are a few bottles, though but a few, of good old Madeira wine, introduced in the country through your agency, and some of it the fruit of your bounty. But here in this great city I have not a single drop of such wine as I have mentioned. Not having fallen into the Sherry heresy, I like a glass of Madeira sometimes myself. But that is not important. There comes our new President, however, and I should like to be able to offer to him and his attendants a glass of what you and I regard as fit to drink.

Therefore, I will be obliged to you to send to me a dozen or two of such a quality of wine as you think likely to make a favorable impression on the taste of our chief magistrate-elect, and I will cheerfully defray cost and charges.

To Mr. March (a little later):

You are always doing me acts of friendship and kindness. I have now to thank you for the boxes of "Ceylon" which you say are on the way, and which will probably arrive today. Remember, it was "Ceylon" which Lord Ashburton used when the Treaty of Washington was in process of negotiation.

To Mr. Charles A. Stetson, Astor House, New York:

The best pair of working oxen on my farm shall set out for your place on Monday. They are seven years old, large, handsome, perfectly well broke, and for common cart-work on a farm, are a team in themselves. I shall send, also, a likely pair of three-year-old steers, which have been somewhat used to the yoke, but are not yet quite so well trained and drilled as a couple of dining-room waiters at the Astor House.

To James Hervey Bingham:

My Dear Old Classmate, Room-mate and Friend: It gives me very great pleasure to hear from you and to learn that you are well. Years have not abated my affectionate regard. We have been boys together, and men together, and now are growing old together, but you always occupy the same place in my remembrance and good wishes. You are still James Hervey Bingham, with your old bass viol with *"Laus Deo"* painted upon it; I hope you have it yet; and I am the same Daniel Webster whom you have known at Exeter, at Lempster, at Charlestown, at Salisbury, at Alstead, at Portsmouth, Claremont, Boston and Washington. . . .

Bingham had written Webster asking him to get him a place in the public service. Webster, a little later, found a clerkship for him in the state department.

To Mr. Blatchford:

I am looking into the latest edition of Boswell's Johnson. I read this book a great many times, formerly, and remember much of it, but with the notes of recent editions it contains new and interesting matter. My life has been an unimportant one, and my stock of information never large. Nor have we had in this country, associations, clubs, &c., where conversation has been cultivated. And yet I have often wished, that what has passed, when I have been with some eminent men on some occasions, could be recalled and preserved.

Mr. Gore, Mr. King, Mr. Mason, the Buckminsters, father and son, Chief Justice Marshall, Chancellor Kent, Judge Story, Mr. Madison, Samuel Dexter, Mr. Gaston, &c., &c., have all said things worthy to be remembered; and yet only some of them have left anything valuable on record. Of Mr. Ames's conversation I am not old enough to have heard much. Jeremiah Mason was perhaps the best talker I have been acquainted with; he was full of knowledge of books and men, had a great deal of wit and humor, and abhorred silence as an intolerable state of existence.

When I first came here there were several old men in Congress whose remembrance of public things went back beyond the Revolution. . . . With these it used to delight me to pass time. I was young and eager to learn; they had well-stored memories and were willing to talk. Egbert Benson was also a very pleasant and communicative man. He delighted to converse about New York things. before and during the Revolutionary War. I ought not to forget John Adams, of whose conversation I heard but little, but that little was always striking. I think if his conversation could be collected it would do him more credit than his writings or his speeches.

In the small and obscure circle of my early days I remember several, both men and women, by whom my attention was always fastened, so that when I could hear them talk I could neither work nor play. John Bowen, of whom you have heard me speak as having been a prisoner with the Indians; Robert Wise, a Yorkshire man who had been round the world in the English service, army and navy; George Bayly, a yeoman of humor and mimicry, and some neighboring women, who had lived on the border from the felling of the first trees. Oh, I shall never hear such story-telling again!

To Mr. Blatchford (five days later):

I write to you today from habit and from pleasure of thinking of you, and speaking a word or two without having anything to say. If I meet a friend in the morning, I say, "How are you?" and offer him my hand, and say five words about the weather, the ladies, &c., without having anything of importance to communicate or expecting to hear any news. If writing and sending were as easy as talking and shaking hands, these morning salutations of friends would be equally pleasant on paper. Perhaps electricity will help us to the means of all this yet; so that when you are giving advice or receiving fees in your office in Hanover street I may speak to you from on board my boat at "Sunk Rock" and tell you when I have a bite.

(A glimpse of the telephone which, in twenty-five years, was to come, and perhaps of the radio.)

To John Taylor, Elms Farm:

I am sorry about the steer, but why do you not tell me how his leg got broken? You must know. I am afraid there was some carelessness, something left out of place. Was there not a cart or a harrow or something else in the yard or in the shed which ought not to have been there? A steer does not break his leg in play or in fighting with other cattle. Why did you not tell me in your first letter what caused the accident? Let me know the whole truth immediately.

To John Taylor:

I have received your letter about the steer. It is all well. I am satisfied there was no carelessness, and that is all I wished to know. But it was a strange accident.

You must now keep the cattle well. All the steers should have a little cob meal to keep them in good heart, before they go to pasture. The old oxen, especially, should be well fed. . . . Be sure to have plows, carts and harrows all in readiness. I shall come to see you as soon as I reach Boston. See that there is plenty of dry wood. Remember that to plant ten acres of potatoes is no small job, and that they must be planted early. Porter Wright will do his best to beat you. But you have the best land.

To Mr. S. A. Appleton, his son-in-law:

A telegraphic despatch from Fletcher on Friday morning informed us of the death of dear little Constance. . . . From the first moment of her sickness I had a presentiment that she would not recover. I felt that it was destined that she should immediately follow her mother. . . . Never was a daughter loved more than I loved Julia, and never was a bereaved husband commiserated more than I have commiserated you. But you and I and all must submit to the will of God. . . .

To John Taylor:

If you have a couple of wethers in pretty good order already, I wish you to feed them, so that they may be getting fat. We may want a little mutton next month.

To Mr. J. Prescott Hall:

I have confidence in your fidelity to promises and some trust in your judgment of horseflesh. But both must be brought to the test.

I want a riding horse with these qualities, namely: Cheap, stout, gentle, sure-footed, easy, a good walker, a good stander. He may be ugly provided he is free in the fore-shoulder, and high and strong in the hip.

If you can find such a horse so that I can take it along, ten days hence, in the Fall River boat, why, then I shall have a saddle horse; if not, not.

(*Indorsement by Mr. Hall:* I never could find the horse herein described, although I searched for him, by self and agents for a long time. A dealer told me that Mr. Webster had described an animal rarely seen, and his description of what he wanted is that of an almost perfect saddle-horse, so far as good qualities are concerned.)

To Mr. Edward Curtis:

When I last wrote, Mrs. Webster was still upstairs. She came down yesterday morning, quite bright; and as I had little occasion to go out, we had a home-keeping, family day. We dined alone to all visible appearance, but I put a spoon on one side of the table to represent Mr. Curtis, and a decanter stopper on the other, for Mrs. Curtis. We offered to help these guests and to drink wine with them, and

so we made a pretty comfortable Swedenborgian dinner of it. We had shad.

To Porter Wright at Marshfield:

I told you last fall and now repeat that I wish
to plant the whole field with potatoes, or else no part
of it. I want no small pieces. The land must all be
plowed and subsoil plowed, every furrow of it,
and the manure must be spread and plowed in.

If this can be done, I shall be glad; but if it
cannot all be done, let it all alone. I thought you had
teams enough and could get hands enough to do it all
promptly. But if you cannot, let it all alone, and
leave the manure heap where it is. I want very much
to get home, but must stay here a little longer to earn
a little money to pay the expense of putting in a
potato crop. Do you need any money? If so, speak
your mind. Of course sell the pigs as fast as you can
get a fair price for them; don't sell too cheap.
We will not raise any small calves, but keep all the
heifers, and if you find among the neighbors any
large and handsome steer calves fit to make oxen, buy
them. You may sell some of the inferior cows if you
have a chance.

To Porter Wright (six days later):

If you pluck up enough courage to take hold of
the potato field, which I rather doubt, you must be
particular about the seed. The object is to raise such
potatoes as ripen early and bring a good price in the
market. Daniel Wright knows something about this.
. . . I would not plant all of one sort, nor should I
have too many sorts. Get what seed you think best,
even if you have to go to Boston for it.

John Taylor was evidently Webster's favorite farm
foreman. Porter Wright was occasionally the recipient of
sharp letters, but he was still in charge at Marshfield

when Webster died. Webster seldom if ever discharged anybody, on his farms or in the state department.

To Porter Wright (two days later):

I am glad to hear of your progress in farming. You seem to be going on well. . . . You and I may never try so large a plantation of potatoes again. . . .

To Mr. Harvey:

I understand that of the supplies got together for yesterday's feast there remains an uncooked canvas-back duck, and Mr. Tucker proposes to send it to my table today. I wish you would come at three o'clock and try its quality.

P. S. I have escaped headache and hope you have.

III

ON the cold, unpleasant evening of January 21, 1850, there came without preliminary announcement to the door of Daniel Webster the tottering feet of Henry Clay. Clay was in his seventy-third year, and the mark of death was already upon him. He had a devastating cough, and his strength was so low that he could speak but a little while without pausing to rest. The two men had not for years displayed toward each other much more than formal politeness, but Clay considered the national emergency so great that, on this winter's night, he put aside the past to go to his ancient rival for help. He had conceived and was about to introduce in the senate a series of compromises, which he hoped would settle and quiet all of the outstanding differences between the North and the South. What he wanted to know was whether Webster would help him put these compromises through.

Webster replied in the affirmative, reserving only the right, if he should later desire to exercise it, to make slight amendments.

On the twenty-ninth of January, Clay introduced his resolutions in the senate. How great was the need for conciliatory legislation may be judged from the fact that, five days before the introduction of Mr. Clay's resolutions, the Massachusetts Antislavery Society, in session in Faneuil Hall, Boston, had adopted a resolution in favor of breaking up the Union and forming a new republic in which there should be no slavery.

> We do hereby declare ourselves [read the resolution] the enemies of the Constitution, Union and Government of the United States. . . . and we proclaim it as our unalterable purpose and determination to live and labor for a dissolution of the present union . . . and for the formation of a new republic that shall be such, not in name only, but in full living reality and truth.

Nor was Massachusetts the only state in which there were excited groups. Clay said, in introducing his resolutions, that "in the legislative bodies of the capital and of the states, twenty-odd furnaces are in full blast, emitting heat, passion and intemperance, and diffusing them throughout the whole extent of this broad land."

On the fourth of March, John C. Calhoun, sick, old (he was sixty-eight), and with death standing over him preparing to strike, caused to be read in the senate a carefully prepared speech that at least showed how utterly sincere he was in the views that he held. Knowing that the curtain was ringing down upon his life and that whatever was done by the North and the South would concern him not at all, he nevertheless surveyed the situation and closed with the expression of the conviction that, as matters stood, the South could not, with honor and safety, remain in the Union. It was the last formal speech that Calhoun was to make, even by proxy, in the senate.

The next day, Webster visited his old friend to inquire after his health. Calhoun, who was ghastly pale, shook his head sadly, leaving the impression that he considered his days numbered. During the course of the conversation, Webster said that he expected, on March 7, to speak in behalf of Mr. Clay's resolutions. Calhoun said he would like to hear the speech, but did not expect to do so, as he feared he was upon his death-bed.

It was announced on March 6 that Webster would speak on the following day, and the moment the doors of the senate chamber were opened the next morning, the place was packed. Webster had told some of his friends that the speech he intended to make might quite conceivably ruin him politically. What he intended to say was certain to offend the abolitionists, who had long since passed the point where they felt that anybody but themselves had any right on his side. Webster, who believed he could see right on both sides, and wrong on both sides, intended to speak the truth as he saw it, regardless of consequences to himself. In his view, it was as wrong for Massachusetts abolitionists to talk about breaking up the Union as it was for groups in the South to declare the same intention.

Webster had not been speaking long, when into the senate chamber slowly came a tall, gaunt figure, wrapped in a cloak and surmounted with a mass of white hair that reached to the shoulders. It was Calhoun, making his final entry. Webster did not see him.

Webster continued speaking, and shortly after quoted something that Calhoun had once said in debate and expressed regret that serious illness had prevented "the venerable senator from South Carolina from being in the chamber today." Calhoun, with head bent eagerly forward, stirred in his seat as if to rise, but abandoned the attempt. In a little while, Webster again had occasion to mention Calhoun, "the eminent senator from South Carolina whom we all regret so much to miss, from such a cause, from his seat today." Calhoun could stand the strain no longer. Summoning the last of his fleeting energies, he gripped the arms of his chair, slowly raised his body to a half-standing posture, and feebly said: "The senator from South Carolina is in his seat."

Webster was startled. It did not seem possible that the dying old man could have risen from his bed—but there he was. Webster, hearing his voice, quickly turned toward him, bowed low, smiled, briefly expressed his satisfaction, and went on with his speech.

That speech, even at this late day, is worthy of the most careful consideration. It all but wrecked Webster politically, bringing down upon him from certain groups in the North the most bitter denunciation, though it contained nothing that should have brought anything but praise and appreciation. Parton, nearly twenty years afterward, spoke of certain parts of it as "disgusting," and others charged that Webster had "sold out to the South," the price of his perfidy being the Presidency. Men who are otherwise well informed still speak of Webster's "Seventh-of-March Speech" as the pathetic attempt of an old man to truckle his way into the White House.

It was nothing of the kind. It was what Webster himself said it was, "a speech for the Constitution and the Union." Unless it be argued that the Civil War was just what the United States needed at the time, and that any attempt to avert hostilities was a mistake, Webster's

Seventh-of-March Speech cannot be condemned. He was widely misunderstood and as widely censured, because he attempted to play the part of a kindly, impartial judge. He refused to hate and he refused to witness wrong on either side without reproving it. At a time when the extremists of each section thought mostly in terms of hatred, and seemed to care more for their own purposes than for justice, such a speech as Webster made inevitably offended those who differed from him. We can understand why, in such circumstances, hatreds must inevitably arise, but we should be as fair to the memory of Webster as we are to the abolitionists who did the best they could to wreck him.

It was the custom of Webster, when about to begin the discussion of a controversial matter, to lead off with something as to which there was no difference of opinion. In this instance, he began with a brief history of slavery in the United States. With his great faculty for making dead facts sprout leaves of green he soon conjured up an interesting tree of knowledge. He asked senators to bear in mind that, when the Constitution was adopted, the South was more outspoken than the North in denunciation of slavery. Southerners, who took the lead in bringing about the Constitutional Convention, felt so ashamed of slavery that they would not permit the word to get into the Constitution. Neither in the North nor in the South was slavery regarded as inhuman or cruel, but for indefinable reasons, perhaps, it was something to be sloughed off, and both sides were in favor of sloughing it off. It was believed that if importations of slaves were to be prohibited, the birth-rate of the whites would so exceed that of the blacks that slavery would soon extinguish itself. It was proposed that slave importations be prohibited twenty years after the adoption of the Constitution. James Madison, of Virginia, thought twenty years to be too long to permit the traffic to continue.

Webster traced the picture of the past with broad, sweeping strokes. While the Constitutional Convention was in session, congress was passing a law declaring that there should be no slavery in the Northwest Territory; and the only vote cast against it in committee was cast by a northern man, all of the Southerners voting for it.

Then came cotton. When John Jay negotiated his treaty with England, during Washington's administration, cotton was so insignificant an item in the South's affairs that he did not know it was grown in the South at all. When the first shipment was sent to England it was excluded on the ground that cotton could not be grown in the United States. But it could be grown, was grown, and the invention of the cotton gin sent the industry forward. All of which created for the South a new, powerful reason that it should perhaps think twice before abandoning slavery.

The South thought twice and thrice and then some more, but neither became sensitive upon the subject nor definitely determined to cling to slavery. As late as 1832 a proposition gradually to do away with slavery was debated in the Virginia legislature without anyone becoming in the least excited about it. The bad feeling came when attacks upon slavery began to come from the North, and the South, feeling that its right to keep slaves was in danger, began to seek such extensions to slave territory as would insure the continuance of its political power. As a result of abolitionist activity, Webster said, "the bonds of the slaves were bound more firmly than before, their rivets were more strongly fastened. Public opinion, which in Virginia had begun to be exhibited against slavery, and was opening out for a discussion of the question,

drew back and shut itself up in its castle." Webster gave
the abolitionists credit for good intentions, but not for
good sense. During twenty years they had done nothing
that, in his opinion, was good or valuable. On the contrary, they had, by angering and irritating the South,
done much harm.

Let any gentleman who entertains doubts on this
point [said Webster] recur to the debates in the
Virginia House of Delegates in 1832, and he will
see with what freedom a proposition made by Mr.
Jefferson Randolph was discussed in that body.
Every one spoke of slavery as he thought; very
ignominious and disparaging names and epithets
were applied to it. The debates in the House of Delegates on that occasion, I believe, were all published.
They were read by every colored man who could
read, and to those who could not read, those debates were read by others. At that time, Virginia was
not unwilling or afraid to discuss this question, and
to let that part of her population know as much of
the discussion as they could learn. That was in 1832.
As has been said by the honorable member from
South Carolina, these Abolition societies commenced
their course of action in 1835. It is said, I do not
know how true it may be, that they sent incendiary
publications into the slave states; at any rate, they
attempted to arouse and did arouse, a very strong
feeling. . . . I wish to know whether anybody in
Virginia can now talk openly, as Mr. Randolph,
Governor McDowell and others talked in 1832, and
send their remarks to the press? We all know the
fact and we all know the cause; and everything that
these agitating people have done has been, not to
enlarge but to restrain, not to set free but to bind
faster, the slave population of the South.

The South complained, he said, of the violence of the
northern press. Webster admitted the truth of the charge,

but added that the press everywhere was violent. He characterized the conduct of a part of the press on each side as "outrageous," but added that a free press is worth whatever it costs and such exaggeration was a part of the cost. He suggested that the violence of the press was perhaps caused by the violence sometimes displayed in congress.

As to the Fugitive Slave Law, Webster took toward it exactly the ground that Lincoln later took in his first inaugural address. The law was authorized by the Constitution and, so long as it remained, must be administered by the government in good faith and respected in the North, even by those who did not believe in it. States had no right to make it a felony to enforce this Federal law. Some states having thus fallen short in their duty, Webster agreed with Clay that it became the duty of the Federal Government to enact a supplementary measure that would give the South this right to which, under the Constitution, it was entitled.

Webster then took up the political phase of the question and related how the South, intent upon holding a right that abolitionists denied, had sought to increase its political power by the addition of slave states. First, there had been the annexation of Texas, then the war with Mexico, then the treaty of peace, which brought into the Union great territories out of which it was hoped to carve more slave states.

This phase of the discussion gave Webster an opportunity to make stinging criticism of certain political enemies of his in the North who called themselves northern Democrats. They now taunted him with a tendency to truckle to the South; but what did Webster do and what did the northern Democrats do when southern statesmen, in control of the government, were putting through legislation to bring in more territory out of which to make more slave states? What did Webster do when it was proposed to annex Texas? He voted against it, but northern Democrats united with southern defenders of slavery and brought it in. Webster voted against the peace treaty with Mexico, which brought in more territory, while northern Democrats voted for it. Against the protests of Webster, northern Democrats had made their bed and, having made it, did not wish to lie upon it. Nor was that all. Having made the mischief, they now called themselves "Free-Soilers" and taunted Webster because he insisted that the constitutional rights of the South should be respected. He saw no peaceful way out except for each side to obey the law.

And what were some of the rights of the South, so far as new slave states were concerned? One of these rights was to make four more states out of Texas, free to become slave or not but with a certainty that they would become slave. The Free-Soilers who had helped bring Texas into the Union shuddered at the thought. What was Webster's position? He said there was but one thing to do—obey the law. In admitting Texas, the Government of the United States had entered into an agreement with Texas to permit the new states to be made whenever their population should become great enough to entitle them to such distinction. Was this agreement to be broken? Was the Government of the United States to stand forth as an acknowledged pledge-breaker? Not with Webster's consent. He believed the word of the Government of the United States should always be worth a hundred cents upon the dollar. Against his wishes, he would carry out the agreement with Texas merely because it had been made.

As to California and New Mexico, he would not

ruffle southern feeling—which was already far more troubled than safety permitted—by enacting a law that these states should come in only as free states. His reason for taking this position was that, in the very nature of things, California and New Mexico could never be any-thing else but free. Soil and climate had combined to make cotton growing and therefore slavery impossible. Webster would not try to reenforce an act of God by an act of congress. While congress was talking, California adopted a free-soil constitution, asked for admission and was admitted.

Everything else having been said, there remained the subject of secession. Did some southern men believe what they said when they talked about breaking up the Union. Some Southerners had even talked about "peaceable secession."

Peaceable secession [said Webster]! Sir, your eyes and mine are never destined to see that miracle. The dismemberment of this vast country without con-vulsion! The breaking-up of the fountains of the great deep without ruffling the surface! Who is so foolish, I beg everybody's pardon, as to expect to see any such thing? . . . I will not state what might produce the disruption of the Union; but, sir, I see as plainly as I see the sun in the heaven what that disruption must produce; I see that it must produce war, and such a war as I will not describe, in its twofold character. . . .

I know, although the idea has not been distinctly stated, there is to be or it is supposed possible there will be, a Southern Confederacy. I do not mean, when I allude to this statement, that anyone seriously contemplates such a state of things. I do not mean to say that it is true. . . . Sir, I may express myself too strongly, perhaps, but there are impossibilities in the natural as well as in the physical world, and I hold the idea of a separation of these states . . . as such an impossibility. . . .

Sir, I am ashamed to pursue this line of remark. I dislike it, I have an utter disgust for it. I would rather hear of natural blasts and mildews, pestilence and famine, than to hear gentlemen talk of secession. To break up this great government! To dismember this glorious country! To astonish Europe with an act of folly such as Europe for two centuries has never beheld in any government or any people! No, sir, no, sir! There will be no secession. Gentlemen are not serious when they talk of secession.

If not secession, what? What was to be done to solve the slavery question? Here Webster modestly put forward the idea of "compensated emancipation" that was later suggested by Lincoln.

I will say, however [said Webster], though I have nothing to propose, because I do not deem myself so competent as other gentlemen to take a lead upon this subject, that if any gentleman from the South will propose a scheme to be carried on by this government on a large scale, for the transportation of free colored people, to any colony or any place in the world, I should be quite disposed to incur almost any degree of expense to accomplish that object. Nay, sir, following an example set more than twenty years ago by a great man then a senator from New York [Mr. Rufus King], I would return to Virginia, and through her to the whole South, the money received from the lands and territories ceded by her to this government, for any such purpose as to remove, in whole or in part, or in any way to diminish or deal beneficially with, the free colored population of the southern states. . . . There have been received into the treasury of the United States eighty millions of dollars, the proceeds of the sales of the public lands ceded by her. If the residue shall be sold at the same rate, the whole aggregate will exceed two hundred millions of dollars. If Virginia and the South see fit to adopt any proposition to relieve themselves of the free people of color among them, or such as may be made free, they have my full consent that the government shall pay them any sum of money out of the proceeds of that cession which may be adequate to the purpose.

When Webster finished speaking, Calhoun struggled to his feet:

Mr. Calhoun: I cannot agree with the senator from Massachusetts that this Union cannot be dissolved. Am I to understand him that no degree of oppression, no broken faith, can produce the destruction of this Union? Why, sir, if that becomes a fixed fact, it will itself become the great instrument of producing oppression, outrage and broken faith. No, sir, the Union *can* be broken. Great moral causes will break it, if they go on; and it can only be preserved by justice, good faith, and a rigid adherence to the Constitution.

Mr. Webster: The honorable member asks me if I hold the breaking of the Union, by any such thing as the voluntary secession of states, as an impossibility. I know, sir, this Union can be broken up; every government can be; and I admit there may be such a degree of oppression as will warrant resistance, and a forcible severance. That is *revolution*— that is *revolution!* Of that ultimate right of revolution I have not been speaking. I know that law, of necessity, does exist. I forbear from going further, because I do not wish to go into a discussion of the nature of this government. The honorable gentleman and myself have broken lances sufficiently often before on that subject.

Mr. Calhoun: I have no desire to do it now.

Mr. Webster: I presume the gentleman has not, and I have quite as little.

Twenty-four days later, Calhoun was dead and, in a little time, his body was brought into the senate chamber and placed upon the spot where he had so often spoken. The first of the great triumvirate was gone, the second was about to go, and the third had but a little time to linger.

For making this speech, Webster, a year later, was barred from Faneuil Hall and denounced generally by abolitionists. It is true that the mayor and aldermen of Boston who barred him from the "Cradle of Liberty" did not represent the feelings of most of the people, as they discovered the next year when they came up for reelection and were defeated, but it is nevertheless true that they faithfully represented the feelings of abolitionists. The speech was like oil upon the troubled waters of the South, where it was received thankfully and appreciatively. Throughout the North, except in abolitionist circles, it was generally well received, but the abolitionists were so energetic and so vindictive that their opposition, relatively small as it was, was felt by Webster.

IV

ON July 17, 1850, Daniel Webster spoke in the senate for the last time. Thirty-seven years before he had, as a young man, entered congress almost unnoticed and now, at the age of sixty-eight, he was, by the irony of Fate, to go out as quietly as he had come in. Nobody knew it was to be his last speech. He himself did not know it. Eight days before, Death, by knocking at the White House door, had set in motion a train of events that quickly removed from the senate the most towering figure that had ever appeared in it—or was destined to appear in it, at least during the next eighty years.

DANIEL WEBSTER
As Secretary of State

Webster's last speech in the senate was worthy both of him and of the occasion. During the four months that had elapsed since the delivery of his famous Seventh-of-March address, he had been much troubled by what seemed to be the inability of fanatics to understand what he had said. He had even appealed to a newspaper friend to help him out. "Do please write one column opening up the matter to the comprehension of such men as Mr. ———. Pound hard upon the enormous thickness of their skulls. . . . There is no inconsistency between my late speech and anything said in my speech in 1845."

There was no inconsistency, because before Texas was admitted, under an agreement to permit her to subdivide into four additional states, it was proper to object to the admission of Texas as a slave state. After Texas was admitted, objection to the making of four more states out of Texas became improper, since it involved repudiation of an agreement that the national government had made. To Webster this was plain, but notwithstanding his repeated explanations the abolitionists continued to make the charge that he had "sold out to the South."

"It is difficult," Webster wrote to his newspaper friend, "to beat the truth into men's heads."

What galled Webster most, perhaps, was that he was being fought by men who had nothing in common except the fact that they hated him. Speaking of the bill that contained Clay's compromises, Webster said in his last speech in the senate:

> Sir, this measure is opposed by the North or some of the North, and by the South or some of the South; and it has the remarkable misfortune to encounter resistance by persons the most directly opposed to each other in every matter connected with the subject under consideration. . . . There are those in

the country who say, on the part of the South, that the South, by this bill, gives up everything to the North, and that they will fight it to the last; and there are those on the part of the North who say that this bill gives up everything to the South, and that they will fight it to the last. And really, sir, strange as it may seem, this disposition to make battle upon the bill, by those who never agreed in anything before under the light of heaven, has created a sort of fellowship and good feeling between them. One says, "Give me your hand, my good fellow; you mean to go against this bill to the death, because it gives up the rights of the South. I mean to go against the bill to the death because it gives up the rights of the North. . . . "

For myself, sir, I propose to abide by the principles and the purposes which I have avowed. I shall stand by the Union and by all who stand by it. I shall do justice to the whole country, according to the best of my ability, in all I say, and act for the good of the whole country in all I do. I mean to stand upon the Constitution. I need no other platform. I shall know but one country. The ends I aim at shall be my country's, my God's and Truth's. I was born an American, and I intend to perform the duties incumbent upon me in that character to the end of my career. I mean to do this with absolute disregard of personal consequences. What are personal consequences? What is the individual man with all the good or evil which may befall a great country in a crisis like this, and in the midst of great transactions which concern that country's fate? Let the consequences be what they will; I am careless. No man can suffer too much and no man can fall too soon, if he suffer or if he fall in defense of the liberties and Constitution of his country.

The curtain fell. Webster, as a senator, had become a part of history.

V

GENERAL TAYLOR died on July 9, 1850, and Vice-President Millard Fillmore, who succeeded him in the Presidency, offered to Daniel Webster the post of secretary of state on July 20. The offer was immediately accepted.

"I never did anything more reluctantly," wrote Webster to a friend, "than taking the office which I have taken. From the time of General Taylor's death I supposed it might be offered, and pressed hard upon me by members of congress. The fear rendered my nights sleepless. . . . "

Webster liked Fillmore.

"The President," Webster wrote to Mr. Ticknor, "is a good-tempered, cautious, intelligent man, with whom it is pleasant to transact business. He is very diligent, and what he does not know he quickly learns. More than all, he has read the Scriptures and knows upon what authority it is said, Be not puffed up."

Webster was secretary of state, but his heart was not in the state department; it was in the senate, where the Clay compromise measures were still pending. What was to be their fate? If enacted into law, would they settle the slavery question and free the nation from the chronic menace of disruption? To his friend, Peter Harvey, he wrote on September 10, 1850:

"Since the 7th of March there has not been an hour in which I have not felt a crushing weight of anxiety and responsibility. I have gone to sleep at night and waked in the morning with the same feeling of eating care. And I have sat down to no breakfast or dinner to which I have brought an unconcerned and easy mind. It is over. My part is acted, and I am satisfied. The rest I leave to stronger bodies and fresher minds. . . . "

The series of agreements that came to be known as the "Compromise of 1850" was passed by both houses of congress and signed by the President in September. Webster's Seventh-of-March speech was what put the compromise through, and, though he came to regard it as his greatest address, nothing else that he ever did brought upon him so much criticism. While the guns of the Civil War were still roaring, Horace Greeley referred to the speech as "deplorable." More than thirty years after the address was made, Henry Cabot Lodge, in writing a biography of Webster, devoted several pages to an attempt to prove that the speech was "wrong in principle and mistaken in policy, " adding that the verdict against it had passed into history and that nothing could ever be written that would change it.

Perhaps Lodge was right. Many an error becomes embedded in history and remains there. But in the United States of America, the memory of Daniel Webster is and always will be entitled to a square deal. In his case, it is worth while and never too late to try to undo a wrong. Such criticism of Webster as there was originated in the blind hatreds engendered by the discussion of the slavery question. When Lodge wrote, in the middle eighties, those hatreds were still smoldering. Forty-five years later, they are all dead. Perhaps Webster can now get the fair hearing to which his memory is entitled.

The first fact to get in mind is that the speech which abolitionists regarded as so deplorable was heartily approved by the great mass of the American people. Lodge himself admits this, by inference. The proof that the American people indorsed the speech is afforded by its results; and of these we will let Lodge speak:

The blow fell with terrible force. . . . The 7th of March speech demoralized New England and the whole North. . . . The Free Soil party quivered and sank for the moment beneath the shock. The whole anti-slavery movement recoiled. The conservative reaction which Webster endeavored to produce came and triumphed. . . . The conservative elements everywhere rallied to his support, and by his ability and eloquence it seemed as if he had prevailed and brought the people over to his opinions. It was a wonderful tribute to his power and influence, but the triumph was hollow and short-lived. He had attempted to encompass the impossible. Nothing could kill the principles of human liberty, not even a speech by Daniel Webster. . . .

Consider the last sentence. Was Lincoln trying to "kill the principles of human liberty" when he repeatedly expressed his eagerness to end the war with slavery intact if only the Union were preserved? Was Lincoln moved to emancipation by the clamor of the abolitionists or by military necessity? Were the people of the North fighting to free the negroes or to preserve the Union?

The correct answers to these questions are known to everybody. If Webster, in his Seventh-of-March Speech went wrong, Lincoln also went wrong in his first inaugural address. From this conclusion there can be no escape, because they both said the same things.

Speaking of the Fugitive Slave Law, which Webster defended, not because he liked it, but because it was sanctioned by the Constitution, Lodge said:

The legal argument in support of that right was excellent, but the Northern people could not feel that it was necessary for Daniel Webster to make it.

A curious revelation of a certain type of mind. With such minds in motion, in both North and South, can one

wonder that the Civil War came? In other words, while
the South was entitled, under the Constitution, to the
benefits of the Fugitive Slave Law, let it find this·out for
itself and get such benefits if it could! Webster, as a
senator, was a Federal official, and it was as much his
business to see that the South got all of its constitutional
rights as it was to see that the North received all that was
its due. Lincoln, as a Federal official, certainly did not
think it was not his business to take precisely the same
position with regard to the Fugitive Slave Law that Webster had taken. In his reply to Douglas, at Peoria, Illinois,
on October 16, 1854, Lincoln said:

> When they remind us of their constitutional
> rights, I acknowlege them—not grudgingly but
> fully and fairly; and I would give them any legisla-
> tion for the reclaiming of their fugitives which would
> not in its stringency be more likely to carry a free
> man into slavery than our ordinary criminal laws are
> to hang an innocent one.

Lincoln, in his first inaugural, quoted that part of the
Constitution which authorized a Fugitive Slave Law,
and said that members of congress were as much obli-
gated by their oaths of office to support that part of the
Constitution as they were to support any other part.

Why did not Lodge censure Lincoln, too? The question answers itself. Lodge did not dare. Webster was fair
game. Lincoln was not.

Lodge complained because Webster's speech "pleased
the South." A strange criticism. What was Webster to do
—offend the South still more? Would that have been the
way to pour oil upon the troubled waters and avert war?
Webster was trying to bring the two sections of the country together. Was that a mistake? It was, from the abo-

litionist point of view. But Lincoln was never an abolitionist; and while the Emancipation Proclamation that he
ultimately issued pleased abolitionists it was not issued
because they had convinced him that they were right.
It was issued solely because he believed it would cripple
the South's military power. Lincoln, like Webster, hated
slavery, but he did not free the slaves because he hated
slavery.

Lodge said that Webster, between 1822, when he delivered the Plymouth Oration, and 1850, when he
delivered the Seventh-of-March Speech, had "changed."
In his early days he was against all compromise; later he
was for it.

Webster never changed in his opposition to slavery.
He always regarded it as wrong. At Plymouth he lashed
Boston hypocrites who, with one hand on the Bible, were
using the other to make shackles for the use of importers
of slaves. Such hypocrisy, based solely upon a desire to
reap profits, did not appeal to him.

As to the charge that Webster shifted from "no compromise" to "compromise," it is true—but what does it
prove? It certainly does not prove that he had smothered
his conscience and decided to do wrong. Between 1822
and 1850 conditions had vastly changed. The prospect of
civil war had become alarming. If bloodshed were to be
averted, something must be done and done quickly. Webster could see wrong on both sides. The northern abolitionists were utterly wrong except in their hatred of
slavery. They could not wait to end it constitutionally.
They must end it at once, and violently.

The more the Seventh-of-March Speech is studied,
the more evident does it become that all of the controversy it created arose from differences of opinion as to
whether it was worth while to end slavery at once, even

at the cost of civil war. Lodge sneered at Webster because he seemed content to leave the solution of the whole matter "to Providence." What Webster meant by this, of course, was that, while he could not at that moment see a way peaceably to end slavery, such a way might later be seen and adopted. What was wrong with that? Are not statesmen today taking the same position with regard to much smaller matters? Is there an intelligent member of congress today who does not know that, while something can be done for the "relief" of the farmer, real relief must be left to the slow working-out of events —in other words, to Providence? Must a high official, to be a statesman, always be able to solve every problem on the spot?

Webster did not believe it was worth while to have a civil war to free the negro. Was he wrong? The Civil War set the South back fifty years. It left the American racial stock poorer, by taking from it some of its best blood. Better that slavery had lasted until now than that it should have been ended at such a price. Now slavery, if it were still here, could be put down by constitutional amendment. The votes to do it exist. The common sense of mankind has asserted itself. Was Webster so far wrong in trying to keep the peace until Providence could show a way out? When Webster was young he was like most young men—he would not compromise. When he became older he learned, as most men do, that in order to achieve larger ends, compromises are sometimes necessary.

Lodge said:

> The rise and final triumph of the Republican party was the condemnation of the 7th of March speech, and of the policy which put the government of the country in the hands of Franklin Pierce and James Buchanan.

If so, why did the Republican party nominate a man for President (Lincoln) who agreed with Webster in his attitude toward slavery and the problems that grew out of it? The answer, of course, is that the quoted utterance of Lodge's is untrue. The names of Lincoln and Webster may appropriately be bracketed, but the names of Webster, Pierce, and Buchanan cannot be. Webster wanted peace, but if the Union could in no other way be preserved, he was always prepared to fight—as we shall see, a little later, when we read what he said to an audience in Virginia. Webster was loyal, through and through, to the Union. Pierce in 1860 and Buchanan in 1850 wrote letters to Jefferson Davis, egging him on. Pierce told him the North was so divided in sentiment that if war should come there would be much bloodshed among Northerners. Buchanan urged Davis to come out, even more strongly, for southern "rights."

Nobody ever found such a letter with the name of Daniel Webster signed to it. Webster was true blue; and when, after his death, the war came that he did not want, his only remaining son, Fletcher Webster, thrilling with the spirit of his father, went to the front as the colonel of a Massachusetts regiment and was killed.

Lodge tried to show that Webster, after the Seventh-of-March Speech, realized that he had made a terrible mistake; in proof of this assumption he referred to Webster's letter to Peter Harvey, dated September 10, 1850, in which Webster said that since March 7 there had not been an hour when he did not feel a "crushing sense of anxiety and responsibilities." Lodge, it would appear, could not be fair enough to assume that Webster's feelings had something to do with his anxiety lest the country be plunged into war. Nor did Lodge seem to know (though he must have known) that on September 27, 1851, Webster wrote to Edward Everett: "My speech of the 7th of March, 1850, is probably the most important effort of my life, and as likely as any other to be often referred to."

The only weak spot in the speech was the confident assertion that it was unnecessary to bar slavery from the territories acquired from Mexico, because the Creator, by making the growth of cotton in them impossible, had already barred it. Of course slaves can work in mines as well as in cotton fields—they can work anywhere that labor is required. But Webster was trying to save the feelings of the South as much as he could, and, believing that this region would be free, anyway, considered it good strategy not to press the point. Unfortunately, the reason that he gave for not doing so was a poor one.

To sum up, the question of whether Webster's Seventh-of-March Speech was good or bad depends upon whether one does or does not believe that it was worth while, as the abolitionists believed it was, to go to war in order that slavery might at once be ended. But if Webster, in taking the view he did, was wrong, so was Lincoln. The two must stand or fall together.

VI

WEBSTER was now almost sixty-nine years of age and his health was beginning to break. He had been, for many years, a sufferer from hay-fever, which eventually developed into an asthmatic cough, and to which were added other complications of a serious nature. He lost color, weight, and strength, and during the autumn, when the hay-fever was at its worst, was all but prostrated. So, in October, 1850, he went to Marshfield for a month. Fletcher went with him, and while there they selected a place where Fletcher's mother, his two brothers, and his two sisters were to be buried. This done, Webster, without saying a word to his son, pointed to a spot. Fletcher nodded. Webster wished to be buried where he pointed, and a stone bearing only his name now marks the place. Webster wrote to President Fillmore about this, adding:

"I dwell on these things without pain. I love to see a cheerful old age; but there is nothing I should dread more than a thoughtless, careless, obtuse mind, near the end of life. Of course it makes no difference, in our future state, on which spot we mingle again with our parent earth, but it sobers the mind, I think, and leads us to salutary reflections, to contemplate our last resting-place."

Webster's body was breaking, but his mind would not stop and, so far as it could do so, his mind drove his body forward. Not until he actually broke down did Webster quit, and during most of the last eighteen months of his life he was more active, perhaps, than he had ever been in his life. He was secretary of state and, as such, had the usual duties of the office to perform; but his activity was by no means confined to the state department. During 1851, he made a great number of important political speeches, each one of which was devoted to an attempt to drive home the thought that the people of the United States had, in their government, something worth preserving. Wherever he went, that was the burden of his message—the Union! Without question, Webster drove the idea of nationality deep into the mind of the North. His speeches put into northern hearts the love of country that ultimately saved the Union.

In the midst of such activities, word came that a fugitive slave arrested in Boston had been freed by a mob. Webster wired to the United States Marshal for a report, and let him understand that action was expected. What else could he have done? The abolitionists were attempting to nullify a part of the Constitution. Twenty years before, when Calhoun was preaching nullification in South Carolina, Webster had come out against him. Was not nullification always to be treated the same, regardless of where it might raise its head? Webster thought so, but of course the abolitionists did not agree with him.

In May, 1851, Webster felt it to be his duty to accompany President Fillmore to the western part of the state of New York to attend the ceremonies marking the completion of the Erie Railroad. As the news spread that he was to go, invitations to speak came from every city and almost from every village along the way. At Buffalo, a tremendous crowd had gathered from the city and surrounding country. For an hour and a half Webster addressed this crowd during a drenching rain. Never was he in better form. Never did his words go more directly to the mark. The closing paragraphs of his speech explain why the crowd stayed to the end, unmindful of the storm:

Gentlemen, I regret that slavery exists in the southern states, but it is clear and certain that congress has no power over it. It may be, however, that in the dispensation of Providence, some remedy for this evil may occur or may be hoped for hereafter. But in the meantime I hold to the Constitution of the United States, and you need never expect from me, in any circumstances, that I shall falter from it; that I shall be otherwise than frank and decisive. I would not part with my character as a man of firmness and decision and honor and principle for all that the world possesses. You will find me true to the North, because all my sympathies are with the North. My affections, my children, my hopes, my everything, are with the North. But when I stand up before my country, as one appointed to administer the Constitution of the country, by the blessing of God, I will be just.

Gentlemen, I expect to be libeled and abused. I have not lost a night's sleep for a great many years from such a cause. I have some talent for sleeping. And why should I not expect to be libeled? Is not the Constitution of the United States libeled and abused? Do not some people call it a covenant with hell? . . .

Gentlemen, will you allow me, for a moment, to advert to myself? I have been a long time in public life; of course not many years remain to me. At the commencement of 1850 I looked anxiously at the condition of the country, and I thought the inevitable consequence of leaving the existing controversies unadjusted would be civil war. . . . I saw these things and I made up my mind to encounter whatever might betide me in the attempt to avert the impending catastrophe. And allow me to add something that is not entirely unworthy of notice. A member of the house of representatives told me that he had prepared a list of one hundred and forty speeches which had been made in congress on the slavery question. "That is a very large number, my friend," I said. "But how is that?" "Why," said he, "a northern man gets up and speaks with considerable power and fluency until the speaker's hammer knocks him down. Then gets up a southern man and speaks with more warmth. He is nearer the sun and he comes out with the greater fervor against the North. He speaks his hour and is, in turn, knocked down. And so it has gone on until I have got one hundred and forty speeches on my list." "Well," said I, "where are they and what are they?" "If the speaker," said he, "was a northern man, he held forth against slavery; and if he was from the South he abused the North, and all of these speeches were sent by the members to their own

localities, where they served only to aggravate the
local irritation already existing. No man reads both
sides . . . and the speeches sent from Washington,
in such prodigious numbers, instead of tending to
conciliation, do but increase in both sections of the
Union, an excitement already of the most dangerous
character."

Gentlemen, in this state of things I saw that something must be done. It was impossible to look with
indifference upon a danger of so formidable character. I am a Massachusetts man, and I bore in mind
what Massachusetts has ever been to the Constitution
and the Union. . . . As I honored and respected her,
I felt that I was serving her in my endeavor to pro-
mote the welfare of the whole country.

And now suppose, gentlemen, that on the occasion
in question I had taken a different course. . . .
Suppose that on the 7th of March, 1850, instead of
making a speech that would, so far as my power
went, reconcile the country, I had joined in the general clamor of the anti-slavery party? Suppose I had
said: "I will have nothing to do with any accommo-
dation; we will admit no compromise. . . ."

Now, gentlemen, I do not mean to say that great
consequences would have followed such a course on
my part; but supposing I had taken such a course,
how could I be blamed for it? Was not I a northern
man? Did I not know Massachusetts' feelings and
prejudices? But what of that? I am an American.
I was made a whole man and I did not mean to make
myself half a one. I felt that I had a duty to perform
to my country, to my own reputation; for I flattered
myself that a service of forty years had given me
some character, upon which I had a right to repose
for my justification in the performance of a duty
attended with some degree of local unpopularity. I
thought it my duty to pursue this course and I did
not care what was to be the consequence. I felt that
it was my duty in a very alarming crisis to come out,

to go for my country and my whole country, and to exert any power I had to keep that country together. I cared for nothing, I was afraid of nothing, but I meant to do my duty. . . . And, gentlemen, allow me to say that if the fate of John Rogers had stared me in the face, if I had been at the stake, if I had heard the fagots already crackling, by the blessing of God I would have gone on and discharged the duty which I thought my country called upon me to perform. I would have become a martyr to save that country.

And now, gentlemen, farewell. Live and be happy. Live like patriots; live like Americans. Live in the inestimable blessings that your fathers prepared for you; and if anything I may do hereafter should be inconsistent, in the slightest degree, with the opinions and principles which I have this day submitted to you, then discard me forever from your recollection.

After speaking in Albany and a number of other cities, Webster, late in May, returned to Washington. After a month at the state department he went to Capon Springs, Virginia, where he delivered a notable speech to a great crowd, composed in part of persons who had traveled in wagons as much as fifty miles to hear him. Webster was now in his seventieth year, but the intensity of his desire to keep the Union together drove him on. He sat down with the farmers to a great public dinner that they had prepared for him. From the beginning, it was a love-feast. William L. Clark of Winchester, in introducing Webster, turned to him and said:

"We have given you, sir, not only our admiration— that the world gives you—but we have given you our affections. Long ago you enchained our understandings; now you have thrown a spell over our hearts.

"You came among us suddenly and, I can add, unexpectedly. We have neither pomp nor circumstance to give you; but we have a deep and abiding sense of the inestimable service that you have rendered to our beloved country; and we have sought and do now most earnestly seek to impress your mind with that conviction."

Webster began in a manner intended to make every Virginian present still more his friend. He had a purpose in this because he intended, before he sat down, to say things to them that they would take only from a friend. So he began by expressing generous appreciation of pretty much everything he had seen in the state. The mountains —wonderful! The Shenandoah Valley; where was there another wheat country like it? Nowhere. Virginia women —none better.

Gradually, he switched to politics. He modestly disclaimed having done anything in defense of the Constitution except what he had been able to accomplish in cooperation with far abler men. He had worked hard all his life, he said, devoting most of his years to the public service, and if he had not accumulated much of a worldly estate, he tried to console himself with the thought that he had made a reputation that, as an inheritance, would "not be entirely disreputable" to those who should come after him. As he uttered this sentence he was almost overcome by emotion, and the crowd, now thoroughly in harmony with him, cheered him wildly.

From politics in general, he concentrated his attention to the Union in particular. What states had led in the making of the Union? Why, Virginia and Massachusetts—their state and his. What a blessing it had always been! The sunshine, too, is a blessing, but human beings have become so accustomed to it that sometimes they forget how important it is. Some persons, too, seemed to have forgotten the importance of the Union. They were talking of breaking it up. Here, for the first time, he used the word "secession." He was coming to his point. What did secession offer? "A region of gloom and morass and swamp—all fever and ague." Cheers, laughter, approval. He was carrying his audience along with him.

"Those who assail the Union today," he said, "seem to be persons of one idea only, and many of them of but half an idea."

Back came the crowd with its applause.

"The secessionists of the South," Webster continued, "are learned and eloquent, they are animated and full of spirit, they are high-minded and chivalrous; they state their supposed injuries and causes of complaint in elegant phrases and exalted tones of speech. But these complaints are all vague and general. I confess to you, gentlemen, that I know no hydrostatic pressure strong enough to bring them into any solid form in which they can be seen or felt. If I may be allowed to be a little professional, I would say that all their complaints and alleged grievances are like a very insufficient plea in the law; they are bad on general demurrer for want of substance."

Laughter and applause served to inform the speaker that his audience was still with him. At this point, Webster apparently felt that the time had come to say what he wanted the whole South to hear.

"Let these things go on," he said. "The whole matter, it is to be hoped, will blow over and men will return to a sounder mode of thinking. But one thing, gentlemen, be assured of. The first step taken in the program of secession, which shall be an actual infringement of the Constitution or the laws, will be promptly met. [Great applause.] And I would not remain an hour in any administration that should not immediately meet any such violation of the Constitution and the law effectually and at once. [Prolonged applause.] And I can assure you, gentlemen, that all with whom I am at present associated in the government entertain the same decided purpose. [Renewed applause with cheers.]"

One of the reasons that the Civil War came was because some men in the South did not believe the North would fight. On this day, Webster told the South that, if the Union were attacked, the North *would* fight. The audience at Capon Springs cheered him because they felt that he meant to be just.

"I am as ready to fight and fall for the constitutional rights of Virginia," he said, "as I am for those of Massachusetts. I pour out to you, gentlemen, my whole heart and I assure you these are my sentiments. [Cheers.] I would no more see a feather plucked unjustly from the honor of Virginia than I would from the honor of Massachusetts. [Great applause.] It is said that I have, by the course I have thought proper to pursue, displeased a portion of the people of Massachusetts. That is true, and if I had dissatisfied more of them, what of that? [Great and continued applause.] I was in the Senate of the United States and had sworn to support the Constitution of the United States . . . and my vote was to bind the whole country. I was a senator for the whole country. What exclusive regard had I to pay to the wishes of Massachusetts upon a question affecting the whole nation, and in which my vote was to bind Virginia as well as Massachusetts?"

Webster had no more than returned to Washington before he had to deliver the oration at the laying of the cornerstone of the addition to the Capitol, on July 4th. But on the second of July, he stopped long enough to write the following letter to John Taylor, his boss-farmer:

I have returned and find your letters. I cannot lay out a dollar in horseflesh, and the rule is, you know, to have no trading in horses. Your horses have worked well enough together heretofore, and I hope will do so still. Keep your own team, do your own work, do not trouble yourself about the Sawyer place, give your whole attention to your own farm and your own business—then everything will go well. Never mention the word horse to me. I expect you to hire all the labor which may be necessary to carry on the farming briskly—hoeing, haying and all the rest. Employ good men at fair prices, and their pay shall be ready when the work is done, or as it goes on. I enclose one hundred dollars to pay for labor. Go ahead! I hope you and your family are well.

D. W.

On the Fourth of July, Webster turned from horses to the cornerstone of the Capitol. He made a speech, either the preparation or the delivery of which would have been beyond the powers of most men in their seventieth year. He ranged the wide world over in tracing the growth of the democratic idea and the search for liberty. He inserted, here and there, quotations from ancient poets and other writers who had joined in the pursuit of liberty. He presented a tabulated statement of the nation's growth since Washington, fifty-eight years before and standing upon the spot where Webster then stood, had laid the cornerstone of the central part of the Capitol. He resorted to the same oratorical device that he had once employed upon John Adams and, after picturing Washington picking his way along the trunk of a fallen tree to cross a stream to get to the Capitol site, put words into his mouth and made him speak:

"Ye men of this generation," he made Washington say, "I rejoice and thank God for being able to see that

our labors and toils and sacrifices were not in vain. . . .
Cherish liberty as you love it. . . . Maintain the Constitution. . . . Preserve the union of the states. . . ."

Henry Lunt of Boston was so moved by Webster's
picture that he at once wrote to him a word of praise.
Lunt said he had seen Washington lay the cornerstone,
later in the day had seen him eat dinner in a tavern in
Georgetown, and added that "Washington was most
happy."

But Webster did not stop with his dramatic imperson-
ation of Washington. Having made the picture of American progress under the Constitution, he asked the people
of each section of the country what they thought about it:

"Ye men of the South . . . are you or any of you
ashamed of the great work of your fathers?

"Ye men of Virginia . . .

"Ye men of James River and the Bay . . .

"Ye men beyond the Blue Ridge . . ."

It was a moving appeal for the preservation of the
Union. Beneath the cornerstone that he laid that day
he placed a document, written with his own hand, in
which he said that if it should be the will of God that
the Capitol should sometime be destroyed and the contents of the cornerstone box opened to the eyes of men,
he, as secretary of state, certified that on July 4, 1851, at
any rate, the Union stood firm.

After the laying of the cornerstone, Webster went
to Marshfield for the summer and early autumn. He
remained until October, but gout and hay-fever kept
him from going fishing more than once; the rest of the
time he kept close to the house. Marshfield seemed not
the same, because he was not the same. Old age was
shutting down upon him and upon his friends. Philip
Hone was not there. He had died in the preceding May.

A coming event was already casting its shadow across the lawn and down to the sea.

The autumn found him again upon the treadmill of the state department, plagued with many problems, most of which were petty. Still, they must receive attention. Kossuth, the Hungarian patriot, who was in the country, had to be pleasantly received by Webster, promised nothing—and given what he was promised. The Minister from Brazil who, at a private dinner in Webster's house, had been assigned a seat at the table below the British Minister, whom he claimed to outrank, had to be told, in reply to his protest, that the dinner was private and that the rules of precedence laid down in the Treaty of Vienna therefore did not apply to his case.

On February 24, 1852, Webster went far afield to deliver an address. Notwithstanding his age, poor health, and many burdens, he yielded to the request of the New York Historical Society and spoke on "The Dignity of Historical Compositions."

"If I make a poor figure in this intended address," he said to a friend, "no matter; everybody knows that I know nothing but law and politics." This was pure Websterian irony, probably uttered for the benefit of unkindly critics who had perhaps discussed rather freely his supposed limitations. At any rate, he delivered a lecture on literature that revealed a knowledge of its history that could not today be equaled by one man in a hundred who regards himself as a "literary" person.

Webster was a wonder at such exploits. He had an enormous faculty for making an intensive study of a subject and, after a few hours, presenting it as if he had been gathering the material throughout life. Early in his congressional career, he made a speech on Greece that contained more facts about Greece than most Greeks knew.

Edward Everett gathered the material for him, and Webster arranged and breathed life into it. Gathering material was not in Webster's line; too much like drudgery. But, once the materials were dumped on his doorstep, his flair was for arranging them and presenting them in the best manner. That was what he did in the Dartmouth College case, and very likely it was also what he did in the erudite address he made to the New York Historical Society.

The following month, Webster went to Trenton, New Jersey, to argue a case for the Goodyear rubber interests. This was the case, already mentioned, which he at first refused but later accepted when he was offered a retainer of ten thousand dollars with five thousand more if he should win. Webster was heavily in debt and needed the money. The case was exceedingly difficult, involving, as it did, a thorough knowledge of a highly technical subject, including the patent laws pertaining to it. To make matters worse, the attorney on the other side was Rufus Choate, an old friend of Webster, and a very able lawyer. But Webster put his mind to the matter, mastered it, went to Trenton and won the verdict over Choate, who later wrote a letter certifying that the rumors pertaining to the supposed decline of Webster's intellectual powers were all wrong. He said that physically Webster was not the man whom he had first seen thirty-four years before, but that, his mind had never been better.

When Webster closed his books that day and walked out of the courtroom, he had completed his career as a lawyer. He did not know he was through, but never again was he to plead a case. A wealth of experience and of achievement lay between that day and the earlier occasion when, before his own father, sitting on the bench, he had uttered his first word in court. Between these dates, he and John Marshall had practically made the Constitution of the United States; that is to say, they had determined how, in most of its chief characteristics, it was to be construed. Gouverneur Morris, who wrote the Federal Constitution (though at the Hartford Convention, he was almost ready to destroy it) knew the importance of such work. When he returned from the Philadelphia convention in 1789 and a friend sought to compliment him by telling him that he seemed to have assisted in making a good constitution, Morris replied that it all depended upon how it should be construed. More than any other man, Webster was responsible for bringing about the acceptance of the idea in the North that the United States was a nation and not a mere group of states.

This year of 1852 was the year in which Webster was to die. It was also the year in which another President was to be elected. In a number of states, Webster's friends moved to bring about his nomination by the Whigs. Webster neither helped nor hindered the movement. That he did not hinder it was apparently because the old flame that had so often burned within him flared up again. Certainly, he was too old and too infirm to consider the Presidency. At any rate, the Whigs again sacrificed everything else to "availability" and nominated General Scott, a military figure, who had nothing to recommend him but his war record. When Webster heard the news, he was, for a time, much depressed. He told Peter Harvey that Franklin Pierce would defeat Scott and that the Whig party would disappear as a national party, in which prediction he was exactly correct.

During April, Webster made speeches in Harrisburg and Annapolis, each filled with the old fire of devotion to the Union. Always, he was for peace, provided a certain line were not crossed. At Annapolis, he said:

"Let them drink in secession many days and inwardly

digest it. And, so far as I have any voice in the councils of the country, this meditation of theirs shall never be disturbed; not a breath shall ruffle their sensibility *until it comes to a point where something is done that amounts to an actual conflict with the Constitution."*

Webster always knew what, in certain circumstances, he would do. Southerners might talk about secession, but they must not act upon it.

While Webster was thus employed at conducting the state department and making public speeches, he was keeping up also an incessant fusillade of letters to his farm bosses at Marshfield and Franklin, New Hampshire. Never before, perhaps, or since, were such letters written to men engaged in the tilling of the soil. To John Taylor, at Franklin, whom he frequently addressed as "Brother Farmer," he quoted poetry having to do with the breaking up of winter and the coming of the time for farm activity. In one such letter, having quoted a few lines of poetry, he said:

> John Taylor, when you read these lines do you not see the snow melting and the little streams beginning to run down the slopes of your Punch-brook pasture, and the new grass starting and growing in the trickling water, all green, bright and beautiful? And do you not see your Durham oxen smoking from heat and perspiration as they draw along your great breaking-up plow, cutting and turning over the tough sward in your meadow in the great field? The name of the sensible author is Virgil, and he gives farmers much other advice, some of which you have been following all this winter without even knowing that he had given it:
>
> But when the cold weather, heavy snows and rain
> The laboring farmer in his house restrain,
> Let him forecast his work with timely care,
> Which else is huddled when the skies are fair;

Then let him mark the sheep and whet the shining share,
Or hollow trees for boats, or number o'er
His sacks, or measure his increasing store;
Or sharpen stakes and mend each rake and fork,
So to be ready, in good time, to work—
Visit his crowded barns at early morn,
Look to his granary and shell his corn;
Give a good breakfast to his numerous kine,
His shivering poultry and his fattening swine.

And Mr. Virgil says some other things that you understand up at Franklin as well as he ever did:

In chilling weather, swains enjoy their store,
Forget their hardships and recruit for more.
The farmer to full feasts invites his friends,
And what he got with pains with pleasure spends;
Draws chairs around the fire and tells once more
Stories which often have been told before;
Spreads a clean table with good things to eat,
And adds some moistening to his fruit and meat;
They praise his hospitality and feel
They shall sleep better after such a meal.

John Taylor, by the time you have got through this you will have read enough. The sum of all is, be ready for your spring's work as soon as the weather becomes warm enough, and then put your hand to the plow and not look back.

A few days later, Webster began another letter to John Taylor:

Go ahead. The heart of winter is broke, and before the first day of April all your land may be plowed. Buy the oxen of Captain Marston if you think the price is fair. Pay for the hay. I send you a check for $160 for these two objects. Put the great oxen in condition to be turned out and fattened. You have a good horse-team and I think in addition to this, four oxen and a pair of four-year-old steers will do your work.

On June 1, 1852, Webster wrote:

John Taylor: By this time, I suppose, you have committed the greater part of your grains to the earth, and the rest remains to the providential arrangements of the season.

Be gracious, Heaven, for now laboring man
Has done his part. Ye fostering breezes, blow!
Ye softening dews, ye tender showers, descend!
And temper all, thou world-reviving sun,
Into the perfect year.
D. W.

No accounts of receipts and expenditures on the farms, no books kept of any kind, but plenty of poetry for the farmers.

VII

WEBSTER was living his last weeks upon earth but did not know it. Physically speaking, his sins had found him out. Cirrhosis of the liver had laid firm hold upon him, as had also stomach and intestinal ailments that of themselves were enough to kill him. Like Franklin, he had three fatal diseases, but unlike Franklin he did not congratulate himself that he had no more, because he did not know he had these. Between bad spells, he pushed forward with his various activities. Early in May, he was the victim of an accident that, while it did him no good and may possibly have hastened his end, would have been a minor matter to a younger man in better health, or even to a man of his age in good health. While driving with his secretary from Marshfield to Plymouth, a distance of thirteen miles, the bolt broke that was intended to hold together the body of his carriage and the front axle, the horses ran away, overturning the carriage, and Webster was thrown to the roadside, somewhat cut and bruised, but not seriously hurt. Webster had foreseen the possibility of such an accident and had fixed every other carriage he owned, except this one, so that if the bolt broke, nothing would happen.

The news of the accident, coupled with Webster's age and the status of his political affairs, seems to have produced a peculiar psychological effect throughout New England. All at once, everybody but himself seemed to realize that his career was at an end, that he had already become, in a sense, an historical figure, a part of the past. As an evidence of the overflow of good feeling that was produced by this realization, Webster was invited to speak, late in May, in Faneuil Hall. He had not yet entirely recovered from his accident, and really should have declined the invitation; but feeling as kindly toward the people of Boston as they did toward him, he accepted.

The richness of his mind was seldom better illustrated than it was in this speech. He had prepared nothing. He said nothing about politics, which was his stock in trade. He spoke for more than an hour. Yet his speech was never dull and reads well today. History, humor, philosophy, and a variety of happy illusions filled his discourse. He told how the Royal Court Gazette of Madrid, desiring to honor the American Secretary of State, had attributed to him the authorship of Webster's Dictionary. A bit of philosophy was offered in the form of a quotation from Locke to the effect that "time is measured by the passage of ideas through men's minds." In a day of clocks and watches, that is an odd way to measure time, and odder now, when a watch may be bought for a dollar—but is it not still true? Webster's Faneuil Hall speech, aside from the entertainment that it offered, gave his audience something solid about which to think. Webster was that kind of man. Closing, he quoted an old line:

"Ye solid men of Boston, make no long orations.

"This I take to myself, and am bound to obey the injunction. The concomitant line falls in remarkably with the prevailing spirit of these times and this place:

"Ye solid men of Boston, drink no strong potations.

"Let us all give heed to these admonitions."

Before going to Faneuil Hall, Webster's physician had advised him to drink a glass of wine, which Webster, saying that he had just begun to learn the value of temperance, refused to do.

Boston had suddenly come to feel so great a tenderness toward Webster, and so few had been able to get into Faneuil Hall to hear him, that immediately there came a demand for him to speak on Boston Common, where thousands could hear him. This he did on July 9. Cannon were fired when he left the house of a friend, where he had stayed the night before, and he rode to the Common in a carriage drawn by six gray horses. Cannon along the route were fired as the procession that he led passed along the streets, while the ringing of countless church-bells served to inform everybody that Daniel Webster was on his way to deliver—his last speech in Boston. It was a good speech, too, though not so good as the one delivered in Faneuil Hall. His diseases were slowly closing in upon him. But he had not yet lost the easy, flowing style that characterized all of his oratory, and the tens of thousands that packed the Common remained with him to the end. Most of them could not hear him, but to see him was worth while. He had become a great historic figure.

On June 29, eleven days before Webster spoke in Boston Common, an old man, full of coughs, weaknesses, disappointments, and infirmities, had died. The man was Henry Clay, the second of the great triumvirate to go. Years before, Webster had said that he "never liked Clay." Webster of course heard of Clay's death, but in all the letters that he wrote that summer there is no reference to it. Perhaps he could not forget. He had forgiven many a man who had actually wronged him, which Clay had never done. But Clay had done something that is more difficult to forget than a wrong. He had deeply hurt Webster when he came out for Fillmore for President. Having supported Clay many times, Webster believed he was entitled to Clay's support, and Clay did not give it.

During the midsummer of 1852 Webster made occasional plunges into the overheated atmosphere of Washington only to return to Marshfield each time a little weaker. When he alighted from the train at Kingston, nine miles from his home, on July 25, he suddenly discovered that his neighbors had arranged a surprise for him. Everybody in eastern Massachusetts, it seemed, was at the train, waiting to escort him home. Webster at once inquired of a servant what plans had been made. As to this, the servant was not quite clear; all he knew was that if the crowd came to Marshfield they would tear up the lawn and make the place a mess. He was for keeping them off the lawn and leading them to a place back of the house where they could do no harm. Webster quickly negatived this. "I don't care," he said, "if they tear up the avenue and grounds six feet deep. These people all want to go to the house and they must go."

Go they did—a procession of vehicles two miles long

followed by more than eighty men on horseback. Webster's secretary, Charles Lanman, tells what happened:

Upon a hill, in the immediate vicinity of the mansion, the great concourse came to a halt, and they delegated an orator to welcome him with a speech. To the many, his reply was beautiful and appropriate, but to the few who lived in his shadow, there was a tone of sadness in all he uttered. He finished his address just as the sun was setting, and it was the last he ever uttered to a public assembly. After the crowd had dispersed, he entered his house, fatigued beyond measure, covered with dust, and threw himself into a chair. For a moment his head fell upon his breast, as if completely overcome, and then he looked up, like one seeking something that he could not find. It was the portrait of his darling but departed Julia, and it happened to be in full view. He gazed upon it for a time in a sort of trance, and then wept like one whose heart is broken. "Oh, I am so thankful to be here," he said. "If I could only have my will, never, never, would I again leave this home."

One by one, Webster's activities were coming to an end. In the preceding March he had closed his career as a lawyer. In early July he had spoken in Boston for the last time. Now at Marshfield, before the close of July, he had delivered his last public address. On August 4, he went to Washington to resign as secretary of state, but President Fillmore persuaded him not to do so, urging him to remain at Marshfield and conduct the state department as best he could by correspondence. When Webster took the train to go home he was not to see Washington again. He expected to return and resume his duties, but he never did. Almost to the end he kept up the business of the state department and wrote several letters a week to President Fillmore, but steadily his strength declined.

THE "BROTHER AND SISTER TREES" AND THE SECOND WEBSTER HOME
The trees in the foreground were the elms which Webster planted a few years before his death in memory of his son Edward and his daughter Julia

VIII

ONE thing Webster still could do and that he did, which was to entertain company. The social side of his nature was the last to be submerged by his infirmities. To his house in mid-September came Professor Felton, whom Webster drove about the estate, discoursing volubly upon a great variety of subjects. He told how he had been helped throughout life by the criticism that a newspaper had made of a Fourth of July oration delivered when he was a boy. Part of the address, the newspaper had said, was "mere emptiness." Webster said that when he read this criticism it at once occurred to him that it was true, and he thereupon resolved nevermore to use words that had no thought behind them. He regretted that he had seldom had an opportunity to enjoy for any length of time, the society of literary and scientific men. "I have kept very bad company," he said with a laugh. "I have lived among lawyers and judges and jurymen and politicians, when I should have lived with Nature and the students of Nature."

While Webster and Felton were out together they sometimes came upon neighboring farmers. To them Webster talked crops, and to one who inquired about his health, replied:

"I am not good for much. My strength is nearly gone. I am no match for you now. I am scarcely a match for your grandson, yonder."

As soon as Professor Felton left, Webster, by this time seriously concerned about his health, went to Boston to consult a physician. He did not remain long, because while there he learned that George and Anna Ticknor desired to visit him.

George and Anna Ticknor! Twenty-odd years before, the three had spent that delightful week visiting Madison and Jefferson in their homes. Many memories must have come to them as they gathered this time at Marshfield. The best the place afforded was set upon the table for the guests; Webster could eat only gruel and not much of that. But even if he could not eat, he could tell stories; and this is one that he told:

There was an old lady in New Hampshire with whom we were very intimate many years ago, and to whom we generally paid a visit about once a year. The children called her Aunt Howth. She was a famous housekeeper and always kept her house in perfect order. But she had a fashion of always apologizing for the disorder of her establishment, and never would allow anyone to suppose that she thought things were as they should be. One day, when we arrived there, she received us very hospitably, and immediately began the usual apologies. She was dreadfully sorry that we should find her house in such disorder—and we had this story over three times. At last, Julia, who had been listening all the time, spoke up: "Well, it doesn't matter much, aunt; it doesn't look very nice, but I wouldn't say any more about it." "How dare you say so," Aunt Howth exclaimed, "how dare you say so, you little wretch? You never saw a house in such nice order since you were born!"

Somebody brought up the subject of John Adams. Webster said he had a very uneven mind, sometimes moving along almost sluggishly and then suddenly bursting forth with great power. Adams reminded Webster of Concord River, which a fellow lawyer once used to illustrate the traits of a certain man. The gentleman's reasoning, the lawyer said, might be profound, but, like the Concord, it was so deep that one could not tell which way it was running.

Webster was not well enough to accompany his guests about the place (there were others present beside the Ticknors), but he sent them to see his fat oxen and cattle. In the evening he joined them a little while at whist, but did not play well and soon went to bed. The next morning, they were served what Mr. Curtis called a "very luxurious breakfast," every item of which was prepared at Webster's order, but none of which he could eat. Webster had arranged entertainment for everybody for the day, but remained at home himself. At dinner, he was in excellent spirits and told a number of good stories. One was about a man named Huntington.

> He had been chosen lieutenant-governor of Connecticut [Webster said] and a committee of the legislature was sent to Hartford to announce it to him. He was in the field, and they waited in the best room while he was summoned and put on his Sunday clothes. The chairman of the committee very solemnly announced the honor which had been conferred upon him, to which Mr. Huntingdon with equal solemnity replied that he accepted it with great distrust of himself, but not without hope that he might be able to fulfill, in some degree, the duties it imposed upon him, as he had held a similar office for nearly forty years in his own family.

When the guests were preparing to leave, Webster called Mr. Curtis aside, told him that, while his health was improving, he did not care to have the news get abroad, for such a report would bring too many visitors. He said he meant to take things easy at Marshfield during the remainder of the autumn and get in trim to return to Washington for the winter. That was on the twenty-fifth of September. When Curtis bade Webster good-by he never dreamed his end was so near.

When these friends left Marshfield, Webster's career as a host was at an end; never again were guests to cross his threshold. But he could still write an occasional letter, and one that he wrote a few weeks before his death is of peculiar interest. An article had appeared in a Boston newspaper about an old man in Gloucester who had told a reporter that in his youth he had been the schoolmaster of Daniel Webster. Many incidents were related by the old man: among them his offer of a jack-knife one Friday afternoon as a prize to the pupil able to repeat on Monday the most verses from the Bible. When the test came, many pupils did well, but Daniel, as he proceeded to repeat verse after verse, soon astonished both teacher and classmates. After he had repeated sixty or seventy verses, the teacher called upon him to stop, telling him that he had already won the jack-knife by so wide a margin that it was unnecessary to go on. Daniel replied that he was prepared to repeat three or four more chapters.

When Webster read this story he was, for a moment, no longer the sick old statesman, but a boy again. He remembered the teacher perfectly; he was James Tappan, now eighty-six years old. Webster wrote to Tappan, telling him how glad he was to learn that he was still alive; and in writing he did an odd thing that all men do when they meet one of their old school teachers. His mind clicked back into the old relationship of a junior addressing a senior, as evidenced by the fact that following a custom of boyhood, he addressed him as "Master" Tappan. Regardless of how great a boy may grow to be, the relationship between him and his teacher never changes. The teacher, however unrenowned, always regards himself as still the superior in wisdom, and the "pupil," however celebrated he may have become, momentarily seems, as Webster did, to admit it. Webster sent the old man twenty dollars, which was the last that Master Tappan ever heard from Daniel Webster.

IX

WEBSTER, on October 24, was to die. On September 30, he wrote to President Fillmore:

"Dr. Jeffries has been down and stayed two nights, and has freely conversed with Dr. Porter, our local physician. Their statement is more favorable than I expected, for I have been much alarmed and that alarm has not all subsided yet."

Webster did not know half the truth. His physicians saw that only a few more days were left for him. Dr. James Jackson, who came down from Boston about this time, told Webster's family there was no hope.

Down in his heart Webster must have known that he was doomed, but for a few more days he tried to create the illusion that nothing much was the matter with him and that he would soon be well. For a week he struggled with dictation, in a pathetic effort to direct the state department. And when, two weeks before his death, his old friend Peter Harvey came to see him, he made a last desperate effort to seem, not merely strong, but gay.

Peter Harvey was a man of whom Webster once said: "He never denied his friend." Fletcher Webster had named one of his sons after him, and Webster thought the world of him. Harvey came on a Sunday—that day of all days in New England, when families are accustomed to get together around the dinner table, exchange good cheer, and generally rejoice that they are alive.

What Webster intended to do was perhaps precipitated by the thought of a flock of sheep at which he had asked Harvey to look that morning.

"I suppose they are carrying their heads pretty high now," he said, laughing, "and they begin to think that nobody in Marshfield can now eat mutton; but one of these days, Friend Harvey, we will make them laugh out of the other side of their mouths. We will make them sing a different song."

What he said seemed to have given him an idea. His thoughts turned to Monica, the cook, a colored woman, now grown old, who had been in his service thirty years, dating from a time when, in Washington, he had bought her out of slavery and given her freedom.

"Monica," he said, "is roasting as nice a leg of mutton as was ever put upon a man's table. It was ripe today. It is the ninth day since it was slaughtered and it has hung in a place where it has kept all its juices and arrived at just the right condition. I have ordered it cooked. Friend, it is for your dinner; and I am going down to dine with you today off that mutton."

"It would give us great pleasure to see you down to dinner," said Harvey, "but I suppose you are joking."

"I never was more in earnest in my life," replied Webster.

"But wouldn't it be injurious to you?" asked Harvey. "Wouldn't it hurt you?"

Harvey was dismissed and William Bean, Webster's valet, was called. Bean, like Monica, was a negro whom Webster, many years before, had bought out of slavery.

For the next two hours, the valet went to his work. He shaved Webster and dressed him with that minute attention which Webster always demanded, dressed him in blue coat with gilt buttons, buff vest, black pantaloons, white cravat with collar turned down, and fancy black shoes. Bean, while he was working, wore the same kind of suit himself. Webster always gave him his old clothes.

While these things were going on upstairs, Mrs. Webster was in a flutter. She did not at all approve her husband's contemplated action, but knew him too well to put in a word against it.

A little before three o'clock, steps were heard descending the stairs. Webster, dressed as if for a party, was coming down, leaning heavily on Bean's arm. As soon as he saw Harvey, a smile that Harvey described as "beautiful" came over his face, and he said to his colored valet: "Now William, I will dispense with you; you may leave me."

Harvey approached him, Webster grasped both of his hands, kissed him on the cheek, and said: "Now, then, if you will give me your arm, we will proceed."

Webster took Harvey's arm and slowly they walked through the music room to the library, in which a grate-fire was burning. Mrs. Webster, believing that her husband would not feel well enough to go to the table, had arranged a sofa, with a pillow nicely nestled at one end of it, before the fire. Attention was called to the pillow by Mrs. Webster, and he was urged to lie down. Webster straightened up a little and looked at her. "I don't want any pillow," he said. "I came down here to dine with my friends. Roll back the sofa," he said to a servant. "Replace the chair."

The chair of which he spoke was a large overstuffed affair. He tried to walk around it to go to the dining-room, but could not. His strength gave out, and he sank down, apparently completely exhausted. For a minute he said nothing. His eyes were closed. When he opened them, he said:

"This is better than all the medicine of the doctors— the countenances of one's friends. What is so consoling? What can give such comfort to a sick man?"

A servant entered the room and announced that dinner was ready. Webster asked Mr. Paige, his first wife's half-brother, to take his place at the dinner table. To Harvey he said:

"My friend, will you hand Mrs. Webster to the dinner table? I will not go just now. I will come in a few minutes, but do you go now."

Nobody ate much, and that little was eaten in silence. Webster never entered the room. When the meal was finished he sent word to Harvey to come to him in the library. For a long time he talked politics—Scott's nomination and the impending disintegration of the Whig party. Then his mind drifted to his wife and Fletcher, and what would become of them when he was gone. If he could only get two more fees like the Goodyear fee he could die free of debt, which was his ambition. He would have liked to leave Mrs. Webster better taken care of financially, but he had something to leave her. She had property of her own, and would be able to get along fairly comfortably. Julia's children were provided for, because their father was wealthy. But Fletcher— what was to become of him? He had talents, Webster said, but he had never seemed to have the knack of making money. "Poor Fletcher and his family," he said; "when I think of them my heart bleeds. I am sure my friends will not see my own son driven to the necessity of begging his bread."

Darkness had long since come on. It was nine o'clock

in the evening. Mrs. Webster, worried lest he talk too long, finally opened the door.

"Give yourself no uneasiness," Webster said to her. "I have sought this conversation and, whether it makes me worse or not, it has relieved me. You, my friend Harvey, must go tomorrow morning, but come and see me again just as soon as you can."

Webster sent for Monica and Porter Wright. Monica came first.

"Monica," said Webster, "Mr. Harvey is going home tomorrow morning. I don't want him to go without the best breakfast he ever had, and you know how to give it to him."

"I do, indeed, Mr. Webster."

"Tomorrow morning, Monica, have the table spread and a little fire built in the dining-room. Let me see. In the first place, give him the best cup of coffee you can; then some toast; broil a steak; give him a bit of ham and a boiled egg; bake a potato, and put all of these things, smoking-hot, on the table at precisely half past five by the Shrewsbury clock."

"It shall be done just as you say, sir," she replied.

"And you, William, tomorrow morning at exactly five o'clock—right on the moment—take a cup of shaving-water to Mr. Harvey's room, and knock on the door until you get an answer if you have to pound your knuckles off. And when Mr. Harvey answers, set down the shaving-water and ask him for his clothes. Take them out and give them a good brushing. Porter Wright"—Wright had just come in—"Mr. Harvey is going to the depot tomorrow morning. Have the horses harnessed and the carriage at the door at six o'clock, to a minute. Have it at the library door and the coachman on the box.

"Now," said he to Harvey, "I will take your arm and go upstairs."

The next day—October 8—Webster wrote to President Fillmore that the doctors had scrutinized him from top to toe "as if they had been making a post-mortem examination," with the result that they thought they found him a little better. What tales doctors sometimes tell to dying men! All he needed, according to the doctors, was time in which to recover and all the good food for which he could find an appetite. "It is a great while," Webster wrote Fillmore, "since I have been hungry."

About the same time, Mr. G. J. Abbott, a close friend of Webster's, wrote to Mr. Ticknor:

"It is useless to deceive ourselves. The days pass on and with the passage of each, I see a gradual decline. The mind is as bright as ever. Now and then it lights up and reminds me of the old time. A flash of the genial humor of the past brings a smile or a laugh. . . ."

Webster told stories almost to the last. On October tenth, Mr. Abbott wrote:

At his request, his son raised him up in bed that he might affix his name to a letter and envelope which I placed before him, while John Taylor held the candle. Not liking the cramped manner in which he had written his name on the envelope, he asked John "if it did not look squat." John told him it did and he asked for another and wrote his name in a fair hand. He said it reminded him of a story of Judge Smith of Exeter, who, when Governor of New Hampshire and reviewing a regiment of militia, complimented the chaplain on the excellence of his prayer on that occasion. "It would have been much better," said the clergyman, "if I had not been squat for time."

This was the last story that Webster ever told.

The next day was gloomy, foggy and rainy and Webster stayed in bed. He asked Mr. Abbott to read to him from the Bible, commenting from time to time upon what was read.

"If I get well and write a book on Christianity," he said, "about which we have talked, we can attend more fully to this matter. But if I should be taken away suddenly, I want to leave somewhere a declaration of my belief in Christianity. I do not wish to go into any doctrinal distinctions in regard to the person of Jesus, but I wish to express my belief in His divine mission."

What Webster left was an inscription to be placed upon his tomb. His instructions were afterward obeyed. The inscription follows:

"Lord, I believe; help Thou mine unbelief."
Philosophical argument, especially that drawn from the vastness of the universe in comparison with the apparent insignificance of this globe, has sometimes shaken my reason for the faith that is in me; but my heart has assured and reassured me that the Gospel of Jesus Christ must be a living reality.

The Sermon on the Mount cannot be a merely human production. This belief enters into the very depth of my conscience. The whole history of man proves it.

DAN'L WEBSTER

A day or two later when Webster was lying in bed, with eyes closed, he asked a friend who sat near him if there were anyone else in the room? He was told that only William Bean, his valet, was present.

"Very well," he said. "William will tell no tales. I have a secret for you. I want you to go, as soon as it is dark, and hang a lantern at the masthead of my little shallop behind the house and raise the colors. Be sure to keep that light burning every night as long as I live. Don't fail to do this. I want to keep my flag flying and my light burning until I die."

Webster did not tell all that was in his mind. What was happening was that in a vague way he was reaching out to his loved and lost son, Edward—the boy who went away to the Mexican War and never came back. The little shallop had belonged to Edward and, since his death, had been kept in a pond a few rods back of the house, as a memento of him. To the mind of the dying Webster, the sight of the lamp, shining at night at the masthead of his son's ship, undoubtedly stood for something sweet and sacred. The light was a living reminder of his dead boy. At any rate, thereafter, until Webster died, the lantern was duly lighted each night and extinguished the next morning. Each evening, standing in silence before the window, he looked at it. Edward . . . Edward. . . .

More and more Webster was becoming bedridden. He had become much emaciated and looked as if he could not last from day to day. Still, he insisted upon getting up whenever he could and sitting for a while, in an easy chair. One day, about a week before he died, he sent for Porter Wright, his boss-farmer, and asked him to go to the pasture, get about twenty of his largest oxen, and drive them up to the house where he could see them. Webster was friendly toward dogs, admired horses, glowed at the sight of cows—especially if they were large —and loved oxen. Of these he would sometimes buy as many as twenty at a time. Always he had about a hundred cattle in the pasture.

Wright went out, and Webster waited. In a few minutes, the first big ox lumbered up the hill. One by one, others lumbered along after him. Soon, all of them were distributed about the lawn, eating grass. Webster forgot his illness—forgot himself. Porter Wright, in speaking of it afterward, said it was "the last enjoyment Mr. Webster ever had."

On the fifteenth, Webster wrote to President Fillmore:

> I thank you from the bottom of my heart for your kind letter. Your letters are always kind. I have been in great danger. I am attended, nearly every day, by two physicians; and yet, strange as it may seem, when I have got through the night I can sit an hour at the table and write a letter and sign others. I don't foresee the result. I am in the hands of God, and may He preserve you and yours evermore!

On the seventeenth he wrote to the President:

> I have had two comfortable nights on the whole, since I wrote you, though last night I had an excessively painful attack which cost Dr. Jeffries two hours to subdue. I then went to sleep and slept sweetly. This is a beautiful, brilliant but very cold October morning, and now (11 o'clock) I feel uncommonly well and strong; some symptoms are decidedly better. They measure me like an ox and find that there is a small but positive diminution of the distention of the stomach and bowels. We must see now, ere long, what turn these things will be likely to take. . . .
>
> It has been so kind of Mr. Conrad to trouble himself with the concerns of my department, in my absence, that I should be glad to show him some mark of grateful respect. It is a feather in the life of a public man to sign a treaty, and I should be glad that he should have an opportunity of signing one before my return. If you have concluded to submit the copyright treaty to the senate, I propose to you to suggest to him, as from yourself, but with my hearty concurrence, that he sign it. . . .

The next day—the eighteenth—Webster wrote his last letter and it, too, was to President Fillmore:

> By the blessing of Providence I have had another comparatively good night, the afternoon attack coming later and not lasting so long, and then an excellent sleep. At this hour (ten o'clock) I feel easy and strong, as if I could go into the senate and make a speech! At one, I shall sink all away; be obliged to go to bed at three, and go through the evening spasms. What all this is to come to, God only knows. . . . I fear things do not look very well for our side.

The next day he was much worse. Mr. George T. Curtis, a close friend and a lawyer, was called from Boston to make his will.

"Follow the old forms," said Webster, "and do not let me go out of the world without acknowledging my Maker."

When the task stretched over to another day, Webster said that Curtis should consider it professional service and charge for it in the regular way.

"Mr. Webster," said Curtis, "I cannot have *you* for a client. We are of the same guild, you know."

"True," replied Webster, "we are Freemasons enough for that."

Curtis called Webster's attention to a letter from some Whigs who wished him to come out for General Scott for President. While the letter was being read to him, Webster, free from pain, was lying back in a chair with a napkin over his eyes that his ever-watchful colored nurse, Sarah, had put there to shield him from the light which he would not permit to be kept out of the room. At the end, he said:

"I care no more about politics than the jackdaw that

sits on the top of St. Paul's. You remember Cowper's 'Jackdaw':

> "You think, no doubt, he sits and muses
> On future broken bones and bruises,
>   If he should chance to fall.
> No, not a single word like that
> Employs his philosophic pate,
>   Or troubles it at all.
>
> "He sees that this great roundabout,
> The world, with all its motley rout,
>   Church, army, physic, law,
> Its customs and its businesses,
> Is no concern at all of his;
>   And says—what says he?—Caw!"

A day or two later, when he was feeling a little better, his attention was again called to the letter about Scott. He said he would not think of coming out for him.

"This is a matter of principle, and character and reputation with me," he said. "I will die before I will do anything directly or indirectly from which it is inferred that I acquiesce in the nomination made at Baltimore. I ask nobody to vote for me; I expect it of nobody; I find fault with nobody for supporting the nomination. But I cannot and will not say that I acquiesce in it. If I were to do this thing I should feel my cheeks already scorched with shame by the reproaches of posterity."

Curtis read him a letter that had come that morning, urging him not to change his position—to continue to stand against Scott.

"Write to this man," said Webster, "and tell him to look over toward Charlestown and see if the Bunker Hill monument is still standing."

That was the last utterance of Webster with regard to politics.

X

THE activities of the Webster mansion, during these sad days, were not confined to the room in which he lay and the library where Mrs. Webster and a few close friends were assembled. Out in the kitchen were friends, too, who were as gloomy as any of the others and as much given to recalling, in subdued tones, events of the long past in which they had been associated with Webster. Ordinarily the kitchen was not a place in which the cook permitted farm-hands and other workers to assemble, but now it was different. To the kitchen came old Seth Peterson, a strange, red-faced old sailor whom Webster called the "Commodore." Peterson it was who had so often sailed the seas with "the squire"—sometimes until ten o'clock at night—in search of fish. And many a story he told to the group gathered in the kitchen about narrow escapes around sunken rocks while sailing with Webster.

"Before he bought this place," said Peterson, "I was going about with him one day when he said that he must have Marshfield; that he hoped he should lay his bones there, and then added: 'I suppose by the time I get the place and means to make it fit to live in, I shall die and leave it.'"

Peterson said he was once nearly scared to death because of a remark that he thoughtlessly made to Webster. Peterson and his boat were stuck on a bar close to shore. Webster called out to him and asked him if he was making any progress toward getting it off. "Does she get along any?" was the way Webster put it.

"Yes, yes," replied Peterson, "she gets on by hitches as lawyers get to heaven."

XI

AS Webster drew within four days of death the fact
gradually became apparent that a peculiar idea had
developed in his mind. He wanted to see how it felt to
die! He wished, when death came, to be awake with a
clear mind. So much did this desire occupy his attention
that sometimes when he was emerging from the influence
of an opiate it expressed itself in muddled forms. It
seemed as if, when coming back to consciousness, the first
thought that rushed into his mind was his desire to be
awake when he died, but the opiate would not at first
permit him to get the correct answer.

This is the true explanation of what have always
passed for his last words—"I still live." Religious persons
tried to interpret them as an evidence of his belief in the
immortality of the soul, while some of his enemies declared that what he really said was: "I still live—more
brandy." There was never any truth in the brandy story,
and so far as the religious interpretation was concerned,
while Webster believed in the soul's immortality, he was
not thinking about it when he said: "I still live." He
was answering his own question as to whether he had
died without realizing his desire to know how it felt
to die.

Mrs. Baker, his housekeeper said:

Tuesday night, before he died, I watched with
him. He waked up suddenly and said: "I'm dead,
I'm dead." Mrs. Webster ran in and we found that
he felt numb. We rubbed him, and he revived, but
after Mrs. Webster had gone again, he called me to
him and said: "Don't you go to sleep, not a wink for
a thousand dollars. Take the hartshorn and hold it

to my nose every fifteen minutes whether I am awake or asleep. Rub me with spirits and keep hold of my right hand." I think he imagined that he might die suddenly.

Saturday morning, Dr. Jeffries told Curtis that Webster's will must be completed and signed that day. Webster was still alive, in his right mind and able to talk, but Dr. Jeffries was in no doubt as to what was about to take place. Mrs. Webster, down in the library, was crying; the kitchen was strangely still; seldom did anyone speak, and whatever was said was uttered in a whisper. About ten o'clock in the morning, into this gloom came Peter Harvey. Dr. Jeffries told him that nobody was permitted to see Webster. Fletcher Webster, who happened to come along in time to hear the remark, said that Harvey *must* see his father; that he knew his father would want to see him. Harvey was very polite about it all, and begged Fletcher to say no more, but Fletcher insisted, and Dr. Jeffries finally withdrew his objection.

As soon as Mr. Webster saw me [Harvey tells] he exclaimed, in a very distinct voice:

"Why, is it possible that this is you? I thought you would come. Come to me."

I at once passed across the room, very much touched and weeping. When I reached the bedside, he held out both his hands, put his arms around my neck and kissed me. Then he said:

"Kiss me."

"It is distressing to see you suffering so," I said, "and so ill."

"I am not so ill," replied Webster, "but that I know you. I am sick, but I am not too sick to call down blessings on you, faithful friend—true in life, true in death. I shall be dead tomorrow," he added, softly. "Do not leave this room until I am gone. Promise me that you will not."

Time was flying. The morning of what was to be Webster's last day on earth was already far gone. Webster, who had never before spoken of death as an assured, imminent fact, now so discussed it freely. The idea that seemed to be uppermost in his mind was that he had much to do and little time in which to do it. Turning from Harvey to Jeffries, his physician, he said:

"Doctor, you have carried me through the night. I think you will carry me through the day. I shall die tonight."

"You are right, sir," said the doctor, after a pause.

"I wish you therefore," continued Webster, "to send an express to Boston for some younger person to be with you. I shall die tonight. You are exhausted and must be relieved. Who shall it be?"

"Dr. J. Mason Warren."

"Let him be sent for," said Webster.

Dr. Jeffries went to another room to write a note to Dr. Warren. When he returned, he learned that Webster had summoned a servant and given full directions to the messenger—what horse he should drive, what road he should take, and what corners he should turn in Boston.

All of this time, Mr. Curtis had been working in the library on Webster's will, which about four o'clock in the afternoon was completed. Webster asked that his wife and Fletcher go to another room, read it, and then tell him whether it was satisfactory to them. They did so and came back with an affirmative reply.

"Then let me sign it now," said he.

Sarah and Fletcher raised him to a half-sitting posture and propped him up with pillows. Fletcher handed him a pen. Webster took the will and signed it in a clear hand. As he returned the pen to Fletcher, he smiled and said:

"Thank God for strength to do a sensible act."

A moment later, with great solemnity, he said:

"O God, I thank thee for all thy mercies."

After a pause of a minute or two Webster looked around the room as if to see if all whom he wished to address were present. Mr. Curtis, the Boston lawyer who had drawn the will, sensed the fact that Webster was about to speak and, quickly realizing the historic value of anything he might say at such a time, passed to a table upon which there were writing materials. Webster spoke slowly, enabling Curtis to get every word:

"My general wish on earth has been to do my Maker's will. I thank Him now for all the mercies that surround me. I thank Him for the means He has given me of doing some little good; for my children, these beloved objects; for my nature and associations. I thank Him that I am to die, if I am, under so many circumstances of love and affection. I thank Him for all His care.

"No man who is not a brute can say that he is not afraid of death. No man can come back from *that* bourne; no man can comprehend the will or the works of God. That there *is* a God, all must acknowledge. I see Him in all these wondrous works. Himself, how wondrous.

"The great mystery is Jesus Christ—the Gospel. What would be the condition of any of us if we had not the hope of immortality? What ground is there to rest upon but the Gospel? There were scattered *hopes* of the immortality of the soul, running down, especially among the Jews. The Jews believed in a spiritual origin of creation. The Romans never reached it. It is a tradition, if that communication was made to the Jews by God Himself, through Moses and the fathers. But there is, even to the Jews, no direct assurance of an immortality in heaven. There is now and then a scattered intimation, as in Job, "I know that my Redeemer liveth"; but a proper consideration of *that* does not refer it to Jesus Christ at all. But there were intimations—crepuscular, twilight. But, but, but, thank God, the Gospel of Jesus Christ brought life and immortality to *light*—rescued it— brought it to *light*. There is an admirable discourse on that subject by Dr. Barrow, preacher to the Inner Temple. I think it is his sixth sermon. . . .

"Well, I don't feel as if I am to fall off; I may."

Drowsiness seemed to have overcome him. He closed his eyes. But the will to keep awake was, for the moment, stronger than the opiates. He fought his way back to consciousness, looked eagerly around the room and, in a confused manner said:

"Have I— Wife, son, doctor, friends, are you all here? Have I, on this occasion, said anything unworthy of Daniel Webster?"

"No, no, dear sir," they replied.

Immediately he began to repeat the Lord's Prayer. After a sentence or two he felt faint and his voice weakened. "Hold me up," he said. "I do not wish to pray with a fainting voice." More pillows were put behind him and he then clearly and distinctly repeated the remainder of the prayer.

"Where's Monica and the rest of them?" he inquired. "Let me see their faces. Come in here, ye faithful."

The strain, at this point, overcame Mrs. Webster, and, sobbing aloud, she threw her arms around her husband's neck.

"My dear wife," said Webster, trying to calm her, "when you and I were married at the Bowling Green, we knew that we must one day part."

Dr. Warren, for whom a messenger had been sent to Boston, arrived at eight o'clock in the evening. He had

been in the house but half an hour when Webster had a
severe hemorrhage of the stomach. Webster reached out
his arms and asked that he be raised to a sitting posture.
This was done.

"I feel as if I were going to sink right away," he said.
"Am I dying?"

Dr. Warren told him that he was merely faint, and
gave him a stimulant.

Webster knew that his hour was almost at hand when
he would have to devote all his remaining strength to an
effort to retain his consciousness so that he might know
how it felt to die. But before concentrating his mind
upon this final task, he wished to say good-by to all. He
asked that everybody, white and black, file past his bedside and, as they came along, he addressed to each a few
words of affection and consolation. He seemed to have
perfect control of himself.

It was the last time, however, that he was able to
summon his intellect. Flashes of his mind afterward returned, but most of his utterances were muddled. He
dozed, sometimes for an hour, only to awaken suddenly,
apparently much exhausted, and exclaim: "Give me
life, give me life." Twice he awakened thus with a start
and asked: "Am I alive or am I dead?"

A little later, Webster roused up and asked whether
it was likely that his death would be preceded by another hemorrhage of the stomach. Answered in the negative, he asked what the doctors intended to do from then
onward. Dr. Jeffries replied that they would give him
opiates and stimulants as he might require them.

Webster, even in his dying condition, caught the idea.
Whenever they saw him sinking they would give him a
stimulant. Therefore, the giving of a stimulant would
indicate that the doctors detected signs of dissolution.

"Should I not be given a stimulant now?" he inquired.

"No, not just now, Mr. Webster."

"When you give it to me," he replied, "I shall know that I may drop off at once. I will then put myself in a position to get a little repose."

These were Webster's last lucid words. Repose immediately came, never to be broken, except by occasional mumbled utterances which indicated that the desire to meet Death face to face was still coursing through his poor, tired brain. It was about midnight when he said, "I still live." After that, his mind went so far down into the shadows that the question of whether he was alive or dead no longer troubled him. About two o'clock in the morning, he very distinctly uttered the word "poetry" and Fletcher read him a verse from Gray's "Elegy." He did not speak but Curtis said he heard Gray's somber lines and smiled.

Webster spoke no more. Heavy silence fell upon the candle-lighted room. The only sound was the ticking of the great clock in the hall below. Sixteen friends and members of the family were ranged about the bedside, while the colored and other servants were in the background. Peter Harvey, who had promised Webster not to leave the room until he died, was there—faithful unto death, as Webster said he would be. Dr. Jeffries held one of Webster's wrists with his finger on the pulse. At twenty-three minutes to three o'clock, on Sunday morning October 24, 1852, Webster's heart ceased to beat. Dr. Jeffries held Webster's wrist for a few seconds longer, then dropped it and uttered one word: "Dead."

Between seven and eight o'clock in the morning, the bell of the parish church was rung violently. This meant that during the night someone had died. Next, the bell was rung "three-times-three," as the saying was, or given three raps, then silence and another three, then silence and a final three. This indicated that death had taken a man or a boy. Then followed seventy slow, measured strokes and everyone within hearing said, "Daniel Webster is dead."

On Friday, October 29, ten thousand persons—friends, neighbors, strangers, rich, poor, whoever wished to honor the memory of the great man—came to the house at Marshfield. Out on the lawn, in front, reposed a casket in which lay, as one of his friends expressed it, "all of Webster that could die." Dressed in the familiar blue coat with gilt buttons, and the buff waistcoat, the silent figure seemed almost as if it were itself trying to do honor to the assembled multitude and the gorgeous Indian-summer day.

As the long line slowly filed past the bier, a poorly dressed man whom nobody knew—evidently a farmer from the back country—came to a full stop. For a few seconds he looked wistfully down at the still figure upon which the fading autumn sunlight lingered. "Daniel Webster," he said softly, "the world, without you, will seem lonesome."

THE END

[1 K 376

WITHDRAWN

Em   Library
3   9

E340.W4B35   79980 ✓

Benson, Allan Louis

Daniel Webster.